# In Defense of
# Secular Humanism

# In
# Defense
# of
# Secular
# Humanism

Paul Kurtz

**Prometheus Books**

700 East Amherst St.
Buffalo, New York 14215

Published in 1983 by Prometheus Books, 700 East Amherst Street, Buffalo, New York, 14215.

Library of Congress Card Catalog No. 83-62188
ISBN: 0-87975-221-1 Cloth
     0-87975-228-9 Paper

# Contents

# Preface

Secular humanism has come under sustained criticism in recent years, especially from religious conservatives and the fundamentalist right. Critics have called it the "most dangerous" and "influential" intellectual and religious movement in America in the present century. Basic to the attack is the view that secular humanism lacks a moral framework and that it has contributed to the decay of moral values in modern society.

I think the opposition is profoundly mistaken. For it fails to appreciate the significant role humanism has had in developing a moral position relevant to the present age of rapid scientific advances and social change. Indeed, humanism expresses a set of significant moral values, which focus on fulfilling the best in human beings and are positive contributions to human good.

There are, of course, many forms of humanism, religious and secular. My main interest is in defending *secular* humanism, that is, the point of view that holds that it is possible to lead a good life and contribute significantly to human welfare and social justice without a belief in theistic religion or benefit of clergy. Human beings, as free, autonomous individuals, can discover that life can be good and bountiful. Humanist morality can provide a genuine basis for excellence and nobility. Moreover, it is closely related to developments in modern science, and hence is a naturalistic philosophy.

I have been deeply involved in the humanist movement throughout most of my life, and I have often defended humanism from its critics. Indeed, I have been singled out by many on the radical right for special criticism. My writings on humanism, spanning more than thirty years, have appeared in many different periodicals and books. It thus seems worthwhile to compile in one place many of my statements on humanist philosophy and morality. Accordingly, this book contains much that I have said in developing and clarifying the humanist position. There will no doubt be some overlap, since the articles were written at different times in response to different challenges. This volume contains, for example, *Humanist Manifesto II,* which I drafted in collaboration with many others and which especially has come under heavy criticism, as well as *A Secular Humanist Declaration* (also endorsed by many intellectuals). I have included many other articles in which I have attempted to provide a framework for humanist ethics, and I comment on religion, politics, science, and the paranormal as well. Some of the essays appear here for the first time. I hope that this collection will contribute to free inquiry and the clarification of secular humanism. There has been widespread, vociferous, and unwarranted criticism of humanism. *In Defense of Secular Humanism* is an effort, however modest, to provide a reasoned response, to offer a philosophical, scientific, and ethical view that is relevant to the human condition today.

*PART ONE*
# Responding to the Critics

# Defending Humanism Against Its Fundamentalist Critics

ecular humanists are no doubt surprised to hear from the fundamentalists about their alleged influence in American society and the world.
Tim LaHaye in *The Battle for the Mind,*[1] for example, maintains that
"most of the evils in the world today can be traced to humanism, which has
taken over our government, the United Nations, education, television, and
most of the influential things of life." According to him, "humanism is not
only the world's greatest evil but until recently the most deceptive of all
religious philosophies."

Who is Tim LaHaye? A Baptist minister, founder of the Creationist
Institute in San Diego, and one of the leaders of the Moral Majority. Chairman of what is called the Conservative Council, which includes fifty of the
leading conservatives in the United States, LaHaye is a man of considerable
influence. He claims that the humanists control America and that there is an
interlocking network that includes the American Civil Liberties Union, the
American Humanist Association, National Education Association, SIECUS
(Sex Information and Education Council of the United States), the unions,
the universities, the "porno magazines," the textbooks, the foundations,
and so on. He asks: "America is supposed to be a free country, but are we
really free? We are not free to turn on television and find an unshackled
anti-moral pro-humanist thinking. For humanists literally control the TV networks." (The fact, of course, is that the fundamentalists' influence in religious
broadcasting far outweighs the humanist point of view in America.) LaHaye
continues: "We are not free to send our children to school where they are safe
from violence, drugs, and anti-American teachers. . . . In fact, to provide
our young with the high caliber education that includes an emphasis on
basics and character building, we must pay tuition to send them to a Christian school or to other private schools, while paying taxes to subsidize the
religion of humanism in our public schools."

LaHaye's book is something of a best seller in religious publishing and
has been widely read. There has been a spate of such books, all arguing a
similar theme. For example, *Secular Humanism: The Most Dangerous Religion in America* by Homer Duncan has a preface by Senator Jesse Helms,

---

This article is based on an address delivered to the Fellowship of Religious Humanists, Oct.
1981, and was published in *Religious Humanism* (1982).

who comments: "When the US Supreme Court prohibited children from participating in voluntary prayers in public schools the conclusion is inescapable. That the Supreme Court not only violated the right of free exercise of religion for all Americans, it also established a national religion in the United States, the religion of Secular Humanism." According to Duncan and Helms, "The only way to save America is to root out the humanist from all walks of life."

Humanism has thus become the scapegoat of the fundamentalist right. Practically every newspaper carries letters to the editor and column after column repeating the same litany of charges. Fundamentalist critics have attacked the primary humanist organizations, which are very few in number: the American Ethical Union, the American Humanist Association, the Fellowship of Religious Humanists. And they attack the documents that they consider to be the most wicked of the twentieth century, *Humanist Manifestos I* and *II*. They also indict "atheism," "liberalism," "libertarianism"—all as part of the humanist philosophy. But they are not simply attacking secular humanism, they are assaulting the free society. Claiming that secular humanists dominate the establishment, they are thus attacking virtually all of the institutions of the United States. There is also an intensified effort under way to censor books in libraries and schools in the fields of literature, the arts, and the sciences. Attacking the teaching of evolution in the schools, they are demanding equal time for creationism. Two states have passed a bill mandating equal time,[2] and other states are considering it. The fundamentalists also attack sex education in schools, for which they blame humanists; they accuse humanist educators of undermining the morality of the young; and they are critical of programs in values clarification and moral education. They insist that schools should not teach morality, which is appropriate for only the church or the family.

Fundamentalists have introduced a curious legal argument to demonstrate that secular humanism has been established as the religion of the United States. The most important article in this regard is by Whitehead and Conlan.[3] In a lengthy article of sixty-six pages they offer a line of argument that has been taken up now by the disciples of fundamentalism: Since the Supreme Court has said that America must be neutral in regard to religion, neutrality implies humanism; therefore, humanism is the dominant religion throughout American institutions as well as in the public schools! The fundamentalist right is *radical,* for it is attempting to change the political, social, and moral structure of American democracy. Tim LaHaye says, "The battle for the mind is the great battle of our century, for the rest of the century, and the task is to root out secular humanism and provide a true American morality which is basically Judaic and Christian in character."

What should be the humanist response to this massive assault? First, we must recognize that we are being subjected to a new kind of McCarthyism. In the fifties Senator McCarthy attacked fellow travelers and Communists; in the seventies and eighties secular humanists have become similar scapegoats—and guilt by association is being used to defame characters and organizations.

Nevertheless, I think that some of the criticisms made by the Moral Majority have some validity. We cannot simply reject the Moral Majority and say that nothing they claim is meaningful. Although much of what they say is basically mistaken, it seems to me that they are concerned about many things that we should be concerned about: for example, the breakdown of the family in American life. Many humanists consider the family an important human institution. The stability of the family and the bringing up of children in a wholesome family environment is preferable to divorce and separation, but the latter should be a question of choice. The Moral Majority is also concerned about excessive promiscuity, pornography, and the increased use of drugs—as we are too. Humanists believe in freedom, not license or licentiousness. Freedom of choice need not—indeed should not—imply that. Although many of us deplore the Moral Majority, we also need to deplore some of the recent excesses in American life. Or again, the Moral Majority is concerned about the heavy tax burden. This concern is shared by many humanists who as taxpayers are troubled about the growth of government spending and "bracket creep." The Moral Majority is also troubled about the decline in American power in various parts of the world. I know that some humanists disagree on that point, but other humanists—such as myself—are equally concerned about the decline of Western democracy on the world scene and want to restore the American position as a bulwark against totalitarianism. Many humanists who were formerly liberals have become "neoconservatives" or "neoliberals," and many also reject certain aspects of the liberal program as the "ritualistic" application of methods, such as forced busing or the use of quotas to redress inequities of the past, calling them counterproductive and unworkable.

Basically, humanists believe in freedom and pluralistic democracy as virtually our first principle, and we are disturbed by any authoritarian effort to impose one point of view on America. Defense of the open, democratic society should be the first point humanists make in response to the Moral Majority, making it clear that in our reading of the American tradition pluralism is essential. We too are American citizens, nourished like other citizens by the same traditions that go back to the founding fathers, Paine, Jefferson, Madison, and Franklin, who were, in our view, humanistic, anticlerical, and committed to the ideal of a free society. We have to make it clear that the Moral Majority is really shaking the foundations of the American republic. In a free society, diversity of opinion, whether moral, political, philosophical, scientific, cultural or religious, will flourish, and any effort to oppose it is contrary to our deepest roots. The paradox intrinsic to the fundamentalist right is that, on the one hand, it claims belief in "freedom," but yet, on the other, it is all too ready to legislate morality and belief. Perhaps they are talking only about economic freedom, but what about the other freedoms that apply in America? As humanists we need to make clear our uncompromising commitment to freedom of the individual, free inquiry, free culture, free science, philosophy, religion, and conscience. We oppose any tyranny over the minds of men and women, any narrowing of the right to independence of thought.

Our commitment to the separation principle implicit in the First Amendment to the Constitution—that Congress shall make no law respecting the establishment of a religion or prohibiting the free exercise thereof—is a second response to the fundamentalists. According to the Constitution, the state should be neutral in regard to any religion or no religion, protecting the rights of unbelievers as well as of believers. The fundamentalists fail to see that this country includes not simply a variety of Christian and Jewish sects, but also millions of humanists, Buddhists, Muslims, and unbelievers. Thus the separation of church and state is a necessary principle of American society. The basic fallacy fundamentalists make is to say that, because the state is neutral, it is antireligious or establishes a new secular religion. The state takes no position on religion and neither encourages nor discourages it in the public domain, public schools, the courts, legislatures, or other public institutions. This neutrality does not mean, as fundamentalists seem to think, that therefore the state is imposing the religion of secular humanism.

A third mistake that fundamentalists make is to argue that the schools are dominated by secular humanists, a charge that is totally untrue. While there are at least three million teachers in the United States, there are only ten thousand members of humanist organizations. Surely, they do not dominate the schools. (I will not deny that many humanists are among the leading intellectuals of America.) What the fundamentalists actually are opposed to, it seems to me, is *modernism*. What they really want to do is repeal the modern world, turn the clock back. They are opposed to modern science and the scientific revolution of our day. They are opposed to modern literature—everyone from Shakespeare to writers as diverse as Kurt Vonnegut, D. H. Lawrence, and Vladimir Nabokov. (Tim LaHaye even condemns Shakespeare. He also castigates Aristotle as one of the most dangerous men in history and St. Thomas Aquinas—the influential theologian of the Catholic Church—because he was an Aristotelian! He condemns Michelangelo because of his nude statue of David in Florence, as well as other Renaissance art.) The fundamentalists are attacking modern education, including science, literature, the arts, and philosophy. We must grant that the curriculum of modern education expresses secular values. But that is the nature of the modern world; it is not secular humanism per se that is at the root of all evil, as fundamentalists identify it. Surely Catholics, Protestants, Jews, Muslims, Hindus, Buddhists, Confucians, and others may accept the values of contemporary literature and modern science without thereby implying a commitment to the doctrines of secular humanism.

A fourth response to the Moral Majority and fundamentalists is the recognition of their anti-intellectualism. One of their major assaults is not simply upon humanism but upon the humanities. According to an article in the *New York Times,* several volunteers at a parish hospital in Louisiana surprised the hospital administration by resigning in protest against the hiring of a philosopher from Northwestern State University because he was called "a humanist in residence." Regrettably, they misunderstood the nature of the humanities and the fact that a philosopher, historian, classicist, or literary writer is considered a humanist. So they think that humanists dominate all the universities of America. At the same time, in Maine, the federally funded State Humanities Council was defending itself against an attack on its activities by a conservative weekly tabloid. The charge was made that, in supporting the humanities, the state was supporting humanism. According to the *Times* article, Professor Robert Alley resigned as chairman of the religion department at the University of Richmond at the urging of the administration. He came under fire from a local Baptist committee, which condemned his biblical scholarship as "heretical." President A. Bartlett Giamatti of Yale recently said that the attack on the humanities is a kind of know-nothing attack on learning. It is an attack on the very nature of the university — on the idea that you can investigate values independent of the Bible or be concerned with widening the horizons of human imagination by studying literature, the arts, poetry, and other fields of humanistic study.

A fifth objection to fundamentalists is their attack on moral education. They reject those who believe it possible to be moral without a belief in God. That seems to me to be a vital point, one essential to the position of religious and secular humanism. But more, it is an essential feature of humanistic learning in the Western world. Is it possible to be moral without benefit of clergy? Of course it is. We can lead a noble, significant life of excellence and virtue. The whole Western philosophical tradition, from Protagoras, Socrates, and Aristotle through Spinoza, Kant, and Mill down to the present time, is concerned with the autonomy of ethics. Philosophers have said, and humanists have agreed, that it is possible to ground ethical choice in rational intelligence. The orthodox Christian, Jew, or Muslim believes that ethics must be based on divine sanction, on commandments from on high, and that obedience based upon faith is the only ground for morality. Humanist philosophers and even many Christians and Jews have argued that this need not be the case. One can base morality on rational intelligence, moral growth, and development; human beings can lead lives of significance, worth, and responsibility independent of any theological foundations. Indeed, a great number of humanist heroes have done so. The main point we have to make is that no one group in America can claim to have a monopoly on virtue and that individuals may differ in their moral conceptions. Clearly humanists can lead moral lives, be aware of the needs of others, and make contributions to the common good.

A sixth response to the fundamentalist right is to defend tolerance as a basic humanist virtue. We believe in democracy and freedom, which require toleration of different points of view, as well as criticism of sectarian doctrines that engender hatred or absolutist positions tending to divide people against each other.

Having defended humanism against its fundamentalist critics, what is the positive message of humanism? Can we go beyond a mere defensive posture to a constructive statement? In asking anew what is humanism, I wish to make three points. First, humanism presents an outlook on man and nature; second, it is committed to a method of inquiry; and third, it expresses a set of moral values.

First, the humanist outlook today is based primarily upon modern science and has developed rapidly in the modern world. Even though no humanist conspiracy and few humanist organizations exist, humanism is the dominant theme of the modern intellectual world because it provides a perspective on man and nature that is derived from the natural, biological, and behavioral sciences. It is a picture of a universe at least fifteen billion years old in which human life evolved by natural causal pressures. And science constantly adds to our understanding of nature.

Second, humanism is a method of inquiry, which some might even propose as its "first principle"—a commitment to the use of critical intelligence and rational inquiry in understanding the world and solving problems. The hypothetical-deductive method includes some form of skepticism. The humanist recognizes that he is not infallible, that human knowledge is often difficult to discover, that truth is the product of the give and take of competing points of view and, therefore, one may be mistaken in one's point of view. One must constantly be willing to revise one's beliefs in the light of criticism, even radically. Nonetheless, although some skeptical doubt is essential to the method of science, the humanist still believes that knowledge is possible. Knowledge can be constructive, can grow and develop, though it is often a slow process. The scientist considers all beliefs to be hypotheses, tested by the evidence and judged by their experimental consequences and logical consistency.

Third, humanism expresses an ethical philosophy. The Ethical Cultural movement in the United States has focused on that aspect. The ethical humanist insists that life can have meaning without the conception of a supernatural creator or divine purpose. The humanist theory of the meaning of life is thus an alternative to the classical biblical view. While life has no meaning per se, it does provide us with opportunities to enjoy, discover, and create. The great challenge for the humanist is to lead the good life on his own terms and to take destiny in his own hands. Of the many values that the humanist defends, individual freedom is basic: the right of the individual to make up his own mind, to develop his own conscience, and to lead his own life without undue interference from others. Another humanist value is the commitment to creative growth and development. But the humanist does not believe that "anything goes," as critics have charged. He does not believe that there is no right and wrong. That is an absolute libel against humanist philosophy and ethics. I submit that there are, built within each individual, tendencies toward growth. The great challenge of life is to actualize one's talents and satisfy one's needs, while also developing moral awareness and a sense of moral responsibility to others. Other values that humanists emphasize are those of democracy and shared experiences, which entail the belief that a democratic community and cooperative efforts in negotiating differences are the best means of achieving a peaceful and prosperous community.

One might ask: If humanism is a scientific outlook and method and an ethical posture, what is it *not*? It seems to me that humanism is not, nor should it be, identified with a particular political ideology, a specific platform or program. Many twentieth-century humanists err in believing that humanism is irrelevant unless it takes part in social action. Surely, as individuals we should take part in social action and be concerned with social change, both in our own society and in the world at large; that is our task as citizens. But it is not the be-all and end-all of humanism. The danger is that we risk narrowing humanism by making it equivalent to the left wing of the Democratic party or ritualistic liberalism. One can be a humanist and, politically speaking, be a liberal, conservative, neoconservative, socialist, or capitalist. Honest men and women may differ about whether interest rates ought to be higher or lower, or whether nuclear-energy development is good or evil. We can differ about any number of issues in politics and we should. There is no humanist political party but a variety of humanist points of view. Humanism expresses a basic philosophy, an outlook and attitude, a method, and a set of values—but there is room for a wide diversity of opinion. John Dewey, the most important American humanist of the twentieth century, defined liberalism as a method for solving social problems, a method of inquiry and not a specific platform or program. Accordingly, if one is committed to critical inquiry, one should be willing to change one's politics in the light of new evidence and altered circumstances.

One question often asked is: How can humanists get their message across? Let me suggest some ways. First, we need to stand up courageously and say, "Yes, I am a secular humanist." "Yes," I tell people and they are shocked—a "real humanist!" Or, "Yes, I am a humanist skeptic." Or, "Yes, I am a humanist infidel." Humanism expresses a significant historic tradition, not only in America but also in Western civilization, beginning with the Greeks and Romans and continuing through the Renaissance and the Enlightenment to the present. We ought to defend this tradition forthrightly and not be fudging our position. We ought to defend its secular aspect and its skepticism about theism. Although many humanists are *religious* humanists, we should interpret that term in thoroughly naturalistic terms. Religion means a commitment to values, an expression of human ideals. It does not refer to any godhead but to the heightened qualities of moral and aesthetic experience. In addition, many of us should be prepared to openly criticize fundamentalist, biblical, and theistic claims.

One of the great failures in America in the last twenty or thirty years is the virtual monopoly that biblical preachers have had in expressing their point of view without any major challenges to their premises. Many still consider it in "bad taste" to criticize theistic religion, although this was not always the case. In the late nineteenth century there were a great number of freethinkers in America who made no bones about their free thought: for example, Clarence Darrow, Robert Ingersoll, and Mark Twain. Today a strong kind of ecumenicalism prevails. The official religion of America is CAPREW (Catholic, Protestant, or Jew), and it is immune to basic criticism. Most people are reticent in expressing any opposition to it, with the exception, of course, of Madalyn Murray O'Hair. But she is considered by many to be an extremist who may do more harm than good. Yet we must be willing to enter into debate and critically scrutinize biblical claims. We need to ask openly and publicly whether or not Jesus was raised from the dead; whether or not he even existed; whether or not Mohammed was divinely inspired to write the Koran; whether or not Joseph Smith wrote the Book of Mormon. We ought to be willing to defend skepticism, agnosticism, atheism, and all of the various nontheistic points of view in the free market of ideas. We have to make respectable a critique of the claims that are now pouring over the airwaves, unchallenged day in and day out. The electronic church and its preachers—Pat Robertson, Billy Graham, Jerry Falwell, Oral Roberts, and the rest—should not be granted privileged sanctuaries. We need to provide intellectually responsible criticisms of religious claims. But we have to go beyond that to show that humanism is a constructive alternative. One should not simply be negative. We need to demonstrate the vitality of the humanistic message and the validity of its morality.

The practical question can be asked: How do we go about building humanism? We have a vital role to play in America in the future. One direction we might take is to try to influence the opinion-makers, authors, teachers, professionals, and scientists. Tim LaHaye and our fundamentalist critics think we have done that. They affirm that, in the great battle for the mind, we have had an inordinately large influence. I don't think our influence has been extensive enough, but, whatever our role has been in the past, we have to continue to exert it in the media. Another direction for our concern is the vital need to develop humanist leadership. We have a pressing need to interest, train, educate, and inspire a new generation of young people who will become humanist leaders and build humanist institutions. It is not enough to express our ideas and leave it at that. Every generation has to be prepared to wage the same battle for free thought and a free society. That task is unending. If humanism is to prevail in the future, we need to build strong institutions, societies, schools, fellowships, and chapters. We need to begin the hard work of recruiting young people as potential humanist leaders, ones who will understand the nature of humanism and are willing to espouse its message. More importantly, we need to bring up our own children in the humanist tradition. Moral education is still the frontier for humanism. The fundamentalists recognize this fact and are attacking it. They are criticizing programs of values clarification and moral development in the schools such as those advocated by Lawrence Kohlberg; it would be unfortunate if they succeed in weeding these out, for all education is, in a sense, moral. You cannot educate without being concerned with developing character. For those who do not have a religious background or a religious tradition, it is not enough simply to permit individuals to be free. Freedom means nothing unless, at the same time, one cultivates a sense of responsibility and an awareness of the need for others. The development of responsibility should be the task of education, and we ought to be willing to defend its inclusion in the schools. But what should be taught is not necessarily moral education or indoctrination in humanism, but rather the teaching of the common moral decencies. All human beings need to appreciate and share in the moral virtues that are the inherited, collective wisdom of the race. I submit that there are moral truths that can be rationally discovered. Indeed, a reflective and developed moral being comes to appreciate their authenticity. Moral education is vital if we are going to deal with the breakdown of values that sometimes occurs in modern society. The great task of education is neither the simple indoctrination nor the imposition of our point of view on others, but the provision of inspiration and guidance to encourage the development of new levels of moral growth.

Let me conclude with some philosophical reflections about the Moral Majority and the fundamentalist right. In studying American thought we find that at least two cultures have existed side by side throughout our history: the "conservative" and the "liberal" streams. I use these terms with some trepidation, for their meanings are often confused by the ebb and flow of opinion and fashion from colonial days to the present. At one time the liberal stream was the stronger—let us call it the party of freedom. But then the conservative stream dominated—the party of stability and order. Is what we are witnessing now typical of what has happened throughout the entire history of American society? Many humanists and liberals are frightened by the Moral Majority and the fundamental revivalists. One may ask: Is the Moral Majority merely a temporary conservative reaction? Will it in turn be overwhelmed by a liberal tide, or will it become a dangerous, permanent, political presence that will basically alter the character of America and limit the parameters of freedom?

There are no guarantees in history. No one can say with certainty what will happen tomorrow, next year, or during the next decade. We cannot remain complacent, thinking that these latest challenges to freedom will dissipate easily. The fundamentalists have learned how to blend politics and religion. This combination is ominous. Witness what has happened in Iran with the mixing of fanatic fundamentalism and political power or in Northern Ireland, where there is continuing fratricidal warfare. Still, we must remember that there are various kinds of conservatives. Some are as opposed to repressive fundamentalism as we are—Senator Goldwater, for example, has differed strongly with the Moral Majority. In any case, the attempt to use the state to impose a religious and moral doctrine is very disturbing. The fundamentalists may succeed in their efforts, though I seriously doubt it.

One dangerous development, however, is that they have learned how to control the electronic media. Perhaps a good part of the current religious revival can be attributed to that. It would not be so prominent were it not for the fact that the fundamentalists can bring their propaganda right into the living room by means of radio and television. Further, they have developed effective fund-raising techniques, which enable them to acquire enorous sums of money to get their point of view across to the public and help elect or defeat politicians. The fundamentalist right is thus potentially dangerous. Nonetheless, I predict that they will not prevail and are only a passing phenomenon. If we take a broader view, there is some room for optimism. If we examine carefully what they are saying, we find that it is the biblical outlook and ethic of an agricultural and nomadic civilization hardly appropriate to postmodern civilizations. To insist that *all* truths are in the Bible is pure nonsense and a throwback to an earlier age. We live in a highly sophisticated, technologically oriented, space-age society. To think that the primitive doctrine of an ancient tribe of people in the Middle East can be applied in every case to our present problems stretches credulity. I don't see how such a view can, in the long run, prevail. Why? Because technological change is bound to continue. The scientific revolution is the deepest revolution of our time and has transformed the face of the globe. It has broken down frontiers. It has enabled worldwide communication. It has stimulated mobility. The breakdowns in modern society, if there have been breakdowns, have been due primarily to technology, not to secular humanism. This technological revolution will continue. Even the fundamentalists recognize that and wish to use it.

As Americans we need to ask: How would fundamentalism serve the ideals of freedom and democracy on the world scene? What kind of viable message does it provide, as America competes for influence and seeks to defend freedom throughout the world? Even more central is the recognition that absolutistic fundamentalism is alien to an essential aspect of the American heritage. There is a generosity in the American spirit. Whether liberal or conservative, no matter what the point of view, Americans have been basically open and tolerant. If sufficiently threatened, one hopes, the democratic temper will prevail and be defended by the mainstream. All of this suggests that fundamentalism may be a temporary aberration, the last whimper of a dissident though vociferous minority. Inasmuch as more than half of young Americans now go on to colleges and universities, the values of education, high culture, and free inquiry will continue. No doubt, I will be accused of naive optimism. I have not forgotten that vigilance is the price of liberty. Still, the deepest stream of American and human history points in a humanist direction, which means, at the very least, the continued dominance of the scientific outlook and humanist values, goals that the humanist movement cherishes and should continue to espouse and work to attain. Time, I submit, is on the side of humanism.

## NOTES

1. Tim LaHaye, *The Battle for the Mind* (Old Tappan, N.J.: Fleming H. Revell Co., 1980).
2. Federal Judge William Overton has since struck down the law in Arkansas.
3. John H. Whitehead and John Conlan, "The Establishment of the Religion of Secular Humanism and Its First Amendment Implications," *Texas Tech Law Review,* vol. 10, no. 1 (Winter 1978).

# A Secular Humanist Declaration

*Introduction*

Secular humanism is a vital force in the contemporary world. It is now under unwarranted and intemperate attack from various quarters. This declaration defends only that form of secular humanism which is explicitly committed to democracy. It is opposed to all varieties of belief that seek supernatural sanction for their values or espouse rule by dictatorship.

Democratic secular humanism has been a powerful force in world culture. Its ideals can be traced to the philosophers, scientists, and poets of classical Greece and Rome, to ancient Chinese Confucian society, to the Carvaka movement of India, and to other distinguished intellectual and moral traditions. Secularism and humanism were eclipsed in Europe during the Dark Ages, when religious piety eroded humankind's confidence in its own powers to solve human problems. They reappeared in force during the Renaissance with the reassertion of secular and humanist values in literature and the arts, again in the sixteenth and seventeenth centuries with the development of modern science and a naturalistic view of the universe, and their influence can be found in the eighteenth century in the Age of Reason and the Enlightenment. Democratic secular humanism has creatively flowered in modern times with the growth of freedom and democracy.

Countless millions of thoughtful persons have espoused secular humanist ideals, have lived significant lives, and have contributed to the building of a more humane and democratic world. The modern secular humanist outlook has led to the application of science and technology to the improvement of the human condition. This has had a positive effect on reducing poverty, suffering, and disease in various parts of the world, in extending longevity, on improving transportation and communication, and in making the good life possible for more and more people. It has led to the emancipation of hundreds of millions of people from the exercise of blind faith and fears of superstition and has contributed to their education and the enrichment of their lives. Secular humanism has provided an impetus for humans to solve their problems with intelligence and perseverance, to conquer geographic

---

The Declaration was published in *Free Inquiry,* Winter 1980.

and social frontiers, and to extend the range of human exploration and adventure.

Regrettably, we are today faced with a variety of antisecularist trends: the reappearance of dogmatic authoritarian religions; fundamentalist, literalist, and doctrinaire Christianity; a rapidly growing and uncompromising Muslim clericalism in the Middle East and Asia; the reassertion of orthodox authority by the Roman Catholic papal hierarchy; nationalistic religious Judaism; and the reversion to obscurantist religions in Asia. New cults of unreason as well as bizarre paranormal and occult beliefs, such as belief in astrology, reincarnation, and the mysterious power of alleged psychics, are growing in many Western societies. These disturbing developments follow in the wake of the emergence in the earlier part of the twentieth century of intolerant messianic and totalitarian quasi-religious movements, such as fascism and communism. These religious activists not only are responsible for much of the terror and violence in the world today but stand in the way of solutions to the world's most serious problems.

Paradoxically, some of the critics of secular humanism maintain that it is a dangerous philosophy. Some assert that it is "morally corrupting" because it is committed to individual freedom, others that it condones "injustice" because it defends democratic due process. We who support democratic secular humanism deny such charges, which are based upon misunderstanding and misinterpretation, and we seek to outline a set of principles that most of us share. Secular humanism is not a dogma or a creed. There are wide differences of opinion among secular humanists on many issues. Nevertheless, there is a loose consensus with respect to several propositions. We are apprehensive that modern civilization is threatened by forces antithetical to reason, democracy, and freedom. Many religious believers will no doubt share with us a belief in many secular humanist and democratic values, and we welcome their joining with us in the defense of these ideals.

1. *Free Inquiry.* The first principle of democratic secular humanism is its commitment to free inquiry. We oppose any tyranny over the mind of man, any efforts by ecclesiastical, political, ideological, or social institutions to shackle free thought. In the past, such tyrannies have been directed by churches and states attempting to enforce the edicts of religious bigots. In the long struggle in the history of ideas, established institutions, both public and private, have attempted to censor inquiry, to impose orthodoxy on beliefs and values, and to excommunicate heretics and extirpate unbelievers. Today, the struggle for free inquiry has assumed new forms. Sectarian ideologies have become the new theologies that use political parties and governments in their mission to crush dissident opinion.

Free inquiry entails recognition of civil liberties as integral to its pursuit, that is, a free press, freedom of communication, the right to organize opposition parties and to join voluntary associations, and freedom to cultivate and publish the fruits of scientific, philosophical, artistic, literary, moral, and religious freedom. Free inquiry requires that we tolerate diversity of opinion and that we respect the right of individuals to express their beliefs, however unpopular they may be, without social or legal prohibition or fear of sanctions. Though we may tolerate contrasting points of view, this does not mean that they are immune to critical scrutiny. The guiding premise of those who believe in free inquiry is that truth is more likely to be discovered if the opportunity exists for the free exchange of opposing opinions; the process of interchange is frequently as important as the result. This applies not only to science and everyday life but also to politics, economics, morality, and religion.

2. *Separation of Church and State.* Because of their commitment to freedom, secular humanists believe in the principle of the separation of church and state. The lessons of history are clear: wherever one religion or ideology is established and given a dominant position in the state, minority opinions are in jeopardy. A pluralistic, open, and democratic society allows all points of view to be heard. Any effort to impose an exclusive conception of truth, piety, virtue, or justice upon the whole of society is a violation of free inquiry. Clerical authorities should not be permitted to legislate their own parochial views—whether moral, philosophic, political, educational, or social—for the rest of society.

Nor should tax revenues be exacted for the benefit or support of sectarian religious institutions. Individuals and voluntary associations should be free to accept or not to accept any belief and to support these convictions with whatever resources they may have, without being compelled by taxation to contribute to those religious faiths with which they do not agree. Similarly, church properties should share in the burden of public revenues and should not be exempt from taxation. Compulsory religious oaths and prayers in public institutions (political or educational) are also a violation of the separation principle.

Today, nontheistic as well as theistic religions compete for attention. Regrettably, in communist countries, the power of the state is being used to impose an ideological doctrine on the society, without tolerating the expression of dissenting or heretical views. Here we see a modern secular version of the violation of the separation principle.

3. *The Ideal of Freedom.* There are many forms of totalitarianism in the modern world—secular and nonsecular—all of which we vigorously oppose. As democratic secularists, we consistently defend the ideal of freedom, not only freedom of conscience and belief from those ecclesiastical, political, and economic interests that seek to repress them, but genuine political liberty, democratic decision-making based upon majority rule, and respect for minority rights and the rule of law. We stand not only for freedom

from religious control but for freedom from jingoistic government control as well. We are for the defense of basic human rights, including the right to protect life, liberty, and the pursuit of happiness. In our view, a free society should also encourage some measure of economic freedom, subject only to such restrictions as are necessary in the public interest. This means that individuals and groups should be able to compete in the marketplace, organize free trade unions, and carry on their occupations and careers without undue interference by centralized political control. The right to private property is a human right without which other rights are nugatory. Where it is necessary to limit any of these rights in a democracy, the limitation should be justified in terms of its consequences in strengthening the entire structure of human rights.

4. *Ethics Based on Critical Intelligence.* The moral views of secular humanism have been subjected to criticism by religious fundamentalist theists. The secular humanist recognizes the central role of morality in human life. Indeed, ethics was developed as a branch of human knowledge long before religionists proclaimed their moral systems based upon divine authority. The field of ethics has had a distinguished list of thinkers contributing to its development: from Socrates, Democritus, Aristotle, Epicurus, and Epictetus, to Spinoza, Erasmus, Hume, Voltaire, Kant, Bentham, Mill, G. E. Moore, Bertrand Russell, John Dewey, and others. There is an influential philosophical tradition that maintains that ethics is an autonomous field of inquiry, that ethical judgments can be formulated independently of revealed religion, and that human beings can cultivate practical reason and wisdom and, by its application, achieve lives of virtue and excellence. Moreover, philosophers have emphasized the need to cultivate an appreciation for the requirements of social justice and for an individual's obligations and responsibilities toward others. Thus secularists deny that morality needs to be deduced from religious belief or that those who do not espouse a religious doctrine are immoral.

For secular humanists, ethical conduct is, or should be judged by critical reason; their goal is to develop autonomous and responsible individuals, capable of making their own choices in life based upon an understanding of human behavior. Morality that is not God-based need not be antisocial, subjective, or promiscuous, nor need it lead to the breakdown of moral standards. Although we believe in tolerating diverse life styles and social manners, we do not think they are immune to criticism. Nor do we believe that any one church should impose its views of moral virtue and sin, sexual conduct, marriage, divorce, birth control, or abortion, or legislate them for the rest of society.

As secular humanists we believe in the central importance of the value of human happiness here and now. We are opposed to absolutist morality, yet we maintain that objective standards emerge, and ethical values and principles may be discovered, in the course of ethical deliberation.

Secular humanist ethics maintains that it is possible for human beings to lead meaningful and wholesome lives for themselves and in service to their fellow human beings without the need of religious commandments or the benefit of clergy. There have been any number of distinguished secularists and humanists who have demonstrated moral principles in their personal lives and works: Protagoras, Lucretius, Epicurus, Spinoza, Hume, Thomas Paine, Diderot, Mark Twain, George Eliot, John Stuart Mill, Ernest Renan, Charles Darwin, Thomas Edison, Clarence Darrow, Robert Ingersoll, Gilbert Murray, Albert Schweitzer, Albert Einstein, Max Born, Margaret Sanger, and Bertrand Russell, among others.

5. *Moral Education.* We believe that moral development should be cultivated in children and young adults. We do not believe that any particular sect can claim important values as their exclusive property; hence it is the duty of public education to deal with these values. Accordingly, we support moral education in the schools that is designed to develop an appreciation for moral virtues, intelligence, and the building of character. We wish to encourage wherever possible the growth of moral awareness and the capacity for free choice and an understanding of the consequences thereof. We do not think it is moral to baptize infants, to confirm adolescents, or to impose a religious creed on young people before they are able to consent. Although children should learn about the history of religious moral practices, these young minds should not be indoctrinated in a faith before they are mature enough to evaluate the merits for themselves. It should be noted that secular humanism is not so much a specific morality as it is a method for the explanation and discovery of rational moral principles.

6. *Religious Skepticism.* As secular humanists, we are generally skeptical about supernatural claims. We recognize the importance of religious experience: that experience that redirects and gives meaning to the lives of human beings. We deny, however, that such experiences have anything to do with the supernatural. We are doubtful of traditional views of God and divinity. Symbolic and mythological interpretations of religion often serve as rationalizations for a sophisticated minority, leaving the bulk of mankind to flounder in theological confusion. We consider the universe to be a dynamic scene of natural forces that are most effectively understood by scientific inquiry. We are always open to the discovery of new possibilities and phenomena in nature. However, we find that traditional views of the existence of God either are meaningless, have not yet been demonstrated to be true, or are tyrannically exploitative. Secular humanists may be agnostics, atheists, rationalists, or skeptics, but they find insufficient evidence for the claim that some divine purpose exists for the universe. They reject the idea that God has intervened miraculously in history or revealed himself to a chosen few, or that he can save or redeem sinners. They believe that

men and women are free and are responsible for their own destinies and that they cannot look toward some transcendent Being for salvation. We reject the divinity of Jesus, the divine mission of Moses, Mohammed, and other latter-day prophets and saints of the various sects and denominations. We do not accept as true the literal interpretation of the Old and New Testaments, the Koran, or other allegedly sacred religious documents, however important they may be as literature. Religions are pervasive sociological phenomena, and religious myths have long persisted in human history. In spite of the fact that human beings have found religions to be uplifting and a source of solace, we do not find their theological claims to be true. Religions have made negative as well as positive contributions toward the development of human civilization. Although they have helped to build hospitals and schools and, at their best, have encouraged the spirit of love and charity, many have also caused human suffering by being intolerant of those who did not accept their dogmas or creeds. Some religions have been fanatical and repressive, narrowing human hopes, limiting aspirations, and precipitating religious wars and violence. While religions have no doubt offered comfort to the bereaved and dying by holding forth the promise of an immortal life, they have also aroused morbid fear and dread. We have found no convincing evidence that there is a separable "soul" or that it exists before birth or survives death. We must therefore conclude that the ethical life can be lived without the illusions of immortality or reincarnation. Human beings *can* develop the self-confidence necessary to ameliorate the human condition and to lead meaningful, productive lives.

7. *Reason.* We view with concern the current attack by nonsecularists on reason and science. We are committed to the uses of the rational methods of inquiry, logic, and evidence in developing knowledge and testing claims to truth. Since human beings are prone to err, we are open to the modification of all principles, including those governing inquiry, believing that they may be in need of constant correction. Although not so naive as to believe that reason and science can easily solve all human problems, we nonetheless contend that they can make a major contribution to human knowledge and can be of benefit to humankind. We know of no better substitute for the cultivation of human intelligence.

8. *Science and Technology.* We believe the scientific method, though imperfect, is still the most reliable way of understanding the world. Hence, we look to the natural, biological, social, and behavioral sciences for knowledge of the universe and man's place within it. Modern astronomy and physics have opened up exciting new dimensions of the universe; they have enabled humankind to explore the universe by means of space travel. Biology and the social and behavioral sciences have expanded our understanding of human behavior. We are thus opposed in principle to any

efforts to censor or limit scientific research without an overriding reason to do so.

While we are aware of, and oppose, the abuses of misapplied technology and its possible harmful consequences for the natural ecology of the human environment, we urge resistance to unthinking efforts to limit technological or scientific advances. We appreciate the great benefits that science and technology (especially basic and applied research) can bring to humankind, but we also recognize the need to balance scientific and technological advances with cultural explorations in art, music, and literature.

**9.** *Evolution.* Today the theory of evolution is again under heavy attack by religious fundamentalists. Although the theory of evolution cannot be said to have reached its final formulation, or to be an infallible principle of science, it is nonetheless supported impressively by the findings of many sciences. There may be some significant differences among scientists concerning the mechanics of evolution; yet the evolution of the species is supported so strongly by the weight of evidence that it is difficult to reject it. Accordingly, we deplore the efforts by fundamentalists (especially in the United States) to invade the science classrooms, requiring that creationist theory be taught to students and requiring that it be included in biology textbooks. This is a serious threat both to academic freedom and to the integrity of the educational process. We believe that creationists surely should have the freedom to express their viewpoint in society. Moreover, we do not deny the value of examining theories of creation in educational courses on religion and the history of ideas, but it is a sham to mask an article of religious faith as a scientific truth and to inflict that doctrine on the scientific curriculum. If successful, creationists may seriously undermine the credibility of science itself.

**10.** *Education.* In our view, education should be the essential method of building humane, free, and democratic societies. The aims of education are many: the transmission of knowledge; training for occupations, careers, and democratic citizenship; and the encouragement of moral growth. Among its vital purposes should also be an attempt to develop the capacity for critical intelligence in both the individual and the community. Unfortunately, the schools are today being increasingly replaced by the mass media as the primary institution of public information and education. Although the electronic media provide unparalleled opportunities for extending cultural enrichment and enjoyment, and powerful learning opportunities, there has been a serious misdirection of their purposes. In totalitarian societies, the media serve as the vehicle of propaganda and indoctrination. In democratic societies television, radio, films, and mass publishing too often cater to the lowest common denominator and have become banal wastelands. There is a pressing need to elevate standards of taste and appreciation. Of special concern to secularists is the fact that the media (particularly in the United States) are inordinately dominated by a proreligious bias. The views of preachers, faith healers, and religious hucksters go largely unchallenged, and the secular outlook is not given an opportunity for a fair hearing. We believe that television directors and producers have an obligation to redress the balance and revise their programming.

Indeed, there is a broader task that all those who believe in democratic secular humanist values will recognize, namely, the need to embark upon a long-term program of public education and enlightenment concerning the relevance of the secular outlook to the human condition.

## Conclusion

Democratic secular humanism is too important for human civilization to abandon. Reasonable persons will surely recognize its profound contributions to human welfare. We are nevertheless surrounded by doomsday prophets of disaster, always wishing to turn the clock back — they are anti-science, antifreedom, antihuman. In contrast, the secular humanist outlook is basically melioristic, looking forward with hope rather than backward with despair. We are committed to extending the ideals of reason, freedom, individual and collective opportunity, and democracy throughout the world community. The problems that humankind will face in the future, as in the past, will no doubt be complex and difficult. However, if it is to prevail, it can only do so by enlisting resourcefulness and courage. Secular humanism places trust in human intelligence rather than in divine guidance. Skeptical of theories of redemption, damnation, and reincarnation, secular humanists attempt to approach the human situation in realistic terms: human beings are responsible for their own destinies.

We believe that it is possible to bring about a more humane world, one based upon the methods of reason and the principles of tolerance, compromise, and the negotiation of differences. We recognize the need for intellectual modesty and the willingness to revise beliefs in the light of criticism. Thus consensus is sometimes attainable. While emotions are important, we need not resort to the panaceas of salvation, to escape through illusion, or to some desperate leap toward passion and violence. We deplore the growth of intolerant sectarian creeds that foster hatred. In a world engulfed by obscurantism and irrationalism it is vital that the ideals of the secular city not be lost.

*A Secular Humanist Declaration has been endorsed by the following individuals:*

Although we who endorse this declaration may not agree with all its specific provisions, we nevertheless support its general purposes and direction and believe that it is important that they be enunciated and implemented. We call upon all men and women of good will who agree with us to join in helping to keep alive the commitment to the principles of free inquiry and the secular humanist outlook. We submit that the decline of these values could have ominous implications for the future of civilization on this planet.

*(Institutions are for identification only.)*

*UNITED STATES*
George Abell, *University of California at Los Angeles*
John Anton, *Emory University*
Khoren Arisian, *First Unitarian Society of Minneapolis*
Isaac Asimov, *science fiction author*
Paul Beattie, *All Souls Unitarian Church; president, Fellowship of Religious Humanists*
H. James Birx, *Canisius College*
Brand Blanshard, *Yale University*
Joseph L. Blau, *Columbia University*
Francis Crick, *Nobel Prize Laureate; Salk Institute*
Arthur Danto, *Columbia University*
Albert Ellis, *Institute for Rational-Emotive Therapy*
Roy Fairfield, *Antioch University*
Herbert Feigl, *University of Minnesota*
Joseph Fletcher, *University of Virginia Medical School*
Sidney Hook, *New York University; fellow at Hoover Institution*
George Hourani, *State University of New York at Buffalo*
Walter Kaufmann, *Princeton University (deceased)*
Marvin Kohl, *State University of New York at Fredonia*
Richard Kostelanetz, *writer, artist, critic*
Paul Kurtz, *State University of New York at Buffalo*
Joseph Margolis, *Temple University*
Floyd Matson, *University of Hawaii*
Ernest Nagel, *Columbia University*
Lee Nisbet, *Medaille College*
George Olincy, *lawyer*
Virginia Olincy
Willard Quine, *Harvard University*
Robert Rimmer, *novelist*
Herbert Schapiro, *Freedom from Religion Foundation*
Herbert Schneider, *Claremont College*
B. F. Skinner, *Harvard University*
Gordon Stein, *editor,* American Rationalist
George Tomashevich, *Buffalo State University College*

Valentin Turchin, *Russian dissident; City College, City University of New York*

Sherwin Wine, *Birmingham Temple; founder, Society for Humanistic Judaism*

Marvin Zimmerman, *State University of New York at Buffalo*


*CANADA*
Henry Morgentaler, *physician, Montreal*
Kai Nielsen, *University of Calgary*


*FRANCE*
Yves Galifret, *l'Union Rationaliste*
Jean-Claude Pecker, *College de France, Academie des Sciences*


*GREAT BRITAIN*
Sir A. J. Ayer, *Oxford University*
H. J. Blackham, *former chairman, Social Morality Council and British Humanist Association*
Bernard Crick, *Birkbeck College, London University*
Sir Raymond Firth, *University of London*
James Herrick, *editor,* The Free Thinker
Zhores A. Medvedev, *Russian dissident; Medical Research Council*
Dora Russell (Mrs. Bertrand Russell), *author*
Lord Ritchie-Calder, *president, Rationalist Press Association*
Harry Stopes-Roe, *University of Birmingham; chairman, British Humanist Association*
Nicholas Walter, *editor,* New Humanist
Baroness Barbara Wootton, *Deputy Speaker, House of Lords; University of London*


*INDIA*
A. B. Shah, *president, Indian Secular Society; director, Institute for the Study of Indian Traditions*
V. M. Tarkunde, *Supreme Court Judge; chairman, Indian Radical Humanist Association*


*ISRAEL*
Shulamit Aloni, *lawyer, member of Knesset; head of Citizen's Rights Movement*


*NORWAY*
Alastair Hannay, *University of Trondheim*

*YUGOSLAVIA*
Milovan Djilas, *author, former vice-president of Yugoslavia*
M. Markovic, *Serbian Academy of Sciences & Arts and University of Belgrade*
Sveta Stojanovic, *University of Belgrade*

# The Fallacy of the Undistributed Middle

Right-wing fundamentalists are waging a witch hunt to purge the American public schools of the influence of what they call the "religion of secular humanism," which they maintain violates the First Amendment of the Constitution. The argument used by fundamentalists to prove that secular humanism pervades the classrooms perhaps only demonstrates that they sorely need a course in elementary logic.

They reason as follows: Secular humanists believe in the theory of evolution and see value in courses in moral education and values clarification. Many humanists advocate programs in sex education, courses in the social sciences and comparative culture, and the reading of contemporary novels in literature courses. Therefore those teachers and schools that advocate or teach such courses are teaching "secular humanism."

But this argument is patently fallacious. In logic, it is known as the "fallacy of the undistributed middle." For a syllogism to be valid, the middle term, the term common to both premises, must be *distributed*—that is, it must refer to the entire class it names—at least once. We cannot argue a necessary connection between two classes from knowledge of only part of some third class to which they are related. The fallacious argument is as follows:

> All A are B.
> Some C are B.
> Therefore some C are A.

If all secular humanists (A) favor the teaching of evolution, etc., in the public schools (B) and many teachers favor the teaching of evolution, etc., in the public schools (B), it does not therefore mean that those teachers (C) who favor the teaching of evolution, etc., in the public schools are secular humanists (A) or are teaching secular humanism.

The first premise—that *all* secular humanists believe in the teaching of sex education or moral education in the schools—is not necessarily true, since humanists represent a wide range of opinion. But, even if for the sake

---

This appeared in *Free Inquiry*, Fall 1981.

of argument we granted it to be true, this would *not* mean that those teachers in the public schools who favor the teaching of such courses are secular humanists or that they are teaching secular humanism.

If we argued in this way, then we might reason: Fundamentalists (A) advocate the teaching of the three R's in the schools (B). Many teachers (C) advocate the teaching of the three R's in the schools (B). Therefore many teachers (C) are fundamentalists (A) or teach the "religion of fundamentalism."

The fallacy of the undistributed middle is a form of guilt by association. The fact is that many Protestants, Catholics, and Jews—along with secular humanists—believe in and teach the theory of evolution in biology courses. They see the value of instruction in moral education, values clarification, and sex education, and they are against the censorship of books in school libraries and classrooms. They want to provide our children and teen-agers with an enriched curriculum and an appreciation of modern science, ethics, the social sciences, and literature. These are significant fields of knowledge that can be studied without dependence upon a religious commitment or the lack of it. The fundamentalists would have us turn the clock back, repeal the modern world, and thus denude the curriculum. The chief victims of such an impoverished education would be our young Americans, the hope of the future.

As a secular humanist, I believe that the public schools should introduce courses in logic and reflective thinking. Many teachers also believe that courses in logic should be taught in the public schools. Are we therefore to conclude that those teachers who advocate or teach courses in logic and reflective thinking are indoctrinating the "religion of secular humanism"? That is pure nonsense.

# Is Secular Humanism
# a Positive Alternative?

One thing that has become evident is the need to emphasize new directions for humanism. Although its opponents credit secular humanism with dominating modern society, humanists often consider themselves to be dissenters and iconoclasts, rejecting many of the sacred cows of society. Humanists have long been critical of fundamentalist religious institutions and beliefs, particularly when they are imposed upon society. Humanists have long argued for the freedom to develop conscience outside the context of a theistic world view, the tolerance of diverse life styles, and the separation of church and state. There has been a continuous struggle between a theistic view, in which only God can save mankind, and the naturalistic scientific one, in which humans must seek their own solutions. Radically different moral conceptions have flowed from these different views of the universe. Regretfully in these days of revivalism, all too few in the community, the press, or the media are willing to risk attacking biblical indoctrination.

In recent years, humanists have been especially critical of the claims of the paranormal (astrology, UFOlogy, psychic phenomena) and of the bizarre cults of unreason that have proliferated in our society. Humanists more often than not have been out of step with the reigning political or ideological prejudices of their day—whether expounded by hypocritical apostles of free enterprise, nationalistic chauvinists, or defenders of racist doctrines of superiority. Generally affiliated with the "party of progress," humanists have rejected tyrannies committed in the name of progress and have attacked ritualistic liberalism and totalitarian Marxism as readily as conservative intransigence. Indeed, humanists have been their own best critics: self-righteous humanists may on occasion be as strident or dogmatic as their foes. No one has a corner on truth or virtue.

Sometimes humanists are identified with liberalism or radicalism, especially when they are critics of the social order and are working for reform. Other times they are viewed as conservative apologists for the status quo, as when they defend civil liberties or reject so-called "progressive" solutions that may do more harm than good. The salient point is that humanism is committed to free inquiry. Its first principle is to use reason and critical

---

This article was published in *The Humanist*, Nov./Dec. 1978.

intelligence in testing claims to truth or morality and in modifying beliefs and principles, even the most cherished ones, in the light of their consequences. Humanists are wont to expose the gullibility of others and point out the fallibility of human judgment. They are willing to engage in controversy when they believe it has social merit, for truth is often discovered in the give and take of critical debate.

This sometimes leads friends as well as adversaries of humanism to mistakenly infer that humanism is basically negative. Key questions must be raised: Does secular humanism have a constructive role to play? Can it add significantly to the fund of human good? Will humanism ever supplant the theological or paranormal systems of faith that have no foundation in fact? Can humanism provide "spiritual" sustenance and transcending ideals that can stir conviction and commitment? Does life have genuine meaning, and is it worth living? Does humanism represent a viable alternative for society? Can it present significant options?

The humanist believes that the answers to these questions can be in the *affirmative* and that the humanist moral outlook is *positive*. Humanism emphasizes creative fulfillment as the end of life; it is committed to the shared joys of family life, love, work, and career. The humanist wishes to maximize individual freedom and to create a society in which the widest degree of autonomy of choice is present. Humanists have been sympathetic to libertarianism, insofar as it cultivates the conditions that enable individuals to develop and excel. Humanism is not to be equated with irresponsible hedonism; it expresses a genuine moral concern. It is not self-centered or egoistic, but has consistently encouraged an appreciation for the needs of others. This entails the basic ethical principles of democracy: equality and fairness. Humanists have sought to extend this compassionate concern not only to their relatives and neighbors within the same community, but to the entire community of humankind. The ideal is to consider humanity as a whole.

The critics of humanism vehemently maintain that humanism is unable to provide an adequate justification for moral obligation and responsibility, but humanists deny this. Moral decisions may be tested objectively by reference to their consequences in action. Ethics is autonomous, and any effort to deduce morality from religion or theology loses the distinctive qualities of the moral experience. Historically, in any case, religious believers have not been demonstrably more ethical than nonbelievers.

That is one reason why humanists have argued that moral education be taught in the schools. In promoting moral development, or values clarification, the teacher is not necessarily imposing on students the "religion of secular humanism." We believe both in the separation of church and state and in the neutrality of the schools. Ethical inquiry is as old as Western civilization itself and is a field of learning, like mathematics or history, that should be taught.

Yet the question is raised: Can secular humanism itself—free of any illusions about human destiny—provide sufficient inspiration for individuals, for young people adrift, for those seeking purpose in life, for average people who hunger for a deeper meaning to human experience? This is the issue that secular humanism must confront directly: Can humanism help open doors so that individuals, singly and in cooperation with others, can create lives that are rich in enjoyment, eloquent, and meaningful? Humanism as a general philosophical outlook is surely much broader in influence than institutionalized humanism; yet the ultimate test of a philosophical perspective is its relevance to *praxis,* to the concrete experiences of human beings as they are lived.

I have no easy answers about whether secular humanism—which many of the intellectual leaders of our day believe to be an appropriate alternative—will eventually succeed in fashioning symbols and ideals that can inspire commitment and dedication in the ordinary person. Yet it is a decisive challenge. Whether secular humanism will continue as a force in the civilization of the future will depend on how well it can respond to this need.

## PART TWO
# The Ethical Principles of Humanism

# 5

# Humanism and the Moral Revolution

umanists have been debating for years the proper definition of humanism. It is clear that humanism is not a dogma or creed and that there
are many varieties of, and meanings given to, humanism. Nevertheless, one may suggest at least some characteristics that contemporary
humanists emphasize.

Humanists have confidence in human beings, and they believe that the
only bases for morality are human experience and human needs. Humanists
are opposed to all forms of supernaturalistic and authoritarian religion.
Many humanists believe that scientific intelligence and critical reason can
assist in reconstructing our moral values. Finally, humanism is humanitarian, in that it is concerned with the good life and social justice as moral
ideals.

Humanism as a movement is wide enough to include many people who
will agree with some of the above points, but not all. What characterizes an
increasing number of people is a commitment to a moral point of view in
which humankind is viewed as a whole. Such a characteristic does not make
one a humanist by itself. Yet it is an ideal that most humanists share. Humanists may honestly disagree about their political beliefs and about many
social questions. There is no humanist party line. What humanists today
share in common, however, are a concern for humanity, a belief that moral
values must be removed from the mantle of theological dogma, and a conviction that our moral ideals must be constantly reexamined and revised in
the light of present needs and social demands.

The present epoch is a revolutionary one, involving a radical questioning
of basic foundations, structures, beliefs and values. In the present context
humanism has become especially identified with the moral revolution. It is
this aspect that I wish to focus upon.

There have been many kinds of revolution in human history: political,
economic, social, scientific. The revolution that we are experiencing today
is a moral revolution. Although it has many dimensions, at its roots the
revolution is humanistic. It involves a critique of religious, ideological, and
moralistic philosophies that tend to deny or denigrate the most genuine

This essay is from *The Humanist Alternative,* ed. Paul Kurtz (London: Pemberton Books, 1973).

qualities of human existence. And it is an attempt to recover those human aspects of life that have been lost in postindustrial society.

The overthrow of customary morality has occurred in large part because of an explosive technology that has rapidly transformed our culture. A sharp disparity has emerged between the new technology and our inherited moral codes. The latter were encased in custom, enshrined in sacred tradition and supported by the sanction of law. The moral tradition was taken as absolute—unquestionable and beyond the range of critical inquiry. The strains between the received morality and the demands of modern life were too great; the moral "virtues" were out of touch with the world, and practice deviated widely from professed ideals.

Suddenly, the dam has burst and the old moral mythology is now being lampooned. There is a long-overdue demand for reappraisal and modification. A moral reconstruction is proceeding at an accelerated pace.

There are both negative and positive aspects to the current moral reformation. It involves a devastating critique of the hypocrisy and injustice of the Establishment, but it also involves a creative effort to develop new moral ideals more appropriate to the world in which we live. Several ideals are being proclaimed at the same time. These are often unclear and confused.

The basic assumption of the new morality is the conviction that the good life is achieved when we realize the human potential. This means that we ought to reject all those creeds and dogmas that impede human fulfillment or impose external authoritarian rules upon human beings. The traditional supernaturalistic moral commandments are especially repressive of our human needs. They are immoral insofar as they foster illusions about human destiny and suppress vital inclinations.

The moral revolution rejects those impersonal bureaucratic organizations that smother individuality and restrict human autonomy. The new morality is appreciative of the fact that modern technology has provided great benefits for the good life—that it has helped to eliminate the scourges of disease, hunger, drudgery, and misery. But the new morality is especially critical of the dehumanizing and depersonalizing aspects of technology. It attacks the fact that man increasingly tends to lose his sense of responsibility and his appetite for creativity in the highly complex society in which we now live. Human alienation is accentuated by the banality of a consumer-oriented, manipulative economic system that conditions false desires and needs.

Thus the humanistic revolution seeks to rescue the positive qualities of life experience; it seeks to rediscover joy and love, creativity and growth, shared experiences and fraternity, uniqueness and diversity, achievement and excellence. These are human values that must be cultivated anew if we are to overcome the blind forces that threaten the quality of life. A significant life, which fuses pleasure and creative self-realization, *is* possible, says the humanist, and people can again discover ways of enriching experience, actualizing potentialities and achieving happiness. But if human experience is to flower it is essential that normative principles prevail in our social life.

Thus the new morality believes in moral liberation and freedom. This demand for moral freedom is part and parcel of the libertarian ethic; it has roots deep within the liberal tradition of Locke, Paine, Jefferson, and Mill. Classical liberalism tended to focus primarily on political and civil liberty. It defended the rights of individuals to express their beliefs, choose their representatives in government, and influence public policy.

Implicit in a system of values that places freedom high on the scale of human values, however, should be an equal concern for moral freedom. A just society is one that ought to allow individuals to satisfy their tastes, follow their careers, fulfill their moral and aesthetic visions and guide their own destinies as they see fit, without undue social pressure or governmental restriction.

Moral libertarianism expresses itself in many ways. There is today a more tolerant attitude toward sexual freedom and a demand that laws against abortion, birth control, and voluntary sterilization be repealed. There is a change in public attitudes toward pornography and obscenity, an increased acceptance of nudity on stage and in the cinema — especially where artistic values are involved — and a conviction that society should not impose narrow standards of censorship. There is also a more liberal attitude toward the vagaries of sexuality. Sexual relations between consenting adults should be beyond the range of the law.

Moral libertarianism can be positive in impact, for it suggests that a mature society should be tolerant of the wide diversity in human values and that it should avoid the uniform imposition of narrow puritanical restrictions upon all humans. It is interesting to note that both conservatives and radicals have found a common meeting ground in espousing the ideal of libertarianism.

The libertarian demand may assume ridiculous form. If pushed to extremes, it may lead to a flaunting of all standards of decency and propriety; freedom may degenerate into irresponsible and uncivilized behavior. But moral libertarianism need not degenerate. The principle can play a vital role in emancipating individuals from group oppression and in helping to create a humane society. If used with moderation and balance, the principle allows for the development of a reasonable and responsible approach toward life. A mature person recognizes that he can tolerate divergent life styles without necessarily approving of them. In so doing, the horizons of his own personality may be broadened and enriched.

Another principle that is pivotal in the present-day moral revolution is the demand for equal rights, the search for community. It is clear that an individual's freedom can be seriously impaired if he is denied equal treatment by society. Many minority groups have been oppressed and discriminated against, are unable to share in the goods of the affluent society, and have had their freedom of choice and fulfillment impaired. Thus the principle of equality is appealed to in order to help the poor achieve some measure of happiness. It has also been invoked to gain equal treatment for women, students, prisoners, homosexuals, and other groups in society who have been denied equal rights.

The principle of equality is a basic principle of the democratic ethic. Those who appeal to it in a society that professes to be democratic, yet often is not, indict the disparity between democratic ideals and actual deeds. No individual can be free if he is denied certain elementary human rights. An unjust society is one in which obstacles are placed in the path of human realization. When this condition exists, the only recourse may be social reform.

A paradox of the moral life is that the equality principle, like the libertarian principle, can be misused. There is often great confusion as to what the principle implies and how it should be interpreted. If it is abused, individual liberty may be destroyed. The principle of equality should not be equated with egalitarianism. It does not maintain that all men are born equal in talent and capacity. Rather it recognizes the existence of biological and cultural inequalities and it admits differences in individual ability. The principle is not descriptive of what men are, but prescriptive and normative of how they should be treated in the future.

The principle of equality involves at least three ancillary principles: first, that we should grant all human beings equality of consideration and equality of treatment; second, that we grant equality of opportunity by removing all false barriers impeding individual and group advancement; and third, wherever possible, that we satisfy the minimum basic economic and cultural needs of all human beings.

The principle of equality should not necessarily imply a leveling down. It should be sensitive to the plurality of human needs and to the diverse means that may be required for their satisfaction. Nor should the principle mean the destruction of standards of excellence. Thus, for example, while all men and women should have equal opportunity to apply for admittance to a university or college (and, in my judgment, receive free tuition if they so qualify), this does not guarantee their admission if they lack talent, nor does it ensure everyone the "right" to graduate—unless, that is, they demonstrate their competence in performance. The danger of the equalitarian principle is that it will be indiscriminately misapplied by well-meaning moralists, and in the process destroy other meaningful moral principles and values. If properly understood and used, however, the principle can contribute immeasurably to the humanization of life and the development of a genuine community based on trust and cooperation.

Another important principle that has a powerful appeal today is participatory democracy. According to this principle, individuals ought to have some decision over their lives, that is, power ought to be extended to those who are affected by it. "Power to the people" is a slogan that has usually been applied to political democracy; it has meant that governments ought not to govern without the consent of the governed. The moral revolution has now extended the democratic ethic and the ideal of participation to other institutions in society: to the school, church, economy, voluntary associations, and organizations of all kinds. It claims that we need to democratize our institutions, to make them amenable and responsive to the views of those within them. Participatory democracy has thus become a new frontier for social reform.

The principle of participatory democracy was perhaps the most significant contribution of the Port Huron Statement (1962) of the Students for a Democratic Society, which, at its inception, was full of humanistic idealism. Unfortunately, moral ideals often degenerate into mere rhetorical slogans; and participatory democracy has suffered this fate. The demand for participation needs to be balanced against the need to maintain standards of excellence. Democracy should not be construed as preventing those who have talent and competence from exercising leadership. To say this does not commit one to an antidemocratic "elitist" position. How participation works out—in the university, the hospital, the corporation—must be determined in each separate institution, in its own way, so as not to destroy the ability of the institution to function.

Participatory democracy, like liberty and equality, is a vital moral principle. It recognizes that the more a human being can take part in his own institutions, the better will be the quality of his life experience, and the less chance of alienation.

A word of caution: Moral principles when first enunciated may give way to uncritical fervor and passion. There is a tendency for men to be misled or trapped by their moral commitments, to be overwhelmed by fashionable sloganeering. There is always the danger of a new religious romanticism being proclaimed indiscriminately, without reference to the complexities, subtleties, and nuances involved in moral choice. There are many moral principles other than those I have discussed that have claims upon our conscience: peace, cooperation, excellence, achievement, reason, courage, and tolerance are some of them. Any one set of principles must be evaluated and balanced in relationship to other principles and values that we cherish. Principles must be judged by how well they work in practice, how they function in the concrete situations of life experience. In the last analysis, rhetoric must not become a substitute for clarity, nor passion for thought.

Surely we need to reconstruct the moral conceptions we have inherited from a previous age. This reconstruction should be humanistic, that is, it should be predicated upon a concern for individual human beings and their needs. But we must guard our new moral principles to prevent their degeneration into forms of moral mysticism or absolutism.

Compassionate feeling is an essential human good that has a rightful place in human affairs. But it should not be in opposition to reason, rather in unity and harmony with it. A critical morality is one that questions basic assumptions, yet is committed to the use of critical intelligence. Accordingly, moral principles should be treated as hypotheses, tested by how they work out in practice, and judged by their actual consequences. They need to be hammered out on the anvil of reason, not fed by the fires of neoprimitive passion. If so approached, the moral revolution can truly help to create a better life for all men and women.

# 6

# Humanist Manifesto II

*Preface*

I t is forty years since *Humanist Manifesto I* (1933) appeared. Events since then make that earlier statement seem far too optimistic. Nazism has shown the depths of brutality of which humanity is capable. Other totalitarian regimes have suppressed human rights without ending poverty. Science has sometimes brought evil as well as good. Recent decades have shown that inhuman wars can be made in the name of peace. The beginnings of police states, even in democratic societies, widespread government espionage, and other abuses of power by military, political, and industrial elites, and the continuance of unyielding racism, all present a different and difficult social outlook. In various societies, the demands of women and minority groups for equal rights effectively challenge our generation.

As we approach the twenty-first century, however, an affirmative and hopeful vision is needed. Faith, commensurate with advancing knowledge, is also necessary. In the choice between despair and hope, humanists respond in this *Humanist Manifesto II* with a positive declaration for times of uncertainty.

As in 1933, humanists still believe that traditional theism, especially faith in the prayer-hearing God, assumed to love and care for persons, to hear and understand their prayers, and to be able to do something about them, is an unproved and outmoded faith. Salvationism, based on mere affirmation, still appears as harmful, diverting people with false hopes of heaven hereafter. Reasonable minds look to other means for survival.

Those who sign *Humanist Manifesto II* disclaim that they are setting forth a binding credo; their individual views would be stated in widely varying ways. The statement is, however, reaching for vision in a time that needs direction. It is social analysis in an effort at consensus. New statements should be developed to supersede this, but for today it is our conviction that humanism offers an alternative that can serve present-day needs and guide humankind toward the future.

The next century can be and should be the humanistic century. Dramatic scientific, technological, and ever-accelerating social and political changes

The Manifesto was first published in *The Humanist,* Sept./Oct. 1973.

crowd our awareness. We have virtually conquered the planet, explored the moon, overcome the natural limits of travel and communication; we stand at the dawn of a new age, ready to move farther into space and perhaps inhabit other planets. Using technology wisely, we can control our environment, conquer poverty, markedly reduce disease, extend our life span, significantly modify our behavior, alter the course of human evolution and cultural development, unlock vast new powers, and provide humankind with unparalleled opportunity for achieving an abundant and meaningful life.

The future is, however, filled with dangers. In learning to apply the scientific method to nature and human life, we have opened the door to ecological damage, overpopulation, dehumanizing institutions, totalitarian repression, and nuclear and biochemical disaster. Faced with apocalyptic prophesies and doomsday scenarios, many flee in despair from reason and embrace irrational cults and theologies of withdrawal and retreat.

Traditional moral codes and newer irrational cults both fail to meet the pressing needs of today and tomorrow. False "theologies of hope" and messianic ideologies, substituting new dogmas for old, cannot cope with existing world realities. They separate rather than unite peoples.

Humanity, to survive, requires bold and daring measures. We need to extend the uses of scientific method, not renounce them, to fuse reason with compassion in order to build constructive social and moral values. Confronted by many possible futures, we must decide which to pursue. The ultimate goal should be the fulfillment of the potential for growth in each human personality—not for the favored few, but for all of humankind. Only a shared world and global measures will suffice.

A humanist outlook will tap the creativity of each human being and provide the vision and courage for us to work together. This outlook emphasizes the role human beings can play in their own spheres of action. The decades ahead call for dedicated, clear-minded men and women able to marshal the will, intelligence, and cooperative skills for shaping a desirable future. Humanism can provide the purpose and inspiration that so many seek; it can give personal meaning and significance to human life.

Many kinds of humanism exist in the contemporary world. The varieties and emphases of naturalistic humanism include "scientific," "ethical," "democratic," "religious," and "Marxist" humanism. Free thought, atheism, agnosticism, skepticism, deism, rationalism, ethical culture, and liberal religion all claim to be heir to the humanist tradition. Humanism traces its roots from ancient China, classical Greece and Rome, through the Renaissance and the Enlightenment, to the scientific revolution of the modern world. But views that merely reject theism are not equivalent to humanism. They lack commitment to the positive belief in the possibilities of human progress and to the values central to it. Many within religious groups, believing in the future of humanism, now claim humanist credentials. Humanism is an ethical process through which we all can move, above and beyond the divisive particulars, heroic personalities, dogmatic creeds, and ritual customs of past religions or their mere negation.

We affirm a set of common principles that can serve as a basis for united action—positive principles relevant to the present human condition. They are a design for a secular society on a planetary scale.

For these reasons, we submit this new *Humanist Manifesto* for the future of humankind; for us, it is a vision of hope, a direction for satisfying survival.

## Religion

*First:* In the best sense, religion may inspire dedication to the highest ethical ideals. The cultivation of moral devotion and creative imagination is an expression of genuine "spiritual" experience and aspiration.

We believe, however, that traditional dogmatic or authoritarian religions that place revelation, God, ritual, or creed above human needs and experience do a disservice to the human species. Any account of nature should pass the tests of scientific evidence; in our judgment, the dogmas and myths of traditional religions do not do so. Even at this late date in human history, certain elementary facts based upon the critical use of scientific reason have to be restated. We find insufficient evidence for belief in the existence of a supernatural: it is either meaningless or irrelevant to the question of the survival and fulfillment of the human race. As nontheists, we begin with humans not God, nature not deity. Nature may indeed be broader and deeper than we now know; any new discoveries, however, will but enlarge our knowledge of the natural.

Some humanists believe we should reinterpret traditional religions and reinvest them with meanings appropriate to the current situation. Such redefinitions, however, often perpetuate old dependencies and escapisms; they easily become obscurantist, impeding the free use of the intellect. We need, instead, radically new human purposes and goals.

We appreciate the need to preserve the best ethical teachings in the religious traditions of humankind, many of which we share in common. But we reject those features of traditional religious morality that deny humans a full appreciation of their own potentialities and responsibilities. Traditional religions often offer solace to humans. but, as often, they inhibit humans from helping themselves or experiencing their full potentialities. Such institutions, creeds, and rituals often impede the will to serve others. Too often traditional faiths encourage dependence rather than independence, obedience rather than affirmation, fear rather than courage. More recently they have generated concerned social action, with many signs of relevance appearing in the wake of the "God is dead" theologies. But we can discover no divine purpose or providence for the human species. While there is much that we do not know, humans are responsible for what we are or will become. No deity will save us; we must save ourselves.

*Second:* Promises of immortal salvation or fear of eternal damnation are both illusory and harmful. They distract humans from present concerns, from self-actualization, and from rectifying social injustices. Modern science discredits such historic concepts as the "ghost in the machine" and the "separable soul." Rather, science affirms that the human species is an emergence from natural evolutionary forces. As far as we know, the total personality is a function of the biological organism transacting in a social and cultural context. There is no credible evidence that life survives the death of the body. We continue to exist in our progeny and in the way that our lives have influenced others in our culture.

Traditional religions are surely not the only obstacles to human progress. Other ideologies also impede human advance. Some forms of political doctrine, for instance, function religiously, reflecting the worst features of orthodoxy and authoritarianism, especially when they sacrifice individuals on the altar of utopian promises. Purely economic and political viewpoints, whether capitalist or communist, often function as religious and ideological dogma. Although humans undoubtedly need economic and political goals, they also need creative values by which to live.

## Ethics

*Third:* We affirm that moral values derive their source from human experience. Ethics is *autonomous* and *situational,* needing no theological or ideological sanction. Ethics stems from human need and interest. To deny this distorts the whole basis of life. Human life has meaning because we create and develop our futures. Happiness and the creative realization of human needs and desires, individually and in shared enjoyment, are continuous themes of humanism. We strive for the good life, here and now. The goal is to pursue life's enrichment despite debasing forces of vulgarization, commercialization, bureaucratization, and dehumanization.

*Fourth: Reason and intelligence* are the most effective instruments that humankind possesses. There is no substitute: neither faith nor passion suffices in itself. The controlled use of scientific methods, which have transformed the natural and social sciences since the Renaissance, must be extended further in the solution of human problems. But reason must be tempered by humility, since no group has a monopoly on wisdom or virtue. Nor is there any guarantee that all problems can be solved or all questions answered. Yet critical intelligence, infused by a sense of human caring, is the best method that humanity has for resolving problems. Reason should be balanced with compassion and empathy and the whole person fulfilled. Thus, we are not advocating the use of scientific intelligence independent of or in opposition to emotion, for we believe in the cultivation of feeling and love. As science pushes back the boundary of the known, one's sense of wonder is continually renewed, and art, poetry, and music find their places, along with religion and ethics.

## The Individual

*Fifth: The preciousness and dignity of the individual person* is a central humanist value. Individuals should be encouraged to realize their own creative talents and desires. We reject all religious, ideological, or moral codes that denigrate the individual, suppress freedom, dull intellect, dehumanize personality. We believe in maximum individual autonomy consonant with social responsibility. Although science can account for the causes of behavior, the possibilities of individual *freedom of choice* exist in human life and should be increased.

*Sixth:* In the area of *sexuality,* we believe that intolerant attitudes, often cultivated by orthodox religions and puritanical cultures, unduly repress sexual conduct. The right to birth control, abortion, and divorce should be recognized. While we do not approve of exploitive, denigrating forms of sexual expression, neither do we wish to prohibit, by law or social sanction, sexual behavior between consenting adults. The many varieties of sexual exploration should not in themselves be considered "evil." Without countenancing mindless permissiveness or unbridled promiscuity, a civilized society should be a *tolerant* one. Short of harming others or compelling them to do likewise, individuals should be permitted to express their sexual proclivities and pursue their life styles as they desire. We wish to cultivate the development of a responsible attitude toward sexuality, in which humans are not exploited as sexual objects, and in which intimacy, sensitivity, respect, and honesty in interpersonal relations are encouraged. Moral education for children and adults is an important way of developing awareness and sexual maturity.

## Democratic Society

*Seventh:* To enhance freedom and dignity the individual must experience a full range of *civil liberties* in all societies. This includes freedom of speech and the press, political democracy, the legal right of opposition to governmental policies, fair judicial process, religious liberty, freedom of association, and artistic, scientific, and cultural freedom. It also includes a recognition of an individual's right to die with dignity, euthanasia, and the right to suicide. We oppose the increasing invasion of privacy, by whatever means, in both totalitarian and democratic societies. We would safeguard, extend, and implement the principles of human freedom evolved from the *Magna Carta* to the *Bill of Rights,* the *Rights of Man,* and the *Universal Declaration of Human Rights.*

*Eighth:* We are committed to an open and democratic society. We must extend *participatory democracy* in its true sense to the economy, the school, the family, the workplace, and voluntary associations. Decision making must be decentralized to include widespread involvement of people at all levels—social, political, and economic. All persons should have a voice in developing the values and goals that determine their lives. Institutions should be responsive to expressed desires and needs. The conditions of work, education, devotion, and play should be humanized. Alienating forces should be modified or eradicated and bureaucratic structures should be held to a minimum. People are more important than decalogues, rules, proscriptions, or regulations.

*Ninth: The separation of church and state and the separation of ideology and state are imperatives.* The state should encourage maximum freedom for different moral, political, religious, and social values in society. It should not favor any particular religious bodies through the use of public monies, nor espouse a single ideology and function thereby as an instrument of propaganda or oppression, particularly against dissenters.

*Tenth:* Humane societies should evaluate economic systems not by rhetoric or ideology, but by whether or not they *increase economic well-being* for all individuals and groups, minimize poverty and hardship, increase the sum of human satisfaction, and enhance the quality of life. Hence the door is open to alternative economic systems. We need to democratize the economy and judge it by its responsiveness to human needs, testing results in terms of the common good.

*Eleventh: The principle of moral equality* must be furthered through elimination of all discrimination based upon race, religion, sex, age, or national origin. This means equality of opportunity and recognition of talent and merit. Individuals should be encouraged to contribute to their own betterment. If unable, then society should provide means to satisfy their basic economic, health, and cultural needs, including wherever resources make possible, a minimum guaranteed annual income. We are concerned for the welfare of the aged, the infirm, the disadvantaged, and also for the outcasts—the mentally retarded, abandoned or abused children, the handicapped, prisoners, and addicts—for *all* who are neglected or ignored by society. Practicing humanists should make it their vocation to humanize personal relations.

We believe in the *right to universal education.* Everyone has a right to the cultural opportunity to fulfill his or her unique capacities and talents. The schools should foster satisfying and productive living. They should be open at all levels to any and all; the achievement of excellence should be encouraged. Innovative and experimental forms of education are to be welcomed. The energy and idealism of the young deserve to be appreciated and channeled to constructive purposes.

We deplore racial, religious, ethnic, or class antagonisms. Although we believe in cultural diversity and encourage racial and ethnic pride, we reject separations which promote alienation and set people and groups against each other; we envision an *integrated* community where people have a maximum opportunity for free and voluntary association.

We are *critical of sexism or sexual chauvinism*—male or female. We believe in equal rights for both women and men to fulfill their unique careers and potentialities as they see fit, free of invidious discrimination.

## World Community

*Twelfth:* We deplore the division of humankind on nationalistic grounds. We have reached a turning point in human history where the best option is to *transcend the limits of national sovereignty* and to move toward the building of a world community in which all sectors of the human family can participate. Thus we look to the development of a system of world law and a world order based upon transnational federal government. This would appreciate cultural pluralism and diversity. It would not exclude pride in national origins and accomplishments or the handling of regional problems on a regional basis. Human progress, however, can no longer be achieved by focusing on one section of the world, Western or Eastern, developed or underdeveloped. For the first time in human history, no part of humankind can be isolated from any other. Each person's future is in some way linked to all. We thus reaffirm a commitment to the building of a world community, at the same time recognizing that this commits us to some hard choices.

*Thirteenth:* This world community must *renounce the resort to violence and force* as a method of solving international disputes. We believe in the peaceful adjudication of differences by international courts and by the development of the arts of negotiation and compromise. War is obsolete. So is the use of nuclear, biological, and chemical weapons. It is a planetary imperative to reduce the level of military expenditures and turn these savings to peaceful and people-oriented uses.

*Fourteenth:* The world community must engage in *cooperative planning* concerning the use of rapidly depleting resources. The planet earth must be considered a single *ecosystem*. Ecological damage, resource depletion, and excessive population growth must be checked by international concord. The cultivation and conservation of nature is a moral value; we should perceive ourselves as integral to the sources of our being in nature. We must free our world from needless pollution and waste, responsibly guarding and creating wealth, both natural and human. Exploitation of natural resources, uncurbed by social conscience, must end.

*Fifteenth:* The problems of *economic growth and development* can no longer be resolved by one nation alone; they are worldwide in scope. It is the moral obligation of the developed nations to provide—through an international authority that safeguards human rights—massive technical, agricultural, medical, and economic assistance, including birth-control techniques, to the developing portions of the globe. World poverty must cease. Hence extreme disproportions in wealth, income, and economic growth should be reduced on a worldwide basis.

*Sixteenth: Technology is a vital key* to human progress and development. We deplore any neoromantic efforts to condemn indiscriminately all technology and science or to counsel retreat from its further extension and use for the good of humankind. We would resist any moves to censor basic scientific research on moral, political, or social grounds. Technology must, however, be carefully judged by the consequences of its use; harmful and destructive changes should be avoided. We are particularly disturbed when technology and bureaucracy control, manipulate, or modify human beings without their consent. Technological feasibility does not imply social or cultural desirability.

*Seventeenth:* We must expand communication and transportation across frontiers. Travel restrictions must cease. The world must be open to diverse political, ideological, and moral viewpoints and evolve a worldwide system of television and radio for information and education. We thus call for *full international cooperation* in culture, science, the arts, and technology *across ideological borders*. We must learn to live openly together or we shall perish together.

## Humanity as a Whole

*In closing:* The world cannot wait for a reconciliation of competing political or economic systems to solve its problems. These are the times for men and women of good will to further the building of a peaceful and prosperous world. We urge that parochial loyalties and inflexible moral and religious ideologies be transcended. We urge recognition of the common humanity of all people. We further urge the use of reason and compassion to produce the kind of world we want—a world in which peace, prosperity, freedom, and happiness are widely shared. Let us not abandon that vision in despair or cowardice. We are responsible for what we are or will be. Let us work together for a humane world by means commensurate with humane ends. Destructive ideological differences among communism, capitalism, socialism, conservatism, liberalism, and radicalism should be overcome. Let us call for an end to terror and hatred. We will survive and prosper only in a world of shared humane values. We can initiate new directions for humankind; ancient rivalries can be superseded by broad-based cooperative efforts. The commitment to tolerance, understanding, and peaceful negotiation does not necessitate acquiescence to the status quo nor the damming up of dynamic and revolutionary forces. The true revolution is occurring and can continue in countless nonviolent adjustments. But this entails the willingness to step forward onto new and expanding plateaus. At the present juncture of history, commitment to all humankind is the highest commitment of which we are capable; it transcends the narrow allegiances of church, state, party, class, or race in moving toward a wider vision of human potentiality. What more daring a goal for humankind than for each person to become, in ideal as well as practice, a citizen of a world community. It is a classical vision; we can now give it new vitality. Humanism thus interpreted is a moral force that has time on its side. We believe that humankind has the potential intelligence, good will, and cooperative skill to implement this commitment in the decades ahead.

## NOTE

*Humanist Manifesto II* was endorsed by more than two hundred and seventy-five intellectuals of thought and action, including Lionel Abel, Isaac Asimov, Sir Alred Ayer, Paul Blanshard, Sir Hermann Bondi, Francis Crick, Raymond Firth, Betty Friedan, Maxine Greene, Sidney Hook, Sir Julian Huxley, Margaret Knight, Corliss Lamont, Zhores Medvedev, Jacques Monod, Mary Mothersill, Lord Ritchie-Calder, Andrei D. Sakharov, Roy Wood Sellars, B. F. Skinner, and Bertram D. Wolfe.

# 7

# Libertarianism
## *The Philosophy of Moral Freedom*

W hat is the relationship between liberty and morality? Can one coherently espouse libertarianism, yet deny that it presupposes a moral philosophy? To attempt to so argue, in my judgment, is contradictory; for the defense of liberty assumes a set of underlying values. A problem of definition emerges when we attempt to ascertain the meaning of *libertarianism*. It has been taken as an economic doctrine concerned primarily with preserving economic liberty and the free market against the encroachments of government. It has also been used in political philosophy to defend human or natural rights, civil liberties, and the open democratic society. Economic and political liberty are indeed central to the libertarian philosophy, but they are, I submit, derivative from an even more fundamental libertarian ideal: the high moral value placed upon individual freedom of choice.

The classical liberal is concerned with expanding the autonomy of persons over their own lives. This means that social restraints placed upon individual choice should be reduced. These are many, for large-scale governmental power is a primary threat to individual freedom. Twentieth-century "liberals" under the influence of Marx have abandoned the classic libertarian emphasis on individual freedom in favor of a concern for social welfare. They have sought to extend the paternalistic role of the state in regulating the private sector and fulfilling functions that they believe are not being adequately performed by other social institutions. The welfare liberal believes that it is the duty of society to ameliorate the lot of poor persons and to redistribute wealth—all in the name of a theory of "justice," "fairness," or "equity." Welfare-statist mentality has unleashed a self-righteous egalitarianism that has undermined the incentives of productive citizens in favor of the disadvantaged. The principle of equality in its extreme form has led reformists beyond "equality before the law" and "equality of opportunity" to guaranteeing equality of results. They argue that since not everyone has the same access, social policies must equalize the conditions of opportunity. They would force people to be equal against their will. Libertarians thus have rightly pointed out that doctrines of social equality have been counterproductive, smothering

This essay appeared in *Modern Age,* Spring 1982.

individual initiative and in Marxist cultures leading to the infamous Gulags of the spirit.

The libertarian agenda is incomplete, however, if it is only concerned with the evils of government. For government is not the only social institution that can unduly restrain human freedom. Powerful economic corporations can erode human freedom. They can limit an individual's freedom by defining the conditions of employment, fixing prices, driving out competition, and setting the whole tone of social life. I am not taking the Marxists' side here, for I believe that a capitalist society is the best guarantee of human freedom. Wherever the state has a monopoly of power, both economic and political freedom soon disappear. A free market and a strong private sector are thus necessary conditions for political freedom. One needs vigorous competition and a pluralistic economy, in which there are diverse centers of economic decision-making.

Libertarians abhor governmental control of the media of communication. The libertarian seeks a free market of ideas. Yet he must likewise be apprehensive of the de facto domination of the media by powerful corporate interests. Much of the mass media — television, movies, magazines, and newspapers — have been dominated by one point of view — ritualistic liberalism. If conglomerate control of the publishing industry continues to grow, it may tend to push out small publishers and debase the quality of publishing. Still, Western capitalist societies still allow more freedom than others. Thus I do not agree with Marcuse's pessimistic diagnosis outlined in *One-Dimensional Society*. Nevertheless, not all capitalists are libertarians; nor are they necessarily concerned with preserving and extending individual freedom.

The erosion of freedom can also be seen accompanying the enormous growth in size and power of labor unions. The right to work does not exist in industries where the closed shop operates. Of course, there are sound reasons for collective bargaining; the lone individual working for General Motors is no match for the corporation. By entering into a voluntary association with his fellow workers, his ability to bargain collectively more nearly equalizes his economic position. But where unions seek to deny the right to work to those who are not members, they limit choice. No doubt this has been caused by the big hand of government. But government has been able to legislate the closed shop because of the power of the unions and their members.

What I have been saying seems also to be the case in respect to religious institutions. Powerful churches have often suppressed unbelievers. In this regard, religious institutions may function as oppressively as the state, dictating thought and practice, regulating morality and sexuality, on a de facto if not a de jure basis. I am always surprised to discover that some conservatives will defend economic liberty yet readily condone the suppression of religious dissent. Fortunately, American society has had a proliferation of religious denominations and as a result has developed a truce based on the principles of ecumenism. Given the fact of opposing sects, all should have a place in the sun. In some areas—fundamentalism in the South or Roman Catholicism in the North—freedom of conscience in religion and morality are still suspect. There is hardly room left for the secular humanist, free-thinker, or village atheist in a society dominated by religious tradition. The religious liberal thus defends the separation of church and state and liberty of conscience. Yet conformist pressures seek to impose sanctions on those who violate prevailing religious conventions.

Perhaps the most encouraging development in the past two decades on the freedom agenda has been the growth of moral libertarianism. The moral premise is familiar: individuals should have the right to satisfy their tastes, cultivate their values, develop their life styles as they see fit so long as they do not impose their values on others or prevent them from exercising theirs.

Moral libertarianism, as is apparent, has made considerable progress in democratic societies. There has been a noticeable lessening of censorship in the arts, television, movies, the theater, magazine and book publishing. Liberty of expression has been extended far beyond what was imagined only a generation ago—but it has led to the growth of a pornography industry. In sexual morality, there has been a loosening of traditional restrictions; divorce has been made easier and is now widespread. Laws regulating sexual practices have been repealed, as well as those concerned with adultery, anal-oral sexuality, etc. The belief that two or more consenting adults should have the right to pursue in private their sexual proclivities without social or legal interference is now widely accepted by a significant sector of the community. This has led in part to the "gay liberation" movement. Similar changes have occurred in regard to women, who demand that they be treated as persons capable of choosing their own destinies. Permissive attitudes have also developed concerning drugs. If the state permits alcohol and cigarettes, why not marijuana? Today marijuana is as common in some circles as soft drinks and beer, and, regretfully, so are cocaine and heroin.

In one sense these new freedoms—though they liberate people from stultifying customs—have gone too far. Although one may in principle agree that individuals ought to be allowed to do their own thing, in practice this may lead to a breakdown of civilized conduct, indiscriminate promiscuity, violence, drugs, and a lack of moral virtue and excellence. This is particularly the case with many young people. Many college graduates have betrayed the hope and promise placed in them. They are the products of broken homes and a narcissistic morality gone astray. The rejection of the work ethic is widespread. Living off the generosity of relatives, friends, or social welfare, many have abandoned self-reliance and have become self-indulgent. How can one simply defend moral liberty and ignore the loss of virtue? This question is not simply theoretical, but has high practical import for our society. In mass consumer-oriented society, products are manufactured and sold and tastes conditioned without any regard for their moral worth. The immediacies of enjoyment are taken as ends-in-themselves, divorced from the hard work and effort necessary to achieve them. The quality of life has given way to banality.

This is the indictment of the libertarian society that one hears today. It is no doubt overstated. Nonetheless it has an element of truth. If a choice were to be made between a free society and a repressive one, libertarians would opt for the former over the latter, even though they recognize unfortunate by-products as the price of freedom. Moreover, perhaps the only way for some to learn to appreciate responsible freedom is to experience the consequences of their mistakes. Nevertheless, at times liberty may surely lead to license when it should be accompanied by virtue. Is the breakdown of the moral order due to the excessive moral freedom we have enjoyed? May it be attributed to the decline in religious faith and the growth of secular humanism and libertarianism? Can morality prevail only if it is guided by religion?

I do not think it is evident that religious societies are any more moral than nonreligious ones. It may be true that outward displays of sexual conduct and other "immoral" practices are often prohibited in repressive religious communities. Yet they may be masking a hypocritical double standard. Religious societies may be insensitive to other forms of injustice. They may seek to impose order, hierarchy, and the status quo on those who resist it. But more decisively, a libertarian conception of the moral life which has a secular foundation is different from a religious-theistic one. It is not obedience to a prescribed moral code that is the mark of the moral person but the flowering of the free personality.

The libertarian in ethics maintains as his first principle the autonomy of moral choice. And this means the independence of the ethical judgment: that is, values and principles are not to be deduced a priori from absolute rules, but grow out of moral inquiry. Ethical choice requires a sensitivity to moral dilemmas, a willingness to grapple with conflicts in values and principles, rights and duties, as they are confronted in actual life. Authoritarian and legalistic systems of ethics are not based on final or fixed standards. Many traditional religious systems may seek to indoctrinate a set of norms by fiat. This is supposed to guarantee stability and regularity of conduct and inhibit sinful behavior. A religious code such as is found in the Ten Commandments, the Koran, or the Sermon on the Mount may be supported by the authority of clergy and tradition. It may act as a regulative force, guarding against "defiant," "anomic," or "amoral" behavior. But in what sense are these systems moral? There are traditionalist libertarians in the economic sphere who insist that liberty needs to be supported by religious strictures. And they justify religious-moral repression for channeling conduct along approved lines.

A moral libertarian by way of contrast rejects authoritarianism in the moral domain as much as he does political statism or economic regulation.

Yet he is faced with a profound dilemma. For if individuals were suddenly released from all restrictions—political, social, moral, and traditional—what would ensue? Would they be, as the romantic anarchist hopes, noble, beneficent, sympathetic in their relations to other individuals? Would they be temperate and rational in their inner personal lives? Would their choices be truly autonomous and issue from reflective deliberation?

Regretfully, to emancipate individuals who are unprepared for it from all social restraints may indeed result in license. Autonomous choice is not genuine unless individuals are first nurtured to appreciate and handle it. Perhaps the familiar distinction between two kinds of freedom needs to be restated: freedom from restraint is not the same as the developed freedom of a person to realize his potentialities. But there is still another dimension: the full autonomy of choice can only occur in a developed personality.

Some theists attempt to impose authoritarian structures from without by establishing rules of conduct and instilling them in the young, offering no rhyme or reason other than God's commandments. These homilies often do not take hold, for they do not issue from within a person's felt life. Although they may erect defenses against temptation and immorality, they can often be weakened and may collapse. Basically irrational, they do not serve the individual in a changing social world in which new challenges are constantly being presented to him. If they are overthrown, what can the libertarian offer in their place?

The solution to the problem seems to me to be clear: libertarianism in its full sense—that is, the development of autonomous individuals capable of free choice—is not possible unless certain antecedent conditions are fulfilled: a program of moral education and growth is necessary to instill virtue in the young, not blind obedience to rules but the ability for conscious reflective choice. The Thrasymachian man, the absolute tyrant, as Plato long ago observed, is prey to every lust and passion, every temptation of power and ambition. He is buffeted by random irrational drives within, unable to resist or control them, and amoral power conflicts from without. The truly free individual is one whose choices in some sense emanate from a harmonious personality, one with some developed character, a set of dispositional traits, capable of a deliberate process of reasoned decision-making.

This seems to me to be the message of the great philosophic tradition from Socrates and Aristotle to Spinoza, Mill, and Dewey: that rationality and virtue are the source of freedom. If this is the case, to grant freedom without preparation to a child or adolescent, a savage or despot, incapable of reflective choice or mature judgment, unrestrained by a seasoned disposition, is hardly a test of his freedom, for he may be at the mercy of impulses.

Accordingly, freedom makes no sense and is literally wasted unless it is first nourished in the soil of moral growth, where it can be watered and fed. It is as if democracy were suddenly imposed on a people unready for it, or for which it was alien. It can only function effectively where there are values of tolerance, respect for the views of others, a willingness to negotiate and compromise differences; and a sense of civic virtues and responsibilities. Similarly, true freedom for the individual presupposes the concomitant emergence of moral development. It presumes moral education.

What kind of education and by whom and for what ends? These are important questions. Education is a social process. It goes on constantly — in the family, the churches, the schools, business organizations, the media, in the greater society. It is not the sole responsibility of the state, for that may convert it into a form of mere indoctrination. By education, I mean the Greek form: self-actualization. We need to educate individuals so that they can realize their intellectual, aesthetic, and physical talents. And part of moral education is the developing capacity for self-mastery and control. It also involves the maturation of the ability to appreciate the needs of other human beings. In other words, moral education is training in responsibility: first, toward one's self, one's long-range self-interest in the world, learning how to cope with and solve problems that emerge in the environment; and second, toward others, developing altruistic concern for other human beings, an ability to share life's experiences, to help and be helped, to cooperate with others.

Kohlberg and Piaget have written at length about what they consider to be the stages of moral growth. One need not accept the precise theory as presented: from anticipation of reward and punishment, or conformity to social expectations, as motives of moral behavior, to considerations of utility, or the development of a sense of justice, as higher stages of moral growth. Nevertheless, one should surely recognize that there is a process of moral development. For there is a clear difference between the narcissistically self-centered individual (although some self-interest is an important component of a realistic ethics) and the person able to relate to others under conditions of mutual respect and cooperation. One should be more willing to entrust freedom to the latter person, and may be apprehensive about entrusting it to the former. Mill himself recognized that there is an important distinction between the "lower" and "higher" pleasures; the biological pleasures differ in kind from the aesthetic, intellectual, and moral pleasures of a developing human being. As a libertarian he was disturbed by the possible abuse of the hedonic criterion and insisted that pleasures differ on a qualitative scale.

To argue, as I have, that a philosophy of liberty most appropriately should involve a theory of virtue, does not imply that we should deny freedom to those who are incapable of using it in the fully developed sense. Nor should the government or any self-appointed group set itself up as the arbiter of human freedom. One may consistently believe in a free society, yet also recognize that we have a double obligation: to grant freedom to individuals and also to encourage them to acquire a taste and capacity for growth and autonomy. The best way of doing the latter is not by dictate but by means of education and persuasion. Because we tolerate diversity does not mean that we necessarily approve of every style of life, however bizarre or offensive, that has been adopted. We need constantly to keep alive the art of criticism and moral suasion. Liberty does not imply permissiveness. It needs to be accompanied by an ethic that highlights the virtues of the mature personality. This includes *wisdom* (some capacity for intelligent reflective choice), *prudence and moderation* (some concern for one's long-range good) and *responsibility* (a genuine interest in the needs of others). Without virtue, the person freed from restraint may indeed be transformed into a moral monster.

Philosophers of ethics have consistently maintained that in the last analysis intelligence in an ordered personality is the most reliable guide for moral choice. What we ought to do is a function of a deliberate process wherein we examine alternatives, means and consequences and after a comparative analysis make a choice that we consider to be the most suitable in the situation. One of the tasks of moral education is to develop persons who are capable of engaging in moral inquiry.

This will not do, we are reminded by critics of moral libertarianism, particularly those of a nonsecularist bent. Merely to have an autonomous individual is no guarantee that he will behave morally toward himself or others. We cannot educate men to be virtuous, we are told, without the authority of divine sanction. If the only guide is utilitarian ends, whether for the individual or the social good, then anything is possible and all things may be permissible. The critics of secular humanism and libertarianism also attack the effort now under way to develop moral education and values clarification in the schools. They believe this is a "secular religion" that will only further undermine the moral standards of society.

Now it is true that many or most libertarians have emphasized utilitarian considerations in the decision-making process. Moral principles are held to be largely instrumental in the fulfillment of ends or values. The hedonic calculus judges actions by whether they maximize pleasure or happiness in the individual and society. Most libertarians have been relativists, situationalists, and naturalists. Such ethical theories have lacked a well-grounded theory of moral duty and obligation. In my view, however, this need not be the case. Libertarianism is incomplete as a moral philosophy and remains seriously in need of repair unless it is willing to modify its ethical system so that it can introduce deontological considerations.

What I have in mind here is the recognition that there are general ethical principles that ought to prevail in human relationships. These are grounded in human experience, and have been tested in the crucible of history. Moral principles, in my judgment, are not simply an expression of subjective taste or caprice, but may have some empirical foundation. They are amenable to objective criticism. The human decencies are readily recognized by most human societies. We ought to tell the truth, be sincere, honest, and deal fairly with others; we ought to be cooperative, kind, considerate, thoughtful, helpful; we ought not to waste our patrimony needlessly; we ought not to misuse others, be arrogant and unforgiving; we ought not to inflict pain needlessly or cruelly, not be excessively vindictive; we ought to have friends not simply acquaintances; we ought to seek justice and be beneficent.

This list of ethical principles is embodied in the proverbial truths discovered in human affairs. Many or most — but perhaps not all — are transcultural. They are general guides to conduct, not universal or absolute, since exceptions can be made to them on occasion. Nor are they intuitive or self-evident; if they are tested, it is by their observable consequences in conduct. They have some foundation in our sense of reason; and they may be given some strength in our motivation, and be enhanced by emotion and feeling. They involve both our attitudes and beliefs. They are prima facie, for they would seem to express general rules of conduct, which people come to recognize and respect as binding. How they apply and to what extent depends on the context. Sometimes one or more ethical principles may conflict. They may conflict with our cherished values. Moral deliberation is usually difficult, and often we must choose between the lesser of two evils. Or there may be a clash between two goods or two rights, both of which we cannot have.

These ethical principles embody moral truths. We may learn from practical experience that they cannot be easily violated without unfortunate consequences. They may be certified on their own merits without being derived or deduced from questionable theological or metaphysical assumptions. Human experience lends them authenticity.

Thus one may respond to the critics of moral libertarianism in the following manner:

1. Moral conduct is possible without belief in God, or benefit of religion or clergy. (Believers are not more moral than unbelievers.)

2. Reasonable moral choices can be made and moral knowledge discovered in the process of human living and experience.

3. Accordingly, there can be an intelligent basis for moral obligations and responsibility.

One can be a moral libertarian and a secularist without being a libertine or a degenerate, and one may display the marks of nobility and excellence as part of the good life (as exemplified in the philosophies of Aristotle and Spinoza). In this post-Freudian age one may also live a significant moral life, which contains passion and reason, enjoyment and happiness, creativity and responsibility.

Freedom is not simply a claim to be made against society or a demand to be left alone. Freedom is not to be experienced indiscriminately nor squandered stupidly. It is an art to be cultivated and nourished intelligently. The intemperate person is neither autonomous nor civilized in respect to himself or his relations with others. Liberty and moral development go hand in hand; one can enhance the other. There is no complete freedom until there is the developed capacity for maturity in judgment and action. There can be no fully autonomous person unless there is realized growth.

Various forms of libertarianism can be defended independently of a secular focus. One can be an economic or civil libertarian and at the same time a born-again Christian, Buddhist monk, practicing Jew, devout Hindu, or Roman Catholic. We should not insist that secular libertarianism is the only basis for the moral life. I happen to believe that it is the one most in accord with the realities of nature and the promise of individual attainment. In a pluralistic society, those who wish to believe in God or to base their morality on religious faith should be perfectly free to do so. For many moderns, however, God is dead. But to be committed to the secular city does not mean that morality is dead or without moorings. Ethics is a vital dimension of the human condition, and a recognition of the ethical life has deep roots within Western philosophy, antecedent even to the Judeo-Christian tradition. The current attack on secular morality is a display of ignorance about the origins of Western civilization in Hellenic culture and its historic philosophic development. It is an attack on the philosophical life itself.

The charges against moral libertarianism are thus unfounded. Those who now oppose it cannot tolerate moral freedom nor can they stand to see other individuals suffer or enjoy life as they choose. But who are they to seek to impose their values on others? The fact that they assume a mantle of divine sanction for their views does not make them authoritative. Moreover, they fail to appreciate the fact that a moral person is not one who obeys a moral code out of fear or faith but who is motivated to behave morally out of a sense of moral awareness and conviction. The exemplar for the moral libertarian is the free person, capable of choice, yet one who has achieved some measure of moral growth. He is the master of his own fate, responsible for his own career and destiny.

The free person is unlike the obedient servant or slave, who follows a moral code simply because it is commanded by authority or tradition. The free individual is independent, resourceful, and has confidence in his power to lead the good life. Moreover, he can enter into dignified relationships of trust and sincerity with his fellow human beings. He can live a constructive, productive, and responsible life. The moral philosophy of libertarian humanism is thus worthy of admiration. It needs not apologize to those who seek to demean or denigrate its excellence or virtue. In a sense it is the highest expression of moral virtue: a tribute to the indomitable creative spirit of human achievement and personality.

# 8

# The Principle of Tolerance Reaffirmed

Is the principle of tolerance essential to humanism? Conversely, can one maintain a humanistic philosophy and at the same time deny tolerance? Present-day humanism expresses a humanitarian concern for the social good and social justice. Does this humanitarianism require toleration for the rights of other individuals and groups? Or can our obligation to the social good and justice override our obligation to respect differences among human beings?

In this essay I shall argue that tolerance is a fundamental normative principle of libertarian humanism and that any philosophy that contradicts the principle undermines ethical humanism. "Tolerance," "toleration," and "respect" are terms that all point to the same principle: we ought to respect the rights of other individuals or groups to exist and to express beliefs, attitudes, values, and life styles different from our own. The principle of tolerance does not necessarily mean that we must *approve* of the beliefs, values, or conduct of other individuals or groups, nor does it preclude us from criticizing them or attempting to persuade them to modify their beliefs, values, or conduct. It only says that we should not suppress or deny them their right to their beliefs, values, or conduct, nor should they suppress ours. The principle of tolerance implies some commitment to the democratic ethic and to the view that people ought to be allowed to have some measure of freedom to pursue their own interests as they see fit and that we ought to respect their right to do so. This principle, as stated, is very general, and all sorts of qualifications could be made. I shall not attempt a thorough analysis of its meaning or application. Hence, I will focus on only one aspect of the principle—though it is an essential aspect. I will deal with the principle only as it applies to the toleration of beliefs and values. (There are various forms intolerance may take besides those that refer to opposing ideas and values. Among the most familiar are racial, religious, ethnic, nationalistic, class-oriented, or sexual antagonisms and intolerances.)

I wish to argue that a basic principle of humanism we ought to recognize is the moral right of individuals or groups to advocate beliefs or cherish values divergent from those held by me or my group. I am speaking of beliefs

---

This article was published in *International Humanism*, no. 4 (1982).

and values rather than conduct, and do not argue that we ought to tolerate every kind of action. All societies have a need to regulate conduct and to define permissible action in terms of law. We need not permit behavior that violates the law. However, we should distinguish commitment to a value or expression of belief from the performance of an act.

The liberal tradition has clearly enunciated the principle of tolerance as it applies to beliefs and values. In *A Letter Concerning Toleration,* John Locke attempted to convince Christians that they ought to become more tolerant of other Christians, and he opposed the claims of a well-intentioned government to compel "true religion" by force or to establish one sect as "true" in opposition to others. Similarly, John Stuart Mill in *On Liberty* provided a masterful defense of freedom of belief and moral conviction.

The principle of tolerance, of course, has often come under attack — from Plato and the medieval church to Stalin, Mao, and Senator Joseph McCarthy. History is full of attempts to censor opinions considered false or harmful, to prohibit heresy, and to condemn revisionism or unorthodoxy. A recent criticism of tolerance deserves special comment. Herbert Marcuse and others, in *A Critique of Pure Tolerance,* attacked the principle of pure tolerance and questioned its moral basis and its political and social effect. Marcuse again, in *An Essay on Liberation,* raised serious criticisms about the toleration of civil liberties in so-called bourgeois societies. He argued that in some cases it is permissible to withdraw toleration of others. Capitalist consumer economies, he believed, often fraudulently parade civil liberties, which are really forms of "repressive tolerance," for they are used by the power structure to mask its own self-interest and to prevent social change. Presumably, for Marcuse, the left may be intolerant of those tendencies on the right that it finds to be most reprehensible, such as racism or opposition to social progress.

## The Limits of Freedom

This is not the place to evaluate Marcuse's entire thesis. Many of his observations about capitalist societies are astute. So-called free capitalist economies permit advertisers to manipulate values and to inculcate needs and wants that are not genuine. In satisfying these values, they thus develop in consumers a dependence upon the very economic system that seeks to repress them. Humanists need not defend the unlimited freedom of advertisers to do whatever they wish without regard to the social good. But humanists should defend virtually unlimited intellectual and moral freedom. And it is possible to defend pure tolerance not simply on the usual libertarian grounds by deriving the tolerance principle from an individualistic theory of human nature, but rather in terms of a social conception of man and in consideration of the social good. Toleration is prima facie a fundamental normative principle that we ought not to suspend (except possibly in extreme circumstances where a clear and imminent danger regarding actions is involved).

The principle of tolerance is directly relevant to the present-day socio-historical situation and to various kinds of societies that now exist.

1. In capitalist, feudal, or semifeudal societies humanists ought always to work for the extension of civil liberties and for their defense against those who would limit, restrict, or deny them. The cause of tolerance is the cause of human progress.

2. In socialist societies people ought to insist upon the operation of the principle of tolerance. Any effort to deny it is a fundamental contradiction of Marxist humanism.

3. In a rapidly changing political and social situation where one is attempting to bring into being a new society, it is vital that toleration not be abandoned during the transitional period. To do so implies that it is not important and there is the risk that it might never be reinstituted. Moreover, in permitting social intolerance as a way of life, there is danger that the "new man" or "new society" one may wish to bring into being will be intolerant, narrow, and self-righteous in temper and outlook.

## The Basic Justification

I shall present three basic arguments to justify the principle of tolerance; all are based upon consideration of the social good and human progress.

The first argument is derived from the method of science. First, to be intolerant of other points of view or systems of value implies, as Mill observed, that you or your group have the absolute truth, or that your philosophy has reached its final, ultimate, or most perfect formulation. But, as Charles Peirce has pointed out, most claims to infallibility have been falsified in the history of thought, and each effort to define by authority a fixed position, whether ecclesiastical, political, or ideological, has been overturned by some new discovery or daring hypothesis. No single individual or group can claim a monopoly on truth or virtue. Hence the first rule of science is: Do not block the path to inquiry or research. Always leave open the possibility that you may be mistaken and that there may be other points of view that share in meaning and truth.

In any case, social problems are so complex that we need the highest degree of creativity and imagination from all levels of society. Societies that do not allow adventures in thought and invention most likely will stagnate and not be able to resolve their problems as well as those that do. Hence, it is precisely for the social good that one can argue for an open and tolerant society, as a constant source of originality and insight.

The second argument is psychological. Beliefs that are left unchallenged degenerate into mere dogma, dead and ossified prejudices of thought, rather than vital and moving principles. Toleration of opposing critical viewpoints allows for the modification of those beliefs that are false and for the strengthening of those that are true. To test our beliefs by having them contested by contrary opinion enables us to transform blind allegiance based upon fear into genuine and loyal commitment based upon intelligent participation in the decision-making process.

The third argument for toleration is political. No ruling group or class is all-wise or all-good. There is a tendency for those in power to consider their own point of view, especially if left unquestioned, to be true, and to confuse their own self-interest with the common good. Those societies that tolerate criticism and dissent will tend to have less hypocrisy and duplicity than those that are closed and intolerant.

The point is clear: To the extent to which I am receptive to other points of view, I not only allow other individuals and groups to grow and prosper but also I or my group may have a better opportunity to prosper. In being considerate of alternative viewpoints I am able to share in and learn about other kinds of experience and other visions of truth, beauty, and goodness besides my own.

If the foregoing arguments have any merit, then tolerance ought not to be considered a mere luxury, to be dispensed with or permitted under certain social and political conditions, but it should be an essential ingredient of any dynamic, progressive, and humane society. Yet several objections are advanced against the right of toleration. One familiar pragmatic argument often heard from the class in power is that it cannot permit toleration because of the danger of sedition or revolution. In repressive capitalist societies the most common argument is that censorship and strict control must operate because to sanction civil liberties is to court subversion. And in repressive socialist societies there is the similar argument that toleration will lead to counterrevolution. But one must distinguish belief from action; a society should tolerate the former, though it need not permit certain forms of the latter. In the same way, heresy must be distinguished from conspiracy. A heretic may express a point of view in opposition to the official policy, or he may in all honesty disagree with prevailing opinion. This need not mean that he is a conspirator, plotting the violent overthrow of the regime or the social structure. If a government opposes conspiracy, it should nevertheless permit heresy, tolerate opposing points of view, and appreciate the need for critical inquiry.

Another objection to toleration is that it only has meaning in relation to certain historical traditions of a society, and hence it is not possible in some societies that are intolerant of diversity and whose members are extremely insensitive to any criticisms made of them. Thus in some societies it is often difficult to argue for toleration, for to do so is to go contrary to the national grain and the system of cultural values. Yet in response one may say that if one is going to work for a "better" society as an ideal which must overturn deep national habits, then why not at the same time work for tolerance as a moral principle of society?

A classical Marxist objection to tolerance is that, like all moral principles, it is part of the "superstructure" of a society, a reflection of the underlying forces and relations of production, and hence especially applicable to the level of development of liberal bourgeois societies. I think it is a great mistake and a disservice to argue that all moral principles are simply reflective of the mode of production, or class-related, or even expendable in the revolutionary struggle. There are, in my judgment, certain common humanistic principles that transcend their social origins, or at least ought to be so treated since they have important social functions, irrespective of the social structure. Toleration would be one such moral principle.

A particularly strong objection to tolerance widely heard today comes from fundamentalist religious critics—ranging from the Moral Majority in the United States to the Ayatollah Khomeini in Iran. These critics vehemently argue that excessive tolerance and freedom leads to a permissive society and the breakdown of all moral standards. Thus authoritarians seek to censor what they consider "pornographic" literature and films and to prohibit certain kinds of conduct they consider "morally reprehensible," even if privately expressed by individuals or consenting adults who do not interfere with the rights of others. In response, humanists need to point out that, although one may tolerate other points of view and the right of individuals to express their own tastes and values, this does not necessarily mean that one approves of them. Tolerance does not mean that one accepts or condones all of the varieties of human beliefs and values as equally valid or authentic, nor should they be immune to criticism. Libertarianism does not imply licentiousness or libertinism. For the principle of tolerance to function in a society, however, it is essential that those who believe in it attempt by moral education and persuasion to raise the level of taste and appreciation. It means that at the same time we encourage free choice we should cultivate moral growth and virtue. It means that we should seek to develop intelligent and responsible persons aware of the needs of others and capable of appreciating aesthetic, intellectual, and moral pleasures. It means that we should strive to transcend the vulgarities and banalities of mass society by holding forth the possibilities of cultivation and enrichment—but never at the price of abandoning the principle of tolerance or the importance of individual freedom.

## Long-range Gain

Toleration must not be considered in purely formal terms, however, for some societies may preach toleration but not practice it. If the principle is to have some actuality in society, then in addition to the fact that it must be cherished as a moral rule, certain negative conditions that would interfere with its operation must be absent. For example, if tolerance is to be effective, there should not be centralized economic or political control of all media of communication. In capitalist societies every effort by powerful economic or religious interests to control or monopolize the media must be opposed and de facto monopolies should be broken into smaller units. In socialist societies the ministries of information and education should have some independence from political and ideological control, and the right of opposition to official policies in the mass media and elsewhere should be legally recognized. In effect, there should not be only one point of view available within the community, whether of a dominant economic class, political party, religious or bureaucratic group. Otherwise, to claim that toleration of various points of view exists, when in fact only one is heard, is to mouth empty rhetoric. Last, and most important, reprisals must not be taken against those who express heretical intellectual conceptions or nonconformist moral values—whether in the form of economic sanctions, political intimidation, imprisonment, or worse. Where fear is ever present, honest criticism gives way to fawning flattery and objective evaluation to mere cant.

In spite of all this, some may remain unconvinced and believe that patent falsehood (such as black magic or psychic healing) or extremely wicked moral views (such as belief in genocide or racism) should not be permitted. But should we not respond that for the long-range good of society the dangers of a policy of intolerance are far greater than the expression of divergent beliefs, which may be openly combated? I believe it is far better to suffer expressions of falsehood and evil than to attempt to stamp them out, for the cure may be worse than the disease.

Those societies in which the principle of tolerance truly functions will tend to rely upon argument and persuasion rather than force and compulsion as the chief method of social change. Where toleration prevails there is a far better chance that we may develop a just society in which peace and harmony reign instead of hatred and cruelty. Indeed only where there is mutual trust and toleration can we hope to build a society that is truly cooperative.

# 9

# Humanism
# and the Freedom
# of the Individual

Humanism has had a long, though checkered, career in the history of
philosophy. There have been many varieties of humanism appropriate
to the different ages in which they appeared. Though perhaps humanism's highest brilliance can be seen in the Hellenic civilization of classical
Greece and Rome, in the Renaissance and the Enlightenment, and during
the scientific revolution of modern times. In a very real sense the present
day may be characterized as predominantly humanistic, for humanistic concepts and values thoroughly pervade all aspects of life. A number of diverse
and often contending intellectual and philosophical movements may be said
to be humanistic in character: naturalism, materialism, Marxism, positivism,
analytic philosophy, phenomenology, and existentialism. Moreover, many
philosophers influential in the present age are deeply humanistic: Marx,
Nietzsche, Freud, Mill, Dewey, Bertrand Russell, and Sartre, to mention only
some of the most important.

Humanism has had a remarkable resurgence in recent decades. Its critique of classical religion has been very effective. Humanists have continually attacked the inconsistencies and hypocrisies of orthodox religions. As a
result, large numbers of educated people are today unaffiliated with any
organized religious sect and are humanist in outlook and belief. The "God is
dead" movement within theology demonstrates that humanism has been far
more influential on mainstream religion than had been imagined. Many
theologians now accept humanistic premises: Religion must be regarded
essentially as a form of human experience, an expression of human values;
it is empty if it substitutes a dead God for a living ideal of human justice.

Many humanists today believe that the battle against religious orthodoxy has been won, at least in intellectual terms. Accordingly, it is not enough
to debunk faith and dogma without providing a positive set of ethical ideals
in their place. Many are convinced that we must replace the outworn symbols

This paper was read at the 1968 International Congress of Philosophy, Vienna, and was first
published in *Praxis*.

and cliches of an earlier age of protest with more meaningful principles of action. They insist that humanists must overlook any differences that they have had in the past and emphasize instead their common assumptions. The problem that we now face is to build a humanistic ethics that transcends narrow ideological loyalties.

In a very real sense it is in the present century that humankind has become fully aware of itself. There are no longer any isolated cultural regions. All people are involved in the same world and have a common history and heritage. No philosophic or ideological position can escape comparative analysis or critical scrutiny. We have just shed the shackles of theistic theological illusion. We also need to abandon all secular ideologies that degenerate into new forms of intolerant antihumanism.

## I

Is it possible to find a common ground between various forms of humanism? It should be clear that there is no essence to which the term *humanism* corresponds. Rather, any definition of humanism can only be roughly drawn by reference to certain generic philosophical tendencies that humanists have manifested. Humanists, even though of different philosophical persuasions, nevertheless share some basic characteristics. There are, I submit, at least two such minimal principles. First, humanists reject any supernatural conception of the universe; they are sympathetic to one form or another of atheism, agnosticism, or skepticism. Second, humanists affirm that ethical values do not have a supernatural source and have no meaning independent of human experience; humanism is an ethical philosophy in which human beings are central. There are two additional principles to which many, though not all, humanists are attached. Third, there is some commitment to the use of critical reason in the analysis, evaluation, and appraisal of value judgments; and fourth, there is a humanitarian concern for humanity, in both social and individual terms.

### Antisupernaturalism

This first humanist principle, the rejection of the supernatural world view, is shared with materialism and naturalism. Many humanists, however, who vehemently deny that ultimate reality is spiritual or divine, are not necessarily prepared to accept a materialistic or naturalistic framework.

What is essential to all humanisms is the refusal to accept a simplistic cosmic purpose or teleology, the view that God is the ultimate source of all existence and value, or that there is a bifurcation between nature and supernature. The humanist does not exclude a transcendental reality on a priori grounds, nor does he necessarily deny that there may be aspects of the universe that perhaps are beyond investigation now or in the future. He wishes only to maintain that claims to a nonnatural realm have not been confirmed by adequate evidence nor supported on rational grounds. Thus, attempts to prove the existence of God (ontological, cosmological, teleological, etc.) are unconvincing, unverified and even meaningless. The humanist does not simply dismiss the reports of mystical or revelatory experience. But he looks upon these reports as events to be explained and interpreted in natural terms, much the same as other data that we experience. Such events, he finds, can be parsimoniously accounted for without reference to an alleged transcendental reality. In any case, he asks that all claims to knowledge be open to a responsible examination of the grounds by which they are supported; and he does not consider the evidence referred to by the mystic as conclusive.

Most humanists take man as a part of nature, even though man has his own unique dimensions, such as freedom. There is no break between the human mind or consciousness on the one hand and the body on the other, no special status to personality or "soul," and especially no privileged or special place for human existence in the universe at large. Thus, all claims to human immortality or eschatological theories of history are held to be an expression of wish-fulfillment, a vain reading into nature of human hope and fancy. Nature for the humanist is blind to human purposes and indifferent to human ideals.

## Value Is Relative to Man

A second humanist principle, which is basic, is the ethical concern for man and his works. The humanist says that a theory of value cannot be derived from a metaphysics of divinity, that value is relative to man and to what human beings find to be worthwhile in experience. Ethical standards thus are not to be found outside of life but within it. Most humanists have some confidence in the dignity and power of man to discover for himself the sources of the good life. Thus the humanist is an uncompromising critic of the established ethical codes and commandments of orthodox and authoritarian religion. Theistic religions have often suppressed the best human instincts. They have often been dishonest and immoral concerning man's right to truth; and they have frequently censored and blocked free and responsible intellectual inquiry. The humanist, on the contrary, asks that we, as human beings, face up to the human condition as it is. Humanists accept the fact that God is dead; that we have no way of knowing that he exists; or even of knowing that this is a meaningful question.

They accept the fact that human existence is probably a random occurrence existing between two oblivions, that death is inevitable, that there is a tragic aspect to our lives, and that all moral values are our own creations.

To be sure, there have been some humanists who have, in the face of the rejections of the theistic universe of values, become pessimistic. Yet most humanists have found a source of optimism in the affirmation that value is related to man. There must also be an awareness of the challenges and the possibilities that await us. There may be a basis for genuine confidence, not despair and cynicism. For while there is death and failure, there is also life and success. And with life come great and bountiful promises: there are the joys of human love, shared experience and fellowship, the excitement of creativity, the power of reason, and the possibilities that we as human beings have some control over our destinies. If we grant that not all human sorrows and evils can be avoided, the human situation is not even then irremediable; and with some confidence in our power we may help to build a good life.

The theist has not always allowed man to be himself. He has looked outside of nature or human nature, and has created idolatrous religions that worship graven images. He has often frustrated and thwarted independent self-assertion. He has thus contributed to the alienation of man from himself and nature. Man is made to feel dependent upon God, a "sinner" who must renounce and suppress his pride. But the more he exalts God as the Father image, the more he demeans himself. Surely man is dependent upon external forces, some of which are beyond his control (such as death); but why worship or submit to them, and why weaken or belittle man, asks the humanist? Why exacerbate his guilt complex and his sense of sin, and why exalt acquiescence? Man needs to be himself. He needs to affirm his manhood, to develop the courage to persist in spite of all the obstacles that would destroy him; indeed he needs to exceed himself by creating a new life for himself. The challenge for the free man is to realize his possibilities, and to create new ones, not to cower in masochistic denial, nor to withdraw in fear, anxiety, and trembling, nor to look outside of man for help that is not there.

Humanism today can look to the ennoblement and enrichment of human life as an end, whether in individual terms, as each satisfies his ideals and dreams, or in social terms, where he seeks to develop rules and norms of justice. Humanism claims that man is rooted in the soil (nature), that it is the flesh (life) that gives him satisfaction, and that it is in creative fulfillment and social harmony (the "spirit") that he finds his deepest significance.

What is important for the humanist is that there are no absolute values or norms independent of what man individually and socially chooses. Instead, as Sartre has said, man is condemned to make man; we alone are responsible for what we are and what we do. Perhaps this is an overstatement of the case for freedom; at least the humanist asks that man begin to shed the chains of illusion that bind him, and assert himself. What man needs is not renunciation but affirmation, not resignation but confidence— above all, not blind piety and faith but honesty and truth.

The humanist in ethics is usually cautious and tentative in his judgments, and he may even be skeptical about his humanism, recognizing its limitations. He knows that it is difficult to find absolute standards, or categorical imperatives. Yet he suggests that although the human animal finds himself thrust into existence without his permission, he can to some extent define himself and determine who he is and what he shall be. Man can achieve a satisfying and authentic existence here and now. But it is first essential that he cease deluding himself about what is and is not in store for him. The humanist recognizes the rich diversity and relativity of value, as well as the fact that a man may take alternate paths to achieve the good life. He merely claims that it is we who are to choose and that we should not shirk our responsibility to choose, and not escape to a world of dogma and myth.

## Relevance of Reason

Some humanists add to the two principles I have been discussing a third one, which they think is essential to any definition of humanism. They claim that ethical principles are open to rational criticism, that value judgments are capable of some empirical warrant, and that scientific knowledge can be applied to the solution of the problems of man. Such humanists are frequently committed to situational ethics — to the view that ethical principles are not a priori or universal but only general guides to be applied and modified in the light of empirical circumstances and conditions, in terms of means and consequences. This point of view is sometimes known as scientific humanism.

Not all humanists, however, share this faith in the power of reason; nor do they have confidence in the possibility of ethical objectivity. For example, some existential humanists and positivists have emphasized the subjective ingredients in human values, and they have pointed to the basically emotive character of philosophical theories of value. Though all humanisms share the critique of theistic ethics — that it is full of vain hope and illusion — humanistic ethics at the very least involves a rejection of absolutistic ethics as unfounded in reason or evidence.

The whole question of the empirical objectivity and testability of ethical judgments has been vigorously discussed in twentieth-century ethics, particularly by analytic philosophers. It is unfortunate that Marxist philosophers have not, for the most part, taken part in this important metainquiry. Most Anglo-American philosophers have devoted most of their attention to technical metaquestions rather than to practical matters. Within metaethics some humanists (for example, utilitarians and pragmatists) had accepted some version of naturalistic ethics, that is, the view that ethical judgments are empirical or may be supported by scientific knowledge; and they also have had confidence that philosophy might provide help in solving moral and social problems. This point of view, however, has been subjected to a strong criticism by many analytic philosophers.

The key questions that have been raised in metaethics are epistemological, and they concern the definition of our basic moral terms and the methods by which we justify moral principles. G. E. Moore denied that we could define basic moral terms or derive moral conclusions from nonmoral premises without committing the "naturalistic fallacy." The intuitionists agreed that ethical terms were unanalyzable properties and not amenable to empirical testing. And later the logical positivists and emotivists claimed that all ethical terms were expressive and imperative, that attempts to define them were persuasive, and that attitudes being divorced from beliefs, could not be supported scientifically. Many existentialists went in a different direction, though they claimed that our basic values were commitments, absurd, nonrational, and not amenable to any kind of objective treatment. The result was that until very recently many non-Marxist humanistic philosophers seemed reluctant to say anything positive about man's moral life or to recommend any prescriptive ideals; skepticism about normative ethics seemed the only adequate position.

Some have been pleased with the results, likening what has occurred to a "revolution" in ethics. Others have been troubled and have considered it scandalous. One can agree that a powerful advance has been made by developing useful analytic tools, but one can decry the fact that philosophers have ignored the practical moral problems of life. We seem today to be witnessing within philosophy a strong reaction away from the extreme skepticism in metaethics that existed only a few years ago. There is now a recognition that ethical language, after all, does make some sense, that there is a kind of logic of decision making, and that *reason applies to some extent to practice.* Analytic philosophers have had second thoughts about the emotivist's critique; naturalistic philosophers, in rejoinder, have provided revised and more carefully framed theories. We also recognize that philosophers had better not withdraw into a linguistic sanctuary, that there are real problems that human beings face, and that philosophical analysis on the level of concrete experience and in relation to the actual problems of life may have some relevance. Still, philosophers today disagree about the precise role of reason in ethics or the degree of objectivity.

What has been overlooked is that although philosophers may dispute on the technical metalevel concerning linguistic and epistemological issues, they nonetheless may share certain moral principles. Thus many philosophers, including philosophical analysts and logical positivists, are humanists in ethics proper, if not in metaethics. Though philosophers may differ in method and approach in metaethics, many accept in their *own* moral and political lives a general form of humanistic ethics.

## Humanitarianism

Many humanists also wish to add a fourth principle to their definition of humanism—namely, that humanism involves some form of humanitarianism. Most contemporary humanists have a commitment to some form of the greatest-happiness-for-the-greatest-number principle; they consider that the highest moral obligation is to humanity as a whole. This involves the view that since all men are members of the same human family, it is our obligation to further the welfare of mankind.

Now it is possible to be a humanist in the first two senses I have discussed — to reject supernaturalism and to claim that value is basically human — and not accept the third and fourth principles: that is, a commitment to reason or to humanitarianism. Many classical humanists, the sophists for example, have emphasized the perfecting of one's own individual happiness as the highest human good. One can think of Epicurus or Nietzsche as being a humanist without being a humanitarian. Yet today, most humanists are in some way also dedicated to the ideal of social meliorism and a concern for their fellow men. Indeed, a challenge has been hurled at secular humanists by theistic theologians: if man is the sole source of human values, what guarantee do we have that humanists can develop a sense of responsibility to their fellow men and overcome subjectivism and relativism? Can humanism develop not only an ethic of the good life applicable to individuals but an ethic of moral responsibility and obligation appropriate to other human beings or to society at large? If God is dead and if there is no afterlife, does morality have meaning and does man have a basis for moral action? Yes, the present-day humanist insists. Indeed, the notion of a dead and risen God, of a last judgment day, and of the paradox of evil in a world of divine creation, is hardly a "rational" foundation for morality; on the contrary, to the humanist it seems absurd. The *only* meaning that man can find for morality is that which he makes for himself. At least, the humanist and secular view of the universe is more realistic and honest and avoids deception and false hope. Thus humanism, not being based on theistic illusion or obedience, provides man a more secure foundation for the moral life.

Moral imperatives for the humanist are based upon human experience. They are grounded in an estimation of the consequences of our action: Which moral rules, we ask, will lead to the best possible life for all concerned, including ourselves? Humanist morality need not be grounded in unadulterated egoism — although considerations of self-interest are part of the justification one gives for one's moral beliefs. Rather, morality is rooted in a sensitivity to the interests and needs of others, a rational awareness that my good is tied up with the good of others, and a recognition that any happiness I desire presupposes some conditions of order and rules that would make it possible for other human beings besides myself to achieve their ends. If the humanist admits of no absolute foundation for moral sympathy or a priori justification of first principles, he does believe that a reasonable case for morality can be made, a case that all but the extreme skeptic will understand, since it is based upon the common moral experience of mankind.

There is a great variety of humanitarian humanisms, including utopian humanism, liberal humanism, democratic humanism, utilitarian humanism, and socialist humanism. There is a double humanist concern: (1) in individual terms, the ideal of the development of the potentialities of the individual, and (2) in social terms, the ideal of social welfare and justice. If liberal, democratic, Renaissance, and Enlightenment humanism emphasized the perfectability of the individual and had faith in the instrumentality of reason and education, utilitarian, democratic, and especially socialist humanism has emphasized that many or most of man's problems can be resolved by social action, by changing the social system, the underlying economic structure, the forces and relationships of production.

Humanists as humanitarians attack all those social forces that seek to destroy man; they deplore the dehumanization and alienation of man within an industrial and technological world. In effect, they condemn the contradictions of modern life and the failure of modern man to measure up to the full measure of his potential excellence. The problem for the humanist is to create the conditions that would liberate man from one-sided and distorted development, would emancipate him from oppressive and corruptive social organization and from the denigration and perversion of his human talents, and would enable him to achieve an authentic life. Humanists may not agree about the methods of achieving a just and equitable society. But they share a vision of the good life and the goal of its attainment. And they are interested in creating a society in which the fruits of modern technology and automation can be enjoyed and leisure time enriched.

There is, however, an important difference in contemporary humanism between those, such as Marxist humanists, who believe that the problem of man is essentially *social,* and those, such as liberal democratic humanists, who emphasize the need to enhance the qualities of *individuality.*

## II

The fundamental problem for humanism today, as always, is the problem of man. An authentic humanism should not be tied to any particular philosophical ideology, nor to the special social or economic structure of a given historical epoch, nor to a specific program of action. It is true, as we have seen, that humanism has certain minimal general principles. It rejects dogma; it affirms that value is relative to human experience; it uses critical reason; and it has a humanitarian concern for perfecting and enhancing human life. Humanism should be opposed, whatever the source, to that which dehumanizes or destroys man. But humanism is not final in its political formulations, nor absolute in its ethical principles. Humanism must be prepared in any period to change its emphasis. In the Renaissance it was supernaturalism, in the nineteenth century it was rapacious capitalism, and in the twentieth century there are other forms of alienation that need correction.

Humanism is not abstract principle. It must be given an empirical content, and its content, whenever necessary, must be open to modification. Humanism is not simply negative. It has an important affirmative aspect. Marx was no doubt correct when he attacked theoretic atheism for no longer having any meaning, and he defended social humanism as positive and practical in *The Economic and Philosophic Manuscripts* (1844). For Marx the alienation of man had its source in estranged labor, private property, and a class-ridden society. Alienation occurs because labor is coerced, not voluntary, and is external to the worker. It becomes itself a commodity, separated from the process of production. Socialism for Marx was the positive transcendence of private property. Although one might begin with atheism, humanism as atheism is abstract.

Humanism as socialism was "bent on action" and took on "real" dimensions in the world of man because it offered a solution to the problem of alienation.

Marx's positive humanism, though profoundly instructive in its own day, is not the only viable alternative on the current scene. The danger is that Marxist humanism will become ossified, abstract, and theoretic, a form of *pious humanism*—unless, that is, it turns its attention to the solution of present-day alienation. Humanists must cooperate in the continuing task of criticism and reconstruction. Philosophers who are humanists have a special obligation in each age to diagnose that which is destructive of humanity.

If we analyze present sources of friction, we find that racial antagonisms exist in both socialist and nonsocialist societies, that there are competing national sovereignties, and that the dangers of armed conflict and nuclear warfare cannot be explained solely in terms of class struggle. There are genuine human problems we must work on cooperatively: resolution of the disparity between the have and have-not nations and solution of the problems of overpopulation, the pollution of the earth's atmosphere, and the depletion of our natural resources.

The growth of large-scale social organizations constitutes a serious problem in all highly developed technological-industrial systems. The estrangement of the individual within large-scale impersonal bureaucracies—whether the corporation, commune, collective, trade union, or university—is endemic to different economic systems. Marx could not have predicted the new sources of alienation that would emerge after the destruction of the bourgeoisie. The cure of alienation is a challenge to socialist societies; for the problem of alienation is crucial to the Marxist critique of capitalism.

The most sensitive area of disagreement between Marxist humanists and liberal democratic humanists is the question of freedom for the individual. Historically, humanism has had, I submit, a fundamental concern for the creative and autonomous individual—and this is the case not only for Greek, Renaissance, Enlightenment, liberal, and democratic humanists, but also for Marx himself. Indeed, it is difficult to make a sharp differentiation on this point between Marx's humanism and other forms of humanism. Most present-day liberal and democratic humanists in the West have been so influenced by Marxism's desire to emancipate man from an unjust society that it is hard to draw the line between democratic and Marxist humanism, since many or most democratic humanists are at the same time socialist or quasi-socialist in outlook. There are of course, as we are well aware, many interpretations of Marx. Perhaps the real contrast is between democratic Marxism and other forms of Marxism. The issue that I wish to discuss is reminiscent of the debate between the Mensheviks and the Bolsheviks, or between the Leninist interpretation of Marxism and other interpretations. This debate has gone on for almost the whole of this century. The key question concerns the use of nonhumanistic means, particularly by a powerful totalitarian state, to achieve the ideal ends of socialist humanism. In humanist terms today, it leads to the query: In what sense can humanists, who cannot tolerate the inequities of capitalist oppression and inequality, condone in silence socialist oppression?

Surely, aside from anything else, a basic principle of humanism must be a defense of personal freedom. Any humanism that does not cherish the individual, I am prepared to argue, is neither humanistic nor humanitarian.

From the standpoint of the liberal democratic humanist, it is correct to say that man is a social being and that he actualizes his nature largely in social terms. One's biological needs are satisfied by economic and social means; his moral, intellectual, religious, and aesthetic life are sociocultural in origin and function. The language one uses, the clothing one adorns oneself with, one's food and poetry, are all social in dimension. Built upon one's primary biogenic needs are a set of secondary needs, largely sociogenic in character. Humane values can emerge and flourish only because civilization nourishes and sustains them. Yet I would deny that the so-called "essence" of man is equivalent to the sum of his social relations; for aspects of the individual remain that cannot be equated with the social. Although the individual transacts in a sociocultural environment and in relation to other human beings, it is still the individual *agent* that engages in the transaction, and his social role or status can never fully define his nature nor exhaust his being. Man's sociality is no doubt fundamental; and many or most human problems have a social or collective situation—but not all. There are dimensions of personality that cannot, and indeed should not, be smothered.

I am offering here not only a theory of human nature that combines Aristotle and Mill with Marx and that finds creative and autonomous individuals entering into the world and changing it, but a *normative* recommendation that suggests what our attitude concerning individuality ought to be. Thus I am not simply asserting that human beings reserve a degree of individuality for themselves, but that they *ought* to be treated as individuals. Any humanism worthy of the name should be concerned with the preservation of the individual personality with all of its unique idiosyncracies and peculiarities. We need a society in which the full and free development of every individual is the ruling principle. The existence of individual freedom thus is an essential condition for the social good and a necessary end of humanitarianism.

Certain human evils can only be resolved and certain human goods attained only by constant restructuring of the whole society. Yet new and unforeseen evils may emerge in any society so reconstructed. Humanists should be prepared to change those social structures that are unjust and to create new ones—but surely not if this involves the destruction of those qualities of individuality we wish to emancipate from bondage in the first place.

Liberal democratic humanists find this is precisely what has occurred as a result of some socialist revolutions. Moral in aim, the revolution is cruelly betrayed by perverse means, and a new antihumanistic dogmatic theology is resurrected to make excuses for or justify new social inequities. Philosophers should be skeptical of all philosophical systems, including their own; and in particular they should be prepared to criticize philosophical ideas that become enshrined in social institutions and are supported by the authority of a state, party, or class, instead of by the authority of reason and evidence. If humanists condemned medieval Christianity because it used compulsion and censorship to block free inquiry, so must they oppose those ideologies, originally humanist in intent, that are converted into official policies and justified by force, not reason. To suggest that one group has a monopoly on truth and virtue and that all who oppose it have ulterior motives or represent a corrupt social class is to undermine the whole basis of philosophical dialogue. The great danger to humanism is the conversion of genuine humanist philosophy into official dogma and pious cant. If humanism has meant anything, it has meant a respect for free inquiry, an openness to criticism, a toleration of different points of view.

One often hears that freedom cannot be granted because of the danger of counterrevolution and that to create socialism one must first destroy all the fetters of the old society that seek to impede it. But by setting up a closed society, one may destroy the very individuals that one wishes to liberate. In the place of the inequities of class and private property, one may substitute a new bureaucracy and a new class in control of the awesome power of the state, which may result in even greater dangers of alienation. Instead of pluralistic centers of power, all power may be vested in one center, and the condition of the worker may be no better—and perhaps worse—than under older forms of society.

There are inequities in capitalism and in some socialist societies; but this is not what is at stake. The real issue concerns the fundamental difference between democratic and nondemocratic conceptions of society and differing sets of values. Democracy is not a mere bourgeois ruse, a plot of "mendacious liberals" to oppress the masses. The democratic ideal touches at the wellspring of humanism: the enrichment of human individuality. Individual diversity and creativity are positive goods; first, because they are at the very heart of the good life, and second, because they are a precondition for social progress and development. I will argue that an open society in the long run is more likely to find new and ingenious solutions than a closed one. It is rich in discovery and invention, seminal in imagination.

Now I am not in any sense minimizing or demeaning the other important values that socialist humanists have advocated: the need to maintain an adequate standard of living, to get rid of inequalities, the destruction of false class distinctions, equality and fraternity, social solidarity and shared experience, the virtues of a rationally planned social system. These are human goods to be cherished and developed. I am merely saying: Yes, but not at the price of individuality. It is not a question of either individuality or sociality, freedom or justice, liberty or equality; a combination of both is the moral obligation of the humanitarian. For we recognize that an essential condition of freedom is equality.

What do I mean by individual freedom? I am not talking about economic freedom or private enterprise. I believe in some measure of public control. I do not think that it makes much sense to say, as some Hegelians have, that a man is "free" only insofar as he fulfills himself in society. This seems to be a blatant equivocation on the term "freedom." What I wish to emphasize are intellectual, artistic, moral, political, social, and organizational freedoms.

I am arguing first, as humanists have argued against theists, for *intellectual* freedom, for freedom of thought and inquiry. This involves the right of heresy and dissent, including untrammeled freedom of expression. It also involves *artistic* freedom, the right of individuals to express their creative aesthetic visions as they see them without fear of social censorship.

In *moral* terms freedom requires an open society in which individuals may express their own unique talents and pursue their lives as they see fit, enjoy or suffer their tastes, values, attitudes, and beliefs. It means a society in which individuals will have some measure of privacy and be left alone. Freedom includes the right to critically dissent from the prevailing social norms. In recent years this has meant civil disobedience; where the society violates my basic moral values, I may disobey its laws as an act of protest. It is puzzling that civil disobedience is permitted in the Western democracies but not in socialist societies; yet it seems to me an indication of the strength of a society (rather than a weakness) that it can tolerate individual diversity.

In *political* terms, moral freedom cannot exist unless there is some measure of political freedom. This involves the legal right of opposition, elections, petition, recall, the right of assembly. There must exist clearly defined mechanisms for checking political leadership and transferring power. There should be established common legal procedures or a constitutional system guaranteeing individuals due process and equality before the law.

The kind of individual freedom I am talking about is not simply moral and political, but is *social* and *organizational* as well. It entails the right of individuals to participate fully in the social organizations in which they live and function. The demands for self-management by workers' councils or for participation by students and faculty in the affairs of universities recognize the need for individuals to share in the lives of their institutions at different levels of decision-making. Without such decentralization, democracy is not fully operative, nor are human beings saved from alienation.

There are various forces that seek to limit and restrain the individual in capitalist, semicapitalist, or mixed economies. Mass media, advertising, and propaganda all tend to limit individual decision and belief and to dry up effective heresy and dissent.

Human beings are converted into passive consumers and are no longer active, creative doers. Socialist societies face a similar "spiritual" problem, for they also have large-scale technological-industrial forces that tend to dehumanize man. Technology, automation, and highly centralized impersonal organizations all contribute to the impotence and powerlessness of individuals and undermine free choice and self-determination. We need as a corrective widespread democratic participation within organizations by individuals, who, sharing cooperatively with others, shall nevertheless be the masters of their own destinies and capable of ever larger areas of voluntary action.

But, I reiterate, we also need areas of privacy and liberty where no coercive authorities or organizations operate, and where individuals are left alone to direct their own lives and careers in terms of their own inclinations and desires.

Humanism is nothing if it is not a theory of liberation and emancipation of man and if it does not contribute to the enhancement of individual human experience. Perhaps what we need today is a new Humanist Manifesto, written by both Western and Eastern humanists, which spells out the rights of the individual and criticizes all those forces in the modern world that seek to constrain the exercise of these rights.

# 10

# The Democratic Ethic

## The Meaning of Democracy

**D**emocracy is still the most radical social philosophy in the world today—radical because there are so many opposed to it and so few who genuinely understand or believe in it, and because, if adopted, it would mean a fundamental change in human institutions. Nevertheless it is espoused by people from all parts of the political spectrum. Liberals praise democracy; so do conservatives and reactionaries. Even Marxist communists defend what they call "people's democratic republics." Democracy, like other noble ideals, is thought to confer virtue by association. Yet not all those who pay lip service to it are democrats. Democracy has been betrayed by totalitarians and humanitarians of all kinds—by those who believe in government *for* the people, if not necessarily *of* or *by* them—and it has been undermined by apostles of the far right and the far left.

One source of this confusion is that many of those who appeal for democracy are uncertain of its nature, or else choose to misapply it. What is "democracy"? How is it to be applied? Are there any limits that a society calling itself democratic should not exceed? What is essential to democracy?

## The Ethical Dimensions of Democracy

The term "democracy" may be used in different senses. We talk of political, economic, racial, social democracy. The essential factor, in my judgment, is that democracy expresses an ethical dimension. It advocates first and foremost a normative ideal—one that recommends how we shall treat people, and how we should live and work together as individuals in communities. Although the democratic ideal has many different interpretations and applications, it cannot be implemented without recognition of its basic moral foundations.

What are the moral principles that it expresses? The democratic philosophy involves at the very least a commitment to the principles of liberty and equality. But if the principle of liberty is overemphasized, it may lead to an

---

This essay appeared in my *Fullness of Life* (New York: Horizon Press, 1974).

extreme laissez-faire individualism or anarchism, which may deny the rights of others; it may ignore the need for equality of treatment; and it may lead to an unjust society from which large sections of the population are excluded socially and economically. Indeed, the principle of freedom, if allowed to reign alone, could eventually lead to a class society in which some individuals or groups would possess power, with large numbers of people bypassed or excluded from effective involvement. On the other hand, an egalitarian society which is excessively protective of equal rights might so restrict individual freedom that the right of choice and initiative would be thwarted. Societies that emphasize egalitarianism and ignore libertarianism generally tend to become totalitarian, willing to trample on freedom of thought, action, and dissent.

In its concern for the worth and dignity of the individual, democracy recognizes his right to do what he wishes and restricts undue interference in the sphere of individual choice and action. It provides the opportunity and conditions for personal realization and growth.

The democratic ethic recognizes that insofar as we respect an individual's right to personal freedom, we contribute not only to his growth but to our own; insofar as we can appreciate others we can learn to share their stores of experience, wisdom, and truth. In being tolerant of diversity, the democratic approach enlarges our horizons for discovery and insight; it permits creative growth in the community. Insofar as I am willing to listen to another, to consider him as a person entitled to equal consideration and fair treatment, I contribute to both my development and his.

The democratic ethic is also based on the idea of freely given consent; its institutions strive as nearly as possible to base their policies on the consent of the greatest number of people. This consent is not mere acquiescence; it must be freely given, in active approval of the main directions being taken and confidence in the key officials who are to carry them out.

Consent alone is never enough. We should always seek to enlist real participation in the affairs of the state, the sharing of power and responsibility at all levels. Since each person has an equal stake in society and in life, each should have a commensurate role. The true democrat has a measure of faith in the "ordinary man," in his ingrained wisdom and practical judgment, particularly in that which concerns his self-interest. The democratic ethic denies that any group or class has special knowledge or moral virtue that enables it to judge what is good for others better than they can judge for themselves. No claim to power based upon privilege, wealth, prestige, birth or background entitles any group to exercise rule.

There are, of course, many interpretations of cooperative participation. Some believe that democracy requires consensus, even unanimity. Yet, although one tries to arouse wide, if possible unanimous, support for a policy or program, consensus is rarely attained. In small groups where decisions are made face-to-face in daily encounter, it may be possible to reach consensus by persuasion and negotiation. In a large social context, with diversity of opinion, the next best thing is majority rule. Majorities are often lumbering and in error, but they are fairer to a greater number of interests than the minority, even though the minority may be correct.

What is crucial for democracy is the method by which decisions are reached. The most desirable method is that of peaceful deliberation, discussion, persuasion, the widest possible dialogue between opposing conceptions. In recognizing that no individual or group may possess all the truth, democracy leaves open the possibilities for the clash of competing views and thrives on heresy and nonconformity.

## Basic Commitments

Of course, democracy can only survive if its citizens abide by certain rules. Provided that you are willing to listen to me or to those who represent me, and possibly be persuaded to change, I will try to convince you, says the democrat; but if I cannot I will go along in general with what the majority wants. What is essential is the willingness to negotiate differences and to reach common ground. If the democratic method of shared decision making is to be effective, it presupposes that certain concomitant policies and procedures be present. What is of first importance is that there be a common framework of values and ideals; for a democracy to operate people must agree that the ethic of democracy is just and humane. Those who live in the community may dissent from current policies and pursue a plurality of life styles or hold different belief systems; yet they should have some intelligent commitment to the framework, that is, to the methods by which social change is effected, policies enacted, and leaders selected. If large sections of the population do not believe in democracy and are willing to abandon it for a more efficient, or more orderly system, the democratic ethic will break down. And if in an underdeveloped nation there is no heritage of democratic values, people are hardly likely to accept democracy, which presupposes some allegiance to common values.

## An Open Society: Free Education and Information

Public knowledge and access to truth are preconditions of a democratic society. If public decisions are to be made wisely, it is important that state secrets be kept to a minimum and truly concern national security.

Democracy requires some system of universal education. This does not mean that everybody is entitled to pursue programs in any field, or be admitted to any institution of higher education without qualification. What it does mean is that basic opportunities are to be available for all. As John Dewey recommended, we should develop in the young an appreciation for democratic values, the capacity for shared experience and toleration and, most vitally, the arts of intelligence. For an informed citizenry, capable of distinguishing the true from the false, is the most reliable safeguard for a democracy.

If the citizens are to reach their decisions wisely, moreover, it is also essential that there be free access to *all* sources of information. Thus, freedom of opinion, research, investigation, and publication are essential: the key public value is cooperative inquiry. This is not possible where there is no marketplace in which ideas can be examined. We have seen how, in totalitarian societies, the ministry of information controls the sources of information — radio, television, cinema, magazines, newspapers, book publishing, education. And so we must oppose those societies in which the elementary freedom to information is denied, and not be misled by those who label as "democratic" communist societies closed to free inquiry. In capitalist and quasi-democratic societies in the West, on the other hand, it is vital that large commercial interests not be allowed to control the mass media. A genuine threat to freedom of information in the United States has emerged because a few national networks control television, and two or three wire and news services predominate. The development of large conglomerates in book, newspaper, and magazine publishing must also be viewed with alarm.

The problem of free communication and access to information is of course related to economics. If democracy is to be effective, it is necessary that the media be free of undue control by advertisers. It is said that the mass media, based upon the profit motive, need to sell their services to advertisers if they are to survive. But from the standpoint of the public interest, the first duty of the media should be to inform and only secondarily to profit. There can be no quibbling on this point and no compromise. We would surely complain if our public schools were run primarily for profit rather than for service. It is one thing to have the profit motive rule in manufacturing automobiles or selling shoes; it is quite another to allow it to dominate in the sensitive area of ideas, the mainstays of a viable democratic society.

Democracy cannot operate where people fear to express their opinions, or where pressures compel people to behave against their better judgment. In dictatorships the threat of imprisonment and torture effectively prevents expression of ideas, but other forms of sanctions operate more subtly in a democracy to undermine an individual's courage — fear of losing security or status, fear of ecclesiastical excommunication or penance, of social discrimination or racial prejudice.

An increasing peril is the misuse of the mass media. Here too we have seen how dictatorships use them to indoctrinate, to keep people misinformed and docile. The mass media are used in subtle or unscrupulous ways by advertisers, who by conditioning techniques persuade consumers to buy shoddy products. When such techniques are used to sell the presidency or other political offices, the whole fabric of a democratic polity is undermined.

I am not objecting to advertising per se as the informed description of products and services, nor surely to the use of the mass media by contenders for political office. What I do condemn is the increasingly abusive manipulation of the airwaves by political hucksters. The members of modern society are consumers but they are also citizens, and the mass media should not be allowed to cater to one role while they neglect the other. I am not arguing for state control of advertisers and the mass media—we have seen how political power can be as offensive as economic power—but for democratic mechanisms of regulation and support. Consumer unions and groups, for example, should also be allowed to advertise and analyze products sold through the mass media. It is essential that consumers have some power over what is fed to them and that corporate organizations be democratized and regulated so that the public interest will never be overlooked.

## Individual and Minority Rights

If democracy is rule by the people, can the people ever suspend the rights of individuals or of minorities even if they are offensive? If democracy is rule by the majority, can a majority ever abrogate the rights of those with whom it disagrees? Can it suppress recalcitrant minorities? There is considerable confusion here, even among some of the best-intentioned of democrats. After all, if we agree to abide by the majority decision, how can we intervene when it goes against what we like? Must we not suffer in silence, hoping to persuade the majority to reverse itself?

The majority is not sacred; nor does majority rule remain inviolable under every circumstance. Democracy rests upon still more fundamental principles— liberty, equality, toleration, civil disobedience—which are higher on the scale of values. Majority rule does not have an intrinsic value in itself. It is only a mechanism to ensure conditions of social harmony and peace and is used because it entails fewer risks and dangers to social welfare than other methods of decision making. Majority rule is justified only because it safeguards individual rights; it must not be used to suppress them. Opposing minorities and individuals have obligations to the majority—not to impose their beliefs by nondemocratic means. The protection of minority rights is a precondition of any democratic society, in which majorities are free to determine public policy but not to undermine the ethical presuppositions of democracy.

Am I introducing a doctrine of natural rights that are prior to political policy? No, I reject such a notion. Nor do I accept the idea of a social contract. All individual and minority rights are social; they are claims made upon the community, which lay down certain restrictions upon political power. To say that certain liberties and rights should be recognized is to make a normative claim. It is to prescribe or direct future action. How should we regard or treat individuals in society? They are entitled to equal consideration and freedom even if the majority disagrees with them.

How are these principles to be justified? They are not derived from a divine or natural law, nor do they have any special metaphysical status. They are rules offered to govern how we shall behave. They can be justified only by reference to their results. Societies that nourish the rights of individuals and minorities will, in the long run, be happier, more humane, and just. Societies willing to suspend individual rights whenever immediate purposes seem to require it will be liable to disharmony. The respect for those rights is justified because they are more likely to ensure the common good and the conditions whereby individuals may discover the fullness of life.

## The Rule of Law

A democratic society is also based upon respect for due process and the rule of law. There are those who indict "legalism" and "parliamentarianism" and who attack the slow-moving character of democratic societies committed to legal processes, in which policies rest upon precedent. Some are tempted to prefer rule by fiat in order to get things done rapidly, independently of legal tradition or bureaucratic red tape. Yet if there is one conclusion to be drawn from the history of political and social philosophy, it is the collective wisdom of the law. Plato, in *The Republic,* wanted philosopher-kings to rule, and to apply their wisdom and knowledge for the social good. Utopianists and totalitarians ever since have decried laws that have stood in their way and have defended "reason" and "revelation." Yet Plato himself recognized, in *The Laws,* that in the absence of a philosopher-king, laws are the best guarantors of freedom. Alas, such philosopher-kings have not yet been discovered; nor does the easy temptation today to make behavioral scientists our messiahs promise anything better. Laws still seem a more reliable way of running a society. Laws, however, provide us only with general guides for behavior; how they work out depends upon the context. In a just society laws are applied without discrimination. In the absence of law there would be no possibility of security; fear and indecision would be our constant companions. Of course, provisions must be allowed for equity in interpreting and adjusting laws to new situations. Further, a just society should try to minimize the regulation of its citizens' lives, to leave to individuals the widest possible latitude; where regulation is necessary, it should be based upon legal development.

A problem arises when, in the name of civil disobedience and equal rights, some partisans flout the law and argue that it is corrupt. They dramatize crime in the ghettoes, minimize its consequences, and explain it by attributing it to unjust conditions. There is of course a good deal of truth to this claim, particularly for disadvantaged minorities who have often been brutalized by excessive police power and denied their rights. We also need to decriminalize much of the law.

Of course, law does not guarantee freedom. History has taught us how it can be oppressive and arbitrary, especially in fascist or closed societies.

The ideal is for laws to come into being and to be modified by the parliamentary process, and to be applied impartially and humanely. If law is essential to a democracy, it is equally essential that it not become sacrosanct, that it be responsive to the will of the people.

## The Justification of the Democratic Ideal

The foregoing is a mere outline suggestive of some features of a democratic society. Does such a society exist? Obviously not. Democracy is an ideal and any definition of it must be ideal. Naturally there is a descriptive element in the definition. "Democracy" does not refer to some theoretical entity independent of the real world. Many societies have had democratic features, but none has ever been a pure democracy. Hence the concept is comparative, a standard by which we may criticize, classify, and compare existing states, and a guide and incentive to greater democracy in the future. So the definition of democracy is normative and prescriptive for the development of society, and for the ethical principles by which we may evaluate policies and systems and reform them.

We have recently heard indictments of so-called democratic societies. Young idealists accuse them of being hypocritical and of betraying their ideals in practice. It is said that democracy doesn't work. But as I have pointed out, no society — not the United States, nor Britain nor the Scandinavian countries nor ancient Athens — has ever fully implemented the democratic ideal. Then how justify continued commitment to democracy? How would we go about proving its efficacy and power?

One should, to begin with, have a mature and realistic attitude about social systems and ideals. Although there has been immense progress in human affairs, only a pure visionary would expect to see all problems solved or utopia achieved. The justification of democracy is always relative, not rooted in metaphysics or science; it cannot have a deductive or necessary proof. The demand for that kind of justification is, like the demand for the justification of life, an expression of religious need. Democracy can only be justified empirically. For what can be said in comparison with the alternatives — dictatorship, oligarchy, aristocracy? Democracy has a wider concern for a greater number of people; even the lowliest have a stake in it, and so it has a more extensive appeal. But also, in comparative terms, it provides fewer dangers and fewer negative consequences than other systems. There is always the danger that self-interest may be confused with the common good. Power has corrupted and blinded rulers throughout history to their own imperfections; it is dangerous to entrust power to an individual or group without proper checks and balances. This has been the collective wisdom of human experience. Antidemocratic societies, which award power on the basis of class, wealth, military force, or religious authority, tend to degenerate into self-interested rule. Since in a democracy those who are responsible can be called to account, there is less likelihood of excessive duplicity or cruelty. Of course injustices and mistakes occur in a democracy, but at least where a society is open injustices can be examined by the critical eye of the public.

Consequently, in democratic societies muckraking is an important traditional means of exposing graft and corruption, whereas people in totalitarian societies usually live in illusion, far less aware of social problems. It has been said by Marxist critics that the United States and other Western democracies are in decay, whereas the Soviet Union, China, and some Eastern European countries are advancing in many respects. So it may seem to some on the surface, but probably that is due to the fact that the West has great freedom of the press, which tends to dramatize its problems—alcoholism, crime, political corruption, poverty, and racism. It is universally recognized that totalitarian societies, though they have similar problems, withhold them from public view by controlling the press. We need to put things in perspective. At least, free societies can learn about problems that closed societies cannot.

Surely democracy has the potential for the widest realization of happiness for the largest number. It provides the richest soil for both individual development and social cooperation. With a role in society and a stake in the future, man becomes a devoted member of the cause that provides such noble opportunities; his alienation is reduced, his creative commitment and loyalty enhanced. In an age of crisis in religious commitment, democracy is more amenable to meaningful identification with worthwhile goals. It is more likely to be creative and innovative, more receptive to invention and discovery than a closed, hierarchical, or fixed society. Thus, if viewed in terms of desirable consequences, more people will tend to find a more satisfying life in a democratic system than in a nondemocratic one. Democracy presupposes that the experience of freedom in the young will develop an understanding of its responsible application so that it will become ingrained in the mores of the society.

## Political Democracy

This discussion has been a general one, concerning the ideal normative features of democracy viewed in its ethical and social dimensions. But it is the *way* that these principles work out in practice that is important. Some institutions of a society are democratic, some not. With respect to institutions, most democrats believe that an essential precondition for the realization of any genuinely ethical system is political democracy. But many Marxists who claim to be "democratic" deny the importance of this and debunk the definition of liberal political democracy as mere "bourgeois deception."

What is a democratic *political* system? The term "political system" refers primarily to the operations of state and government, the control of decision making and power. In large nation-states, the only feasible method of rule is by means of representation. Although democracy encourages decentralization, enlisting the largest degree of involvement at all levels, some policies cannot be adequately formulated by a local unit and have to be enunciated for the whole society. The only practical way to implement the democratic philosophy is for the people to delegate power by electing representatives to carry out the main programs. In a large society we cannot elect all government officials (the United States, for example, has some twelve million government workers), but only key leaders. Nor can the people, by means of elections, determine all the policies of the state (there are of course many thousands of governmental rules and regulations, many of them highly technical). The presumption is that the major policies are fully discussed before they are adopted. Accordingly, the operation of majority rule, though not a "pure" form of democracy, is the most feasible method of expressing the will of the people. Free elections are the necessary ingredient in a democratic polity—local, state, and federal—as well as in the control of political parties.

Concomitant with this is the legal right of the individual not only to disagree but to make known his opposition to leaders and programs. Where there is no right to oppose the government, to submit its policies to critical scrutiny, and to offer alternatives, there is no democracy. One-party states, where leaders are selected by acclamation, where no alternative programs are available and no mechanisms for making known the views of those in opposition, are not democratic, even though totalitarians attempt to co-opt the term "democracy."

Democracy allows the representatives of the people the right to exercise some independence and autonomous judgment. But since most citizens do not have the time, energy, or interest to be concerned with every decision, a bureaucracy or elite will often emerge. A democracy therefore functions best when there is some intelligent distrust of leaders—if not of motives, certainly of policies and consequences. Excessive criticism, however, and unwillingness to allow them some latitude in judgment and some authority in acting, will undermine their ability to govern, both on the international and domestic levels. On the other hand, the glorification of leaders is antithetical to a democratic milieu. Many who remain in office for ten or twenty years become removed from the people; unresponsiveness sets in. History has taught us how important it is that leadership be renewed.

In the last analysis a political democracy can be effective only if its citizens are interested in the affairs of government and participate in it by way of constant discussion, letter writing, free association, and publication. In the absence of such interest, democracy will become inoperative; an informed electorate is the best guarantee of its survival.

## Social Democracy

However, to talk about the instrumentalities of *political* democracy would be merely rhetorical, if *social* democracy did not exist along with it. What is social democracy? I wish to focus first on two aspects: (1) the elimination of racial, ethnic, and sexual discrimination; and (2) the destruction of a closed class society.

Democracy requires an *open* society. Political democracy by itself is not a sufficient guarantee that the society will be one. Invidious distinctions drawn between individuals and groups prevent the full realization of the ethics of democracy. The most notorious, as we have seen, are the forms of exclusiveness based upon racial, religious, ethnic, or sexual grounds. That such discrimination is undemocratic is universally understood. One may argue that the state should respect free choice, and not force people of different backgrounds and interests to live together if they do not wish to. But in order for the principle of equal opportunity to prevail, false barriers in housing, employment, education, medical treatment, and recreational facilities must be broken down. As I have stressed, the chief method of change should be voluntary and persuasive. I would in principle prefer, for example, voluntary to compulsory busing to achieve racial balance. Where constitutional liberties are denied, however, the courts must intervene to guarantee individual rights and equal opportunity.

Many political democracies, as in Latin America or Europe, may be purely formal. In a closed society, there are strong class lines and a hierarchy, based on wealth, birth, or tradition, making it virtually impossible for one from a lower station in society to break through. An open society would allow full mobility. It would, as far as possible, break down class lines, and thus make interaction, intermarriage, and fraternization possible. In England and France, old class-ridden societies, such mobility has been difficult; in the United States and the Soviet Union there is more mobility.

We are often told that the United States is a class society; hence, its bourgeois democracy is deceptive. What is the meaning of "class"? The nineteenth-century Marxist definition does not seem strictly applicable to the current scene. In an advanced agricultural technology less than 6 percent of the population are now needed on the farms. Hence, farm laborers, who once made up a significant part of society, have virtually disappeared. The percentage of industrial workers engaged in production is also becoming a smaller part of the labor force; skilled labor is replacing unskilled; the expert technician is assuming a more important role; and the number of people in service occupations, the professions, and governmental service is now greater than those in production.

The tendency of corporations to get larger (and we must remember that large-scale industries prevail in socialist as well as in capitalist societies) is harmful to decentralization and democracy. In the United States, where there is a separation between ownership and management, the capitalists alone do not run industry. Consequently, the overly simplified model of the proletarian class on one side of the barricades and the capitalist class on the other is a romantic fiction that Marxists attempt to keep alive, but it has little application to contemporary conditions. In the nineteen-sixties some romantic Marxists had lumped students and blacks into the proletarian class in an effort to increase its size, but this destroys the classical model, for the basis of the distinction is age and race rather than economic interest.

Is class based upon property? Two-thirds of American families own their own homes, and large numbers own stocks or bonds. Is class based upon earnings from interest, rent, dividends? Virtually everyone draws earnings from interest in savings accounts; many people earn money from rent. Millions of workers and retired people own insurance annuities or have retirement plans, drawing dividends and capital gains. One cannot deny the maldistribution of wealth and other inequities in capitalist society, but these do not follow class lines. Presumably, progressive taxation and other kinds of adjustment could rectify these inequities.

The notion of class makes most sense in reference to the existence of a power structure and to distinctions in power and responsibility based upon role and function. There is a power elite that makes decisions and directs the affairs of institutions. But socialist societies have discovered that they too need bureaucrats to direct the large-scale state trusts, industries, and communes, and they are much like the managers in capitalist societies. Given this reality there is a need to democratize the power structure and to see that large institutions come under effective democratic political control. But there is also a need to change the character of elites and the ways of selecting them within these institutions. Antidemocratic tendencies in elites can only be modified when the principles of liberty and equality operate. To have elites is not in itself wicked; indeed, it is hard to see how a complex modern society can exist without them. What *is* important is that membership in an elite group be based upon proven merit and talent, that it be made responsive to public needs, and that it not be laden with privileges and rights that are unavailable to others.

## Competence and the Limits of Participation

General principles are guides for policy and action, to be tested by their consequences and in pragmatic terms. Participatory democracy, though a general principle that I defend, must be applied in context if it is to be meaningful. Individual participation must be related to the functions of the particular organization. Participatory democracy in an army, for example, obviously has its limitations. If a nation wants to win a war, discipline must be enforced and military orders and regulations obeyed; otherwise, chaos will result, and an army will become a mob.

The German General Staff created in the Wehrmacht an army of unquestioning obedience to orders. But it might be argued, in defense of participatory democracy, that if an army's loyalty was based upon intelligent commitment and participation rather than fear, it would contribute to morale and efficiency; that an obedient mass is no substitute for individual initiative, intelligence, and skill; that the stupidities and mistakes of an "infallible" officer class may be unmasked by the practical wisdom of noncommissioned officers and enlisted men; and that a citizens' militia in a democracy is to be preferred to sole dependence upon a professional army cadre. The democratization of the ranks may thus contribute to the performance of the military organization. Yet we all recognize that some limitation on democracy is necessary as long as nation-states and armies exist. One cannot debate whether to go into battle when an opposing army menaces.

A frequent confusion concerning participatory democracy may be seen in the universities, which are for the most part hierarchical organizations made up of three estates: administration, faculty, and students. From one side comes the demand that faculty participate in important policy decisions and wrest power from administrations. The imposition, by boards of regents and trustees, of administrative officials—often success-achievers—upon faculty, and the view that professors are "employees," primarily passive and security-oriented, are archaic notions. As a result faculty members often become ambivalent toward their universities. But what makes a top-flight university, if it is not its faculty? Who should run the university, if not the faculty? The overemphasis upon bureaucracy is to be deplored; the same degree of centralization does not exist in comparable European institutions. Administrators, where necessary, should be elected by the faculty and serve as their representatives, with powers only as delegated by the faculty. The argument of competence or special qualifications does not apply here; one may argue that administrators are no more competent than the faculty, probably less so.

From still another quarter comes the demand that students should participate in all decisions and share power with the faculty and administration. The student often finds the multiversity remote from his interests, hierarchical, conservative, and bureaucratic. From his point of view the faculty often represents an elite whose first commitment is to narrow specialization. The student is considered an unimportant element within the knowledge factory. No wonder that students often have felt alienated, standardized, replaceable, largely irrelevant. The archaic university stands in relation to its students as a parent does, and it can control their conduct to virtually the same extent that parents can. In many universities the student is an outsider whose chief virtue is submission to authority. Students must knuckle under to rules and regulations; those who are "difficult" may be disciplined by suspension or expulsion.

The arguments in favor of granting some measure of personal involvement to students are numerous. An excellent university should not be organized along corporate authoritarian lines but in a way that activates the creative potential in both students and faculty. The two estates should share in the common enterprise of learning and research and thus become a community of scholars in the full sense. What better way for students to learn if not by personal identification with the process of education? What better way to be stimulated toward goals than by participating in creating them? Students are entitled to be treated as adults and individuals, and they should join professors in the effort of developing the university.

Yet, after all is said, the university is a peculiar kind of organization; it is by its nature hierarchical, though this (in theory at least) is based not upon birth, class, or wealth, but upon scholarly attainment. In most universities of quality there are careful processes of selection and standards of tenure; in order to be appointed, promoted, and given tenure, one must demonstrate qualifications in education and experience. Tenure, an essential component in all great universities, protects the academic freedom of the professor, freeing him from fear of censorship or reprisal, and it assures promotion with the highest standards of excellence. There is always the danger that an entrenched oligarchy of senior professors will attempt to keep out new ideas and fresh blood. Junior faculty members need safeguards against prejudicial treatment, and they need a method for redress of grievances.

Freedom and tenure are the essential principles upon which a university committed to the free pursuit of knowledge is based. If the students' right to learn cannot be questioned, however, it does not qualify them for the rights and privileges which faculty members of demonstrated competence possess: to teach and to further research.

Students should be given the opportunity to participate but not to control academic policies. They are not qualified to teach higher mathematics or advanced philosophy, nor can they be responsible for the curriculum. They cannot make up or grade examinations, or set standards for the granting of degrees. They are not competent to judge the quality of a professor's research, though they may judge his teaching to some extent. Learning is the primary responsibility of the student, teaching and research the primary responsibilities of the faculty, and the functions should not be confused. The policy of allowing student and faculty votes to count the same is made even more untenable by the fact that students are transient, whereas educators have a lifetime involvement in education.

There are other dangers. Devotees of an ethical principle may be so carried away by its virtues that they fail to make distinctions. Participation does not mean politicizing the university. It does not mean that the purposes of the university can be dominated by political pressure groups. It does not mean that vocal minorities, or a fortiori suppressive majorities, can intimidate the community of scholarship. It does not mean that force can be used to coerce faculties. It does mean that a university is a place for reason and moderation, for responsible criticism and the free market of ideas, committed to the involvement of students, faculty, and administrators in the educational process.

A crucial question is often asked: If students and faculty share in the common task of education, which decisions are to be made by students and which by faculty? It is clear that students should be primarily concerned with those standards which concern their behavior and moral choices. The doctrine of *in loco parentis* is no longer justifiable. The private lives and social activities of students are their own business, including what they do off and on campuses, within the bounds of civil law.

They should have the freedom to invite speakers to campus, to organize groups, to publish newspapers and magazines. They should have the full protection of those freedoms which are the right of all other citizens in a democracy, all consistent with the idea of an open campus. Students should be permitted to evaluate their professors as a contribution to the improvement of university teaching; they should assist in selecting scholars in residence or visiting professors, within the limits of the budget, and be permitted to suggest new courses and programs. They should be consulted about university facilities, the library, bookstore, cafeteria, transportation, fees, and tuition; they should be involved in all matters that concern their welfare directly.

Certain decisions should be left to the faculty, among them standards for admission and graduation, grading of student performance, curricular content and subject matter of courses, the goals of the university, the character of faculty or university-sponsored research, faculty appointments, promotions, and tenure.

Participatory democracy in those institutions where competence and knowledge are basic does not entail egalitarianism or unbridled liberty. To paraphrase Aristotle, it involves a form of proportional equality, relative to the competence of the participants, which must not be indiscriminately applied. Organizations may claim specialized competence as a basis for excluding personnel from decision making. Such exclusion would be fraudulent in many cases; it may, as we have seen, be meaningful in the university, but only insofar as it furthers learning.

Participatory democracy should allow competence to emerge; it provides the best opportunities for commitment and talent. It does not deny leadership, or the emergence of elites of demonstrated merit, but seeks to make them representative. The premise of the democratic value system is that "he who wears the shoe best knows where it pinches." The most reliable way to direct an organization is to give the people in it a chance to contribute to its functioning.

Society has presented us with a new and complex phenomenon of large-scale organizations able to suffocate the individual. We need to reawaken the sense of democratic community within organizations. There are dimensions of responsibility that can only be expressed by the individual in terms of his hopes and ideals, which cannot be relinquished to any organization. Our humanist concern is based upon a concern for this individual freedom.

To repeat, the institutions of society are judged by whether or not they help individuals express their talents and contribute to the common good. If so, they will help resolve the problems of alienation in the postmodern world.

# 11

# Does Humanism Have an Ethic of Responsibility?

## Freedom versus Responsibility

Does humanist ethics have a theory of moral responsibility? The critics of secular humanism maintain that it does not. There is the familiar argument against "relativistic ethics." Without some belief in God, we are admonished, obligation collapses. This argument is as old as ethics itself. The theist believes that if religion is absent, ethical duty has no source. Many philosophers have been concerned with this challenge. Kant attempted to provide a foundation for ethics without deriving it from God—though he was confronted in the last analysis with moral antinomies.

The view that belief in God is a secure ground for ethical obligation is fallacious. Since there is insubstantial evidence and surely no proof that God exists, the problem of ethical obligation is only pushed one step back to a premise that is itself precarious. The theistic universe presents an ethical order full of inconsistencies: the problem of evil for one, the abandonment of genuine moral freedom for another. If one's ethical principles depended in the final analysis upon the existence of God and His moral commandments, then one's free moral conscience is compromised. Doing something because God commands it, not because it is right or good, is not itself morally worthy. In the Old Testament, God commanded Abraham to sacrifice his son Isaac and he was willing to obey God's command. This illustration of faith and obedience is hardly morally commendable. The fact that God then bade Abraham not to do so is insufficient reason for Abraham's desisting. It was wrong for Abraham to sacrifice Isaac and one does not need a theological system to say so. Ethical judgments should have autonomous grounding in moral experience, and we expect people to be truthful, honest, sincere, and generous whether or not they believe in God. Moreover, individuals who believe in God espouse contradictory moral commandments. Christians and Jews mandate monogamy; some Muslims practice polygamy. Most Protestant sects are for freedom of choice in abortion; Roman Catholicism is opposed. Christians theoretically should turn the other cheek to an offender; Muslims mete out severe corporal punishment. Theological

This essay was published in *Humanistic Ethics*, ed. Morris Storer (Buffalo, N.Y.: Prometheus Books, 1981).

moral codes depend as much or more on doctrines of revelation, church dogma, and a priestly class than on simple belief in divine power. From belief in the fatherhood of God, any number of opposing moral prescriptions — full of stern admonitions of duty — have been drawn.

One can understand the concern of the theist that humanist ethics without religious guidelines and the institutionalization of a code may not provide sufficient support for moral responsibility. Modern secular movements have brutalized man: Nazism and Stalinism as ideological doctrines abandoned traditional norms and ended up by creating infamous Gulags and moral monsters. Surely the humanist cannot be burdened with or blamed for the totalitarian excesses of the twentieth century. Humanists generally have defended human rights and democracy, and they have been among the first to condemn such tyrannies. Theistic religious institutions, particularly where they have had a monopoly of religious power, have not been immune to the suppression of freedom, as the crusades, the Inquisition, and the wars between Muslims and Hindus, Protestants and Catholics, Jews and Muslims vividly demonstrate.

Nevertheless, the humanist is faced with a crucial ethical question: Insofar as he has defended an ethic of freedom, can he develop a basis for moral responsibility? Regretfully, merely to liberate individuals from authoritarian social institutions, whether church or state, is no guarantee that they will be aware of their moral responsibility to others. The contrary is often the case. Any number of social institutions regulate conduct by some means of norms and rules, and sanctions are imposed for enforcing them. Moral conduct is often ensured because of fear of the consequences of breaking the law or of transgressing moral conventions. Once these sanctions are ignored, we may end up with the Thrasymachian man — someone concerned with his own lust for pleasure, ambition, and power, and impervious to moral constraints. The broader question is not whether you can have morality without religious sanctions but whether you can have it without *any* political, legal, or economic restraints, without, that is, any of the rules of law and order that govern a civilized community.

Some utopian anarchists maintain that human nature is basically beneficent; it is restrictive societal laws that corrupt human beings, and not the contrary. Their solution is to emancipate individuals from them; this they believe will untap a natural propensity for altruism. Regretfully, there is no guarantee that this will occur. Human motivation is highly complex and human nature is capable of both good and evil. Love and hate, self-interest and generosity, sympathy and jealousy, cooperation and competition are so deeply ingrained that we cannot be assured that only the best will in the end prevail. Thus we have no guarantee that individual moral beneficence will reign once all institutional sanctions are removed. Moreover, even *if* the world were only full of people with good intentions, they might still differ in an interpretation or application of their moral convictions, and this can be a further source of conflict.

Let me say at this point that I do not believe that a secular humanist, who is supposedly devoted to a philosophy of freedom and social progress, need be any more altruistic or responsible than the nonhumanist or theist. Humanists can be as deceitful and nasty, as full of pride, and as moved by the lust for fame and power — or as beneficent and other-regarding — as anyone else. No one group can claim privileged possession of the moral virtues. There is no moral exclusivity for any one philosophical, religious, or ideological party. Thus there is no assurance that if one is identified as a "humanist" he or she will be moral, especially in regard to the common human decencies. Indeed, some modern-day humanists are prone to an exacerbated moral self-righteousness that may be more wicked than the wickedness they wish to extirpate. Traditional morality, often unthinking, carries with it the smug complacency of the double standard. Humanists are critical of the devout businessman (the modern-day Cephalus) who prays on the Sabbath, yet uses sharp and exploitative business practices during the week, condones conventional morality as sacrosanct, and is insensitive to hypocrisies and injustices. Often pitted against him, however, is the moral reformer, who — though reform is necessary for moral progress — may become an intolerant moral fanatic, willing to destroy those whom he judges to be unjust or disagrees with. Regretfully, some egalitarians are impervious to the complexities of problems and are willing to impose simplistic moralistic solutions to them.

In raising the basic question, "Can humanist ethics provide a framework for responsible action?" I am leaving aside still another challenge that is often presented to the secular humanist: Can humanism adequately answer the question, "What is the meaning of life?" I have addressed myself to this question elsewhere at length.[1] The theist mistakenly believes that life is not meaningful if God is dead, or if there is no divine purpose to the universe. To that I answer, life has no meaning per se, but is full of opportunities. The meanings we discover depend on what we are willing to put into life, the dreams and ideals we cherish, the plans and projects we initiate. Humanist ethics encourages a person to become what he or she wishes. Here one can say that the good life is possible for individuals without the need for an external support system. Such an ethic emphasizes independence and self-reliance, the development of one's potentialities, the cultivation of critical intelligence, and creative self-actualization. For such autonomous persons, an exuberant and full life, overflowing with meanings, is readily available. This does not deny that our fullest happiness involves other persons and presupposes some harmonious relationships with them. But the problem of the ground of moral responsibility is a separate question. A eudaemonistic theory may indeed be self-centered and the desire for one's self-realization egoistic. A central question of ethics thus concerns our relationship to others: What are our responsibilities and duties to our fellow human beings?

## Moral Education

I am persuaded that a humanistic ethic of freedom is not sufficient unless it fulfills at least two further conditions: First, it presupposes the theory and practice of moral education, and second, insofar as reason can be applied to moral choice, it presupposes a set of prima facie ethical principles that should have some claim upon our action.

As I have said, a central humanist value is moral freedom: the freeing of individuals from excessive restraints so that they may actualize their potentialities and maximize free choice. However, such a normative value is hardly sufficient unless moral growth takes place. It is not enough to release individuals from authoritarian institutions, for some individuals may degenerate into hedonists or amoral egoists; thus we need also to nourish the conditions for moral development, in which an appreciation for the needs of others can emerge; and this is dependent upon moral education.

This need seems to be particularly strong in affluent societies today where narcissism is epidemic; many individuals are consumers first and foremost. The entire domain of their universe is immediate self-gratification. The quest for pleasure is located in buying and consuming, using and discarding things, the gluttonous waste of food and drink, the dictates of fashion and adornments, the amassing of trinkets and gadgets to play with and show off. Much of this consumption is not based upon rational use but upon capricious tastes that are conditioned and titillated by advertisers. The never-ending quest of the passive consumer and spectator is to be amused, but ennui always lurks in the background. The heroes of the consumer morality are comedians, show-business personalities, and sports figures, who exemplify the surface character of life: all show, no depth. If affluent societies have solved the problems of poverty and disease for large sectors of their societies—the bane of all societies heretofore—they now have the problem of enhancing the level of taste.

The need for moral education has been recognized by philosophers from Aristotle to John Stuart Mill and John Dewey. This has at least a twofold dimension: first, the elevation of standards of taste and appreciation, the cultivation of qualitative pleasures and creative enjoyments; second, the development of moral virtues and moral character.

There are different pedagogical views about how to develop moral character. The traditionalist opts for training in discipline. He uses Sunday sermons, rote learning, and the threat of punishment to engender good habits. Religious indoctrination has always attempted to instill respect, fear, and love for the moral code. More recently, educational psychologists have argued that moral education in children and young adults involves a process of growth and development. Although at the most elementary level, moral education depends on some training and example, eventually the goal is the cultivation of autonomous agents, free to choose, aware of moral principles, cognizant of their responsibilities to others, capable of some reflective judgment.

The cognitive element in moral education, though, is not sufficient by itself. Morality must enlist the whole person and must address itself to the emotive and aesthetic components of the moral life: to develop attitudes in which some genuine concern for the needs of others is rooted in rational comprehension at the same time that it is fused with sentiment and feeling. Aristotle recognized this in the *Nicomachean Ethics,* when he observed that students would not appreciate his course in ethics and politics unless they had already developed some of the moral virtues through experience and living.[2]

The question of moral responsibility is as much a psychological question as it is a theoretical one: How does one develop an appreciation for others, the moral point of view, a sense of altruism and giving, honesty, truthfulness, sincerity and trust? Some individuals are autistic, self-centered, selfish, concentrating on their own private gratifications. Such individuals lead the lives of crippled moral dwarfs. How does one develop moral growth in them?

Some say by exposing such individuals to the free give-and-take of moral inquiry and by examining moral dilemmas. I agree, though regretfully at times the result may be moral skepticism and nihilism, rather than a developed moral sense. Whether moral sympathy is innate or acquired is difficult to say, given the complexities of human nature.

Psychologists have differed on this point. Some, such as A. H. Maslow, maintain that moral sympathy is intrinsic to human nature and that the inner self which needs to unfold is basically good.[3] Others, such as B. F. Skinner, believe that various forms of moral behavior can be conditioned by operant reinforcement.[4] I believe that both theories have an element of truth: the roots of morality are found in our dependence and reciprocity as social animals, but whether morality is actualized depends in part upon cultural conditions. Surely the schools alone cannot accomplish the task of nurturing moral character, even though they still remain a vital source, for all the institutions of society have a formative role in developing character.

One issue concerns the question of the neutrality of the schools, particularly in pluralistic democratic societies, where opposing sets of values may compete. Should the teacher simply seek to clarify existing values that the student already possesses and has brought to the classroom, or should the teacher attempt to "indoctrinate" (a bad word for libertarians and democrats) new values? Some believe that the school should remain neutral, merely placing value problems under cognitive scrutiny. This is the position of the values-clarification movement.[5] Jean Piaget and Lawrence Kohlberg believe that there are stages of moral development.[6] Whatever one's approach—values clarification or moral development—some values are being assumed by the teacher: intelligence, democracy, and tolerance as a minimum, the quest for fair play or a universalistic criterion as a maximum.

Secular humanist educators have suffered heavy attack, particularly in the United States, at the hands of theists, who maintain that in teaching moral education in the schools, a new religion of secular humanism is being indoctrinated and that this is contrary to the constitutional prohibition against the establishment of religion.

I think this latter charge is unfounded, for if it were generalized the schools could not teach science, contemporary literature, classical philosophy and ethics, or many other fields without being accused of indoctrination in the "religion of secular humanism." What the critics wish to repeal is the modern world; they wish a return to fundamental biblical tradition.

Nonetheless, I believe that the schools need to engage in moral "instruction"—a better term than "indoctrination"—of some kind, since they do it anyway. In one sense virtually all education is moral. Insofar as education strives to expand the horizons of the person, even his intellectual understanding, there is some modification, however subtle, and reconstruction of values going on.

Even in a democracy, the schools can, and should, consciously do this by focusing on the most basic and commonly shared moral values: truth, honesty, sincerity, trust, kindness, generosity, friendship, sharing, concern for others, etc. This can be accomplished without raising ultimate ontological questions of where these values are rooted—in theology or nature. Moral education thus attempts to develop within the child and the young person both an emotive and intellectual basis for character formation. That this should be done is the message of philosophical ethics from the Greeks to the modern world: the autonomy of the moral virtues independent of a religious or nonreligious framework.

Now a good deal of the opposition to moral education in the schools concerns the attempt to offer solutions to specific moral issues that are under dispute in society. Granted, the schools cannot live in isolation from the concrete moral problems that trouble society; but courses in sex education, and discussion of abortion, euthanasia, women's rights, homosexuality, racial integration and intermarriage, war and peace will produce opposing viewpoints. It is enough for the schools to discuss such moral dilemmas, examining alternative positions, without imposing the viewpoints of the teachers or the community. But this is distinct from *the need to root within the psychological makeup of each individual a set of moral dispositions and virtues.* If they are absent, then libertarian societies may be faced with an increase in the number of morally retarded individuals, free to do what they want, insensitive to the hurt they may cause others.

A tragic illustration of the problem faced by democratic societies that do not have programs of moral education is the wanton murders of Charles Frankel, his wife, and two neighbors in Bedford Hills, New York. The Frankels and their neighbors were brutally shot and their homes rifled by thieves. Charles Frankel, an eloquent defender of humanism and democratic freedom, had faith in human intelligence. He was another victim of the excesses of passion and violence unleashed by those in a free society who lack moral virtues.

Some sociobiologists believe that moral turpitude may be in part genetic and that some individuals, particularly hardened criminals, are incorrigible. How, for example, should the penal system deal with repeated offenders? By coddling or punishing them? Should the legal system be rehabilitative or retributive in its approach? The humanist does not wish to give up in his constant effort to reform the institutions of society so that the best that human beings are capable of will emerge. Konrad Lorenz and others, however, maintain that aggression is innate in the human species.[7] Human vices, such as selfishness, laziness, vindictiveness, hatred, sloth, pride, jealousy are so widespread in human behavior that we are all capable of them at times. Perhaps humanists have been overly optimistic about the full reaches of human nature. Perhaps "original sin" — in natural and biological terms — is present in some individuals, who are immune to our efforts at amelioration. What we need is a deeper empirical understanding of human nature, without reading in what our values demand.

The difficulty in postmodern society is that moral education no longer can be entrusted to the family or the schools, and it surely cannot be left to the churches insofar as they preach intangible doctrines of redemption and salvation. In the Western world moral values must compete with other "values" spawned by an economic system that prizes consumer entertainment as the highest value, where the mass media sells violence, pornography, born-again religion, and the paranormal to gullible consumers. I am not simply indicting capitalism nor am I approving governmental regulation of the free market in ideas. What I am pointing to rather is the critical need for some measure of moral education in the larger media of communication. Those who live in democratic societies need to work to influence the content of the media if we are to have any hope of developing moral character. Totalitarian Marxist societies have hardly solved the problems either, for they have imposed in their systems of education and in their mass media encapsulated moral programs. They have abandoned an ethic of freedom in favor of indoctrination in egalitarianism. The result is that the individual is lost. He is dispossessed of his rights; he has only duties to the state but few freedoms from it.

## Prima Facie Ethical Principles

But this still leaves open the question for one committed intellectually to a humanist ethics: Can the question of moral responsibility be resolved? How does one reconcile self-actualization and personal freedom with the rights and needs of others? On the scale of human values, which have higher priority, *my* needs and interests or *yours*?

There is, in my judgment, no ultimate resolution of this problem, no deductive proof of the "moral point of view." It seems to me that some constructive skepticism is a necessary component of moral philosophy; although a reflective person will, in general, come to abide by the moral point of view, it is not universally binding. To some extent, one's own best interest — such as in cases of one's health or survival — ought to have a person's first commitment; in other cases, one's responsibility to other human beings (one's children, family, friends, colleagues, or countrymen) should have a stronger claim. In still other cases, a person recognizes an obligation to consider humanity as a whole and future generations yet unborn (as in questions concerning worldwide pollution or nuclear holocaust). What our duties and obligations are always depends upon the situation at hand and the kinds of questions being raised. We must be prepared to examine and revise our options by means of deliberative inquiry.

Yet I do not think that we need be led to a completely relativistic position in which no general principles are relevant. On the contrary, I submit that a naturalistic and humanistic ethical theory can incorporate general ethical principles that have significance in a situation.

How do we decide what to choose? I do not think that utilitarianism gives us an accurate guide for all moral choices. Surely, we need to take into account the *consequences of our action* in evaluating various alternatives, a pragmatic rather than a strictly utilitarian criterion. The greatest-happiness principle, though relevant in some contexts, is too general to be of much help. If a teleological ethics by itself is insufficient — even though it is essential for any balanced ethical theory — some naturalistic form of deontological ethics should be recognized. Problems of ethical choice for the humanist involves an individual's quest for happiness; he will undertake those things that activate him and contribute to the fullness of his life. But maturity of judgment soon enables one to recognize that his deepest well-being is tied up with others and that *caring* is an essential nutrient in human relationships. Still it is not simply a question of the prudential calculation of one's long-range self-interest. There are general principles of behavior that a developed moral agent will come to accept and these will have some bearing upon his conscience and conduct.

These ethical principles are not derived from God or divinity, nor do they come simply from some moral law implanted within the womb of nature or human nature. Nor indeed are they absolute or final in the sense that they are inviolable. I prefer the term "general" rather than "universal," since they are only approximate guides for conduct and there may be exceptions to them.

W. D. Ross uses the term "prima facie" to denote the fact that some duties are conditionally obligatory, but whether it is our actual duty to fulfill them depends upon a full examination of our obligations within the situation. According to Ross, among the prima facie duties are those that rest upon a person's previous acts, those resting on the acts of others, the contracts and commitments entered into, and the claims made upon us. There are also middle-range duties incumbent upon us: positive duties, such as keeping our promises or paying our debts, and negative ones such as not cheating others. But there are more general duties as well: such as nonmaleficence, not injuring others; justice, attempting to distribute goods as widely as possible; and beneficence, helping to relieve distress where we are able to do so.[8]

I prefer to use the term "principles" rather than "duties," because we can generalize various kinds of action and recognize that these are general prescriptions, rules, and policies we ought to observe. Most of these are part of the proverbial wisdom: "Honesty is the best policy" or "Do unto others as you would have them do unto you."

Now the question that can be raised is: What is the foundation of these prima facie general ethical principles? Many who have defended them have done so on intuitive grounds. They have said that either they cannot be proven and are true without proof, or that they are self-evident to the reflective conscience.

I deny their intuitive character. Such general principles are not mysterious or sacrosanct, but naturalistic and empirical phenomena. They have developed in social relationships over long periods of time—in part because of common human needs and necessities, and in part because they have come to be recognized as imperative in human relationships if we are to realize social harmony. They are tested by their observable effects in human conduct. A relationship between two persons cannot long endure if there is insincerity between them, and a human community cannot long endure in peace if there is widepread duplicity. General ethical principles, however, are not simply justifiable as instrumental; in time they come to have some intrinsic merit, and we come to feel strongly about them for their own sake: they are both means and ends. Those who consider them simply expedient may have no compunctions about breaking or compromising them at will and may be corrupted in the process.

There is an ironic legacy that dependence upon some forms of purely utilitarian or pragmatic moral systems have bequeathed us; that is, some individuals and groups have been willing on utilitarian grounds to justify the use of *any* means to achieve ends they consider worthwhile. The conclusion that Machiavellians have drawn is that if they are to remain in power, they must be ready to employ unscrupulous means. Authoritarian defenders of the status quo have applied the full force of the state, violating human rights, in order to secure their ends; and despots have always employed heinous methods of torture and terror. The paradox of moral compromise— the use of evil means to achieve noble ends—has also undermined Marxism as an ethical philosophy. Marxists are critical of the injustices of capitalism; they wish to usher in a utopian system of ideal values. But some apparently feel that this justifies them in using terrorist means to defeat their opponents, even if it results in the slaughter of innocent bystanders. Totalitarian communist regimes have, on the same ground, crushed dissent and opposition from "enemies" of the party or the revolution.

Humanists are not immune to moral corruption either. I have learned from personal experience in humanist organizations that even those who call themselves humanists will at times use mendacious means to achieve their goals and that they are as prone to vanity, jealousy, vindictiveness, and other foibles as other human beings. Some "humanitarians" and "philan-thropists" make contributions or are devoted to a cause not for the good they will achieve, but for personal power and acclaim. Others will stand by and allow the rape of the moral dignities, on the mistaken assumption that sin is always committed by nonhumanists (bishops, divines, and other such personages), not by the "emancipated." The result is often that the emanci-pated, bereft of all conventional standards, are left without any viable prin-ciples of ethical conduct at all. That is all the more reason humanist ethics needs double rooting. It should have (1) a teleological interest in realizing worthy ends, goods, values, *and* (2) a deontological concern for fulfilling obligations, responsibilities, duties—an ethic of principles, as well as an ethic of ideal ends.

Which of these roots ought to prevail in ethics? Which ought to have the highest priority, the good or the right? I am unwilling to affix an a priori solution to this question. As I have said, it all depends upon the situation at hand. In problems of moral choice, we need to take into account empirical and pragmatic criteria: the facts of the case, the means at our disposal, the consequences of our actions. We also need to consider the prima facie ethi-cal principles that are relevant. Our actual duties, obligations, and responsi-bilities will depend upon the situation and the social milieu in which we live. These are always particular and concrete, growing out of our commitments and values, the contracts entered into, the claims made upon us. Only empirical inquiry can tell us what we ought to do in a given situation.

There is often a conflict between values, and we cannot attain all of them. We may wish to travel widely, raise a family, and have a successful career all at the same time—which may be difficult or impossible. In other cases, there may be a clash between a good to be achieved and a responsi-bility to be fulfilled, as in a conflict between what a man may desire and what others expect of him—and one may have to give way to the other. Similarly, an act may be justifiable, even though in itself evil, because of the preponderant long-range good that will ensue, as when we reluctantly decide to go to war to defend ourselves or others against aggression. In still other situations, all of the alternatives may be bad, and we may be com-pelled to choose the lesser of two evils, as in the case of a person suffering from an incurable disease, who is faced with death, a prolonged and hor-rible one, or euthanasia, but death in any case. The point is, we need to *bal-ance* the competing claims of our values and principles, considerations of the good and the right.

Humanist philosophers have recognized that our ultimate obligation, in the final analysis, is the use of rational thought to resolve, as best we can, such moral dilemmas. What we will decide to do, as I have said, presupposes some moral education and a sensitivity to general ethical principles — an important concomitant of humanist ethics. Still, the autonomous person capable of reflective choice is his own best guide. We need to appreciate at the same time the limitations of absolute moral certitude and the possibilities of moral wisdom. Authoritarian and legalistic moralists will no doubt object to such a conclusion and will wish for something more. Humanist ethics may provide something less than they desire, but this does not mean that ethical choice need be capricious or subjectivistic, or that it is unamenable to some form of objective critical appraisal. Indeed, humanist ethics, although the least pretentious of ethical theories in what it promises, may yet be the most reliable; for it may be best able to allow both the good life to be realized and the moral decencies to prevail.

## NOTES

1. See Paul Kurtz, *The Fullness of Life* (New York: Horizon Press, 1974) and *Exuberance* (Buffalo: Prometheus Books, 1977).

2. Aristotle, *Nicomachean Ethics,* bk. 1, chap. 3.

3. Abraham H. Maslow, *Toward a Psychology of Being,* 2nd ed. (New York: Van Nostrand, 1968).

4. B. F. Skinner, *Walden Two* (New York: Macmillan, 1948).

5. Louis Raths et al., *Values and Teaching: Working with Values in the Classroom* (Indianapolis: Bobbs-Merrill, 1966); Louis Simon et al., *Values Clarification: A Handbook of Practical Strategies for Teachers and Students* (New York: Hart, 1972).

6. See Jean Piaget, *The Moral Judgment of the Child* (London: Routledge and Kegan Paul, 1932) and *The Child's Conception of the World* (New York: Harcourt, Brace, 1929). Also, Lawrence Kohlberg, "From Is to Ought," *Cognitive Development and Epistemology,* ed. T. Mischel (New York: Academic Press, 1971), pp. 131–256; "Stages of Moral Development as a Basis for Moral Education," *Moral Education,* ed. C. M. Beck et al. (Toronto: University of Toronto Press, 1971), pp. 23–92; and "Stage and Sequence: The Cognitive Development Approach to Socialization," *Handbook of Socialization Theory and Research,* ed. D. A. Goslin (Chicago: Rand-McNally, 1969), pp. 347–480.

7. Konrad Lorenz, *On Aggression* (New York: Bantam Books, 1970).

8. W. D. Ross, *The Right and the Good* (Oxford: Clarendon Press, 1930).

# 12

# Moral Faith versus Ethical Skepticism

There are two contrasting approaches to the moral life. The first I shall call "moral faith" and the second "ethical skepticism." Moral faith has been the deepest and most pervasive force throughout the history of human culture, and the proponents of this approach have had the predominant influence. Ethical skepticism has been relatively rare in human history and has been espoused by only a small number of intellectuals. It has always been considered by establishments to be an extremely dangerous position. Its earliest known proponent was Socrates, at least insofar as he questioned the reigning orthodoxy of his age; though his position later became enshrined as part of a new faith.

Of course, there are other postures one may adopt in respect to morality. One may, for example, be largely indifferent to the demands of morality and not take it seriously. One may be a cynic about it, or even assume the role of the nihilist and reject morality entirely. I will not attempt to deal with these positions in this paper, even though some verge perhaps on ethical skepticism. Rather, I shall focus on the two alternative views of morality I have set forth and will attempt to explicate and also defend one variety of ethical skepticism, though skepticism may assume many different forms.

## Moral Faith

The term "faith" is usually employed in reference to transcendent beliefs, that is, beliefs that describe, designate, or point to some existent reality that we cannot demonstrate exists. To say that one has faith usually means that one accepts belief in a state or reality for which there is insufficient evidence, though one has the conviction that this reality exists in some form. Faith is that portion of one's psychological belief-state that transcends the evidence offered for the belief. A moral belief, on the contrary, is normative or prescriptive. It does not simply allege that something is the case, but that it ought to be; and it recommends bringing into being a state of affairs that is considered to be "good," "just," "valuable," "right," or has some other commendable properties. Those who express a moral faith hold it to

---

This essay was first published in the *Journal of Value Inquiry*, vol. 14.

be *true* in some sense of the term; that is, they believe that moral values or principles have some reality independent of the person who espouses them, and that therefore we have an obligation to fulfill or obey them. Those who espouse a moral faith usually also express a deep-seated commitment to that faith. Indeed, the term "faith" implies that a person will defend his moral commitment. It implies that there are deep roots within the individual personality and/or the social institutions that espouse the faith. It is not simply an intellectual commitment on the level of cognition, but involves passion and feeling. It is both *imperative,* in the sense that those who hold the faith believe that what it recommends ought to exist, if it does not yet, and it is *expressive,* in that it evokes an emotional response. But it is not merely emotive, and it is not simply a matter of taste or caprice, for it gives vent to our *deepest* attitudes and longings. Thus a moral faith is generally grounded in one's first principles.

To talk about a person's faith in the area of morality is analogous to talking about a person's faith in religion. When we probe a person's moral roots, we know that we have touched rock-bottom when we are able to elicit a blush or a stammer. Faith is at the core of a person's value structure. Once challenged, it often provokes an intense defensive reaction.

There are at least two fundamental components of a person's moral faith: basic values and moral principles. Though we may distinguish them, values and principles overlap and are intertwined within a personal or social framework. The *values* of a person or a society refer to the things that are found to be good and worthwhile, that are cherished and held dear. In behavioristic terms, values refer to preferential, selective, or teleonomic behavior, the attitudinal-cognitive-conative motives that impel us to achieve goals and purposes. A person has a great number of values, from liking a glass of vodka, a chocolate ice-cream sundae, a melody, or an embrace, to approval of an intellectual position or the long-range quest for happiness. In philosophical language, teleological theories have focused on the ends and goals that are considered to be most enduring and worthwhile. A wide range of experiences has been cherished and diverse ends have been pursued. One's basic commitments, whether to love, piety, science, or the general happiness, express one's deepest values and the kind of world we wish to bring about. For some this refers to ideal ends to be achieved.

A second component of the moral life are moral *principles.* I use the term "principle" here to refer to a rule of conduct, a standard or norm governing action. A principle is usually taken to be universal or general in that it lays down policy guides for future conduct, or it limits or proscribes other forms of human action. It is clearly prescriptive or prohibitive, recommending or advising us how to live or behave. Generally, the philosophical schools that have emphasized this are called *deontological.* They emphasize our obligations and responsibilities to obey or fulfill the principles that serve as moral guides. They underscore the demands of justice and fairness.

We are reminded of any number of moral principles, such as the biblical proverbs: "Love thy neighbor as thyself," "Life for life, eye for eye, tooth for tooth, hand for hand, foot for foot, burn for burn, wound for wound, stripe for stripe," "Do unto others as you would have them do unto you." But there are many other moral principles we recognize: To tell the truth, keep promises, and not cheat, steal, kill, or injure another. Moral principles are often revised and new ones introduced. Two recently enunciated moral principles have aroused intense debate and commitment in democratic societies. There is, for example, the libertarian principle: An individual should be permitted to do whatever he wishes, so long as he does not interfere with the rights of others. And there is the egalitarian principle: All individuals are equal in dignity and worth and entitled to equality of opportunity, equal consideration, or equal deserts. Still other moral principles have emerged today involving the recognition of human rights.

A great variety of moral values and principles have competed throughout history, producing alternative moral codes. The samurai warrior, Christian priest, bourgeois entrepreneur, bohemian poet, scientific investigator, and Marxist revolutionary express different values and principles. Thus there is the familiar problem of cultural relativity. Each social group seeks to inculcate its cherished values and principles. It provides sanctions for those who flout them and rewards those who conform and are considered to be the paragons of virtue.

Moral systems that are rooted in faith generally take their basic values and central moral principles as universal; these are held to express deep truths about the universe of man. Values and principles are not taken as subjective nor are they considered to be merely a matter of taste or caprice; they are allegedly grounded in the nature of things. Thus there are efforts to derive them from religious, metaphysical, ideological, or scientific doctrines. Moral values and principles are not without cognitive support; they are conceptualized and defined, and attempts are made to justify them by an appeal to reason and to defend them against their critics. All of these codes however, have religious or semireligious qualities and elements of faith attached to them.

There are no doubt differences in the degrees of faith with which moral systems are held. On the one extreme is moral absolutism. Here moral principles are considered to be absolute commandments, and they are enforced by the threat of punishment, whether from Jehovah or the state. There is apprehension about flouting them and moral phobias develop; principles become inviolable. Orthodox religious moralities have absolute prohibitions against divorce, adultery, or homosexuality. Such systems can be highly repressive, even tyrannical.

A strongly held faith more often than not involves self-righteousness. There is a fear of heretics, disbelievers, or aliens, who are taken as "immoral" or "wicked" and are condemned as corrupters of the true morality. Adherents believe they have a duty to further the moral faith and to oppose or even destroy offending adversaries. There may be a heightened sense of a cosmic struggle between the forces of good and evil and a conviction that one's side needs all the support it can get in its holy crusade against those benighted souls who reject one's moral point of view or choose to live differently. While these attitudes apply to religious believers—whether orthodox defenders of the old faith or the disciples of a newer cult—they also may characterize entirely secular movements, which may likewise be engulfed by ardor and the need to sacrifice for the cause.

One's moral faith may be considered far more important than one's religious belief; for often it is not what you believe in that counts, but what you do, how you bring up your children and how your women are treated. These matters touch at the very core of one's sense of propriety; and they can arouse intense hatred if they offend it. Public approbation or disapprobation may not be sufficient to support the moral code. If so, other institutions emerge to enforce compliance. A priestly class employs the symbols of God's power and the threat of excommunication or damnation. Or the state becomes the ultimate guardian of morality, for it can enact and enforce the laws. Although the state may legislate morality, all the institutions of society may be charged with inculcating and reinforcing moral conduct: the family, schools, economic institutions, even voluntary associations.

An appeal to the fatherhood of God is a familiar psychological device for sanctifying one's moral principles, but there are the secular equivalents. The twentieth century is all too familiar with secular ideologies that involve ethical-political doctrines and principles held to be implicit within the womb of nature. Instead of God, Marxists appeal to the dialectical laws of history, in which higher forms of social relations struggle to emerge and in which one's highest duty is to assist the oppressed or achieve a classless society. Influenced by Darwinism, Herbert Spencer and others sought to defend free enterprise and the struggle of the fittest for survival. Others defended the idea of inevitable human progress. Gobineau and Chamberlin later provided the basis for Nazi racist policies, but these were based upon mistaken notions of biologically superior and inferior races. No doubt one can indict such simplistic approaches on the grounds that we ought not to commit science to a dogmatic moral faith. Perhaps these theories were not verified, but were forms of pseudoscience. It just shows, however, that scientific theories can be translated into ethical prescriptions and be used as justifications for repression. There are many other illustrations of the uses of science in moral persuasions: the debate about IQ and race, sociobiology and the instinct for aggression, etc. Is science relevant to ethics? Can it function, not as a faith, but in another way?

One fault in these systems, I submit, is that they present a hierarchical structure of values and principles; that is, they take one value or principle and seek to make it all-controlling. This is a common approach in any system of faith. But one should guard against the tyranny of principles, that is, using a principle as an absolute and not admitting any exception to it. To illustrate: Those who argue that it is wrong to take an innocent human life — the fetus is held to be a form of human life and innocent — maintain that any form of abortion is always wrong under any circumstance, even when the fetus is grossly retarded or the pregnancy is due to rape or incest. Conversely, the libertarian defends the principle that an individual should be permitted to do whatever he wants, so long as he does not harm others. Thomas Szasz comes out against any involuntary commitment to mental hospitals, even if a patient is seriously disturbed or schizophrenic. He denies any evidence for the latter. To be consistent, we are told, the libertarian principle means that heroin and other addictive drugs should be legalized — even if this would mean the death or debilitation of a large sector of the population. Thus, for dedicated moral faith, root values and first principles cannot be held in contradiction. Consistency is the ultimate test as to whether one is true to one's principles. A deeply held moral faith can, if pursued to its ultimate conclusion, become ludicrous if it is applied without discrimination.

One's faith is often the product of one's unexamined assumptions. We imbibe our moral faith at our mother's knee and it persists without reflection. It is nourished and fed in the sociocultural context in which we grow and function. It is prerational and affective-conative in character. Some justification for our moral faith-state is sought when it is challenged by others. At that point, appeals may be made to a higher religious faith or moral faith may be derived from an elaborate ideological system. Or we may seek to justify faith by reference to science. Should we equate a moral faith based upon religion or ideology with one based upon science? Is that not stretching it too far? Are there not important differences? I think that there are. Yet I fear that some degree of self-deception lurks under the mantle of science. In its most extreme form there is worship of the faith that "science will save us." The scientific intellectual is not unlike the religious intellectual waiting in expectation of Godot, who never arrives. The scientific believer is waiting for his own Godot, the salvation promised by science.

We should not deceive ourselves into believing that scientific intellectuals are any more fair-minded or impartial than others when it comes to their own cherished values. These often reflect their deepest prejudices. This can be seen vividly in the area of political belief. For many intellectuals, politics often functions religiously. I am often struck by the deep partisan bias — in most cases a liberal-left orientation — and the intense animosities displayed toward individuals or parties that oppose it. Intellectuals are not unique in this regard. Their emotive bias is similar to those who have a conservative right-wing faith, especially business or corporate executives. Alas, all too few intellectuals recognize their political faith for what it is. There is some need for political skepticism about all strongly held partisan positions, whether of the left or the right.

I do not mean to suggest that all moral faiths are intransigent or not self-critical. There are periods in history when, with radical paradigm shifts, new values and principles emerge. Some moral faiths are unyielding; others are receptive to modification in the light of intellectual criticism. And that, as I view it, is the essential role that ethical skepticism can play in reforming and liberalizing preexisting systems and making them responsive to alternative conceptions of the good life or the just society.

## Ethical Skepticism

I do not wish to deny that science is relevant to ethics, but it is important that we be clear about what scientific inquiry can and cannot do. It can never, in my judgment, free us entirely from ethical indeterminacy. Some skepticism is essential to the life blood of the scientific enterprise itself.

What is ethical skepticism? Let me describe it as it developed in the field of twentieth-century metaethics. Interestingly, it has been used most directly against naturalistic and scientific ethics, that is, the confident expectations of philosophers and scientists that we might develop a science of ethics and value.

There are three parts of the skeptical critique: (1) there are inherent logical difficulties in defining our basic ethical terms and concepts; (2) there are epistemological difficulties in testing ethical principles and judgments or of deriving "ought" statements from "is" statements, values and facts; and (3) there are existential difficulties in justifying first principles and root values.

G. E. Moore was among the first to raise serious questions about the meaning of ethical terms and concepts. In particular, he argued that the "good" was indefinable, that all previous ethical theories which had attempted to provide a definition or theory of the good had committed a logical fallacy, which he labeled the "naturalistic fallacy." This fallacy applied to any effort to derive the good or other normative concepts from nonnormative equivalents. Moore leveled his attack at the utilitarians, especially John Stuart Mill, who were influential at the turn of the century. The utilitarians had attempted to create a science of ethics. They sought to derive normative ethics (the good was defined as pleasure or happiness) from a descriptive theory of motivation (psychological hedonism; that is, all humans seek to maximize pleasure and avoid pain). It was a mistake, said Moore, to try to find a nonnormative substitute for "good." He offered his famous "open-question argument." For any definition proposed, one could always ask: But *is* it good, and *why* should I accept your definition? "Good" is "good," said Moore, a "simple nonnatural quality." It is "indefinable," like yellow, though we can know what it is directly and intuitively. Moore's objection applied not only to scientific naturalism but also to any and all efforts at definition. It applied equally to metaphysical or theological definitions — to those in which the good is identified with "God's will," "human progress," the "general happiness," or anything else.

I think Moore was mistaken about much of this. His reasons for rejecting normative definitions were questionable. He thought that the property "good" was a floating "nonnatural" Platonic essence; that is why it was indefinable. We can raise the open-question argument against Moore himself: Why accept his epistemological definitions of "good"? If Moore is correct, then a definists fallacy might apply to *all* scientific efforts at descriptive definition. One could not provide rigorous operational definitions in the sciences for anything. A thing is what it is and not something else.

Other neo-Kantian intuitionists in twentieth-century ethics (Sidgwick, Prichard, Ross, etc.) did not focus on teleological terms, such as "good" or "value," which they thought were derivative and definable, but upon deontological terms such as "right," "wrong," or "justice." These they found nonreductive and indefinable. Although such ethical predicates are knowable, they argued these are not translatable into nonethical terminology. Neither Moore nor the deontological intuitionists were skeptics or subjectivists. They believed that ethical knowledge was meaningful and possible and that there was such a thing as ethical truth.

Of special interest to scientific naturalists are the further perplexing questions they raised: What is the proof of axioms, postulates, and first principles? Mill thought we could not prove first principles. For Mill, the basic point of utilitarianism was that all moral rules are to be tested by their consequences, by whether or not they contribute to the greatest happiness. Mill committed a logical blunder: the only proof we could give that something is visible is that it can be seen, or audible is that it can be heard, and therefore the only proof that something is desirable is that it can be desired. The fallacy here rests in the conclusion that the suffix "-able" implies that a thing *ought* to be desired—not that it can—and this has *normative* force. Thus, Mill's attempted proof of the basic premise of utilitarianism was formally invalid. Whether Mill, one of the leading logicians of the day, had his tongue in his cheek when he wrote is open to debate. The key conclusion that the critics of scientific naturalism drew was that normative judgments could not be derived from descriptive premises. No less an authority than David Hume, the leading skeptic of modern philosophy, is responsible for recognizing the fallacy in attempting to derive an imperative statement from a descriptive one.

There are two key issues here. First, can we define ethical terms and concepts? Second, how can we test ethical judgments? The two other schools in twentieth-century philosophy—logical positivism and existentialism—have further assaulted the foundations of classical philosophy, undermining our confidence in reason and the conviction that we can create a science of ethics or values based on science. The logical positivists agreed with Moore and the intuitionists that we cannot define ethical terms and concepts. The reason for this, they argued, are different from Moore's. Normative terms are nondescriptive and nondesignative. Ethical language has other functions.

It is expressive or emotive in character and imperative in function. The reason we cannot define ethical terms is because they have no identifiable empirical referrents in the world, no sense data to which they refer. Being evocative, they give vent to our feelings and attitudes and seek to arouse similar responses in others. Any effort to provide objective definitions are thus bound to fail and are in the last analysis "persuasive."

The emotivists in ethics drew a threefold distinction between (1) descriptive, (2) analytic, and (3) emotive sentences. The first could be tested by some empirical verification, at least in principle. The second were tautological and formally valid in terms of the rules that governed their use. The third had no identifiable means by which we might confirm them. There were no criteria by which we could determine their truth values. Thus value judgments and ethical sentences had no intersubjective methods of confirmation. They were often prey to indeterminable disputes. This question became pivotal: How could we resolve normative disagreements?

C. L. Stevenson provided us with a modified emotive theory. Many disagreements, he said, were rooted in beliefs. These could be resolved, at least in principle, where factual matters are at issue. Presumably disagreements in the descriptive sciences could be overcome by reference to empirical confirmation or disconfirmation, indirectly if not directly. Ethical disputes, where they are grounded in cognitive beliefs, could be resolved by pointing out the mistakes about factual conditions or the consequences of proposed policies. But ethical disagreements that are rooted in attitudes may be difficult or impossible to resolve. It all depends upon whether or not we share similar attitudes. A science of value thus might reach a hopeless impasse; for whether or not we can solve a moral dispute depends upon whether we share the same moral faith. And when we hit rock-bottom, we may not hold the same ethical convictions.

On this last point existentialism is especially pertinent. For it has maintained that there is a kind of absurdity concerning first principles, and that how we choose to live may, in the last analysis, depend upon a leap of faith. At crucial turning points in life we may be confronted with a kind of radical freedom—to choose or not to choose—and there are no ultimate guidelines. Our first principles are beyond proof. They grow out of and are validated in the process of living; and there is no deductive proof that can be given for one style of life rather than another.

There has been a lot of discussion and analysis since the emotive theory and existentialism burst upon the scene. An extensive critical literature has examined their claims and shown them to be excessive. First, although we may not define ethical terms arbitrarily, their meanings are embedded in our language, and they have a wide variety of uses, which are not simply emotive. Although normative terms are not primarily descriptive, factual considerations are relevant to their definition and uses, and it is by reference to descriptive properties that we apply value terms to objects. For example, if we say "this chair is comfortable," we may use the term "comfortable" because the chair is "soft" or "supportive" and has other descriptive properties.

Second, although value judgments cannot be deduced from descriptive sentences, descriptive sentences are relevant to their verification. There is a logic of judgments of practice, and we employ them in such applied sciences as medicine, engineering, psychiatry, and pedagogy. Value disagreements are not primarily a question of feeling or caprice; there are objective considerations relevant to the context under analysis and the decision-making procedures.

Third, in an ethical dilemma we usually do not have to go all the way back to first principles, but we resolve the problem by dealing with the values and principles that are relevant. The situation generally provides some guidelines and parameters. A return to first principles occurs only in special crisis situations. Normally we deal with principles of the middle-range. Thus there is a kind of practical wisdom that we discover in experience, a kind of objective relativism. What we do is relative to the situation in which we have to make a choice, and these are amenable to some intelligent criticism. Thus there are objective considerations and standards in the field of ethical judgment.

Yet in spite of the foregoing, *some* degree of ethical skepticism remains, and I do not see how we can transcend it entirely. There are, however, two kinds of ethical skeptics. First, there are those who maintain that ethics is entirely capricious and emotive and that no knowledge is relevant to choice. This kind of nihilistic and negative skepticism is self-contradictory and belied by life itself. Some intelligent basis for criticism is necessary, if we are to live and function. Second, there is a kind of modified ethical skepticism, which uses knowledge and data but is never entirely able to prove its first principles or find a decisive verification for its values or principles for those who do not already accept them. Although it rejects moral faith as self-deceptive, it recognizes that the ultimate act of choosing a way of life and the form of being already embedded in a context of values and principles—as the de facto given—are beyond decisive confirmation. We can at best vindicate our basic principles and values and make them seem reasonable to other humans; it is difficult to prove or verify them in any conclusive way.

## A Modified Form of Ethical Naturalism

In what follows I wish to outline a modified form of ethical naturalism. Let me indicate, however, what it can and cannot do: (1) It cannot hope to derive or deduce from our scientific study of nature, society, or human nature a complete set of moral values or principles that everywhere applies. (2) It cannot hope to derive universal values or principles that are objectively verified in the same way as descriptive hypotheses and theories are. What I wish to suggest is a weaker form of ethical naturalism. Simply stated, it is as follows: *Scientific knowledge is relevant to our choices and values and should be part of the evidential and valuational base from which we can formulate ethical judgments.*

Now my underlying premise, which some will no doubt question, is that man is a free, autonomous, and creative agent, at least in the sense that he faces problems and is capable of choosing between alternatives. Knowledge can assist an individual or a community to make wiser or more effective choices.

The basic questions we face are: How shall we choose? What values and principles should guide us? I would suggest the following range of relevant facts:

1. We first have to consider the *factual knowledge* that we have, as drawn from everyday life and the sciences. This refers to:

  (a) the particular facts of the case and the specific circumstances in which we are involved;
  (b) the *causal conditions* that are operative, the social conditions that have led to the present state, the invariant causal regularities;
  (c) the *means* at our disposal, the techniques that are available;
  (d) the likely *consequences* that might ensue, the results or effects of various courses of action;
  (e) the *common needs* of human beings, as preconditions of survival, health, and functioning. All five of these are value-neutral.

2. We also need knowledge of preexisting *values* (teleological ethics):

  (a) comparative knowledge of values that other humans have had, whether in the past or in the present;
  (b) those we are now committed to or that control our lives.

3. We need knowledge of *moral principles* (deontological ethics):

  (a) comparative knowledge of the rules and norms that have governed mankind, empirically based data about the rules of the game;
  (b) the moral principles that are now relevant to the individual and/or the society in which he lives.

What we ought to do is a function of these three conditions: knowledge of (1) facts, (2) values, and (3) principles. The second and third considerations suggest a kind of de facto involvement. These are in one sense contingent and relative to our particular existential situation in history. What we ought to do, how we ought to live is conditioned by our past. But it is also a function of creative inquiry in the present and it entails a balancing of facts, values, and principles in the concrete contexts of choice. I believe there is a role for objectivity, although it is not universal or a priori but is contingent and existential. There is no ultimate justification for the framework in which we happen to exist, or our basic sociocultural perspective. These are semiarbitrary givens. They may be revised or reconstructed, but we are limited by the range of possibilities. Hence, I am skeptical about universalistic ethical systems that ignore actual phenomenological contexts in the real world. There is a kind of irreducible pluralism about human reality and the human condition. Ethics is thus relational to the frames of reference in which we find ourselves. Knowledge is relevant to human choices, but our choices are not simply deducible from propositions or principles. Life precedes thought. Cognition is only one phase of our conative-affective or sociocultural existence.

The universe of man is thus open and uncharted. It is changing, not fixed or final. Life is full of striving and endeavor. It is in part precarious, uncertain, indeterminate. Knowledge can serve us in the ongoing process of living. It is not a substitute for life. Science is a tool, no doubt the most important that we have, but it is not always infallible or reliable. Our existence precedes our essence. Alas, some faith is always present in the act of living—animal faith if you will. Hence, we need some skepticism about even the reaches of science or the possibilities it provides for reforming our moral life, let alone the pitfalls of religion or ontologics or ideology.

Critical scientific inquiry nevertheless, I submit, has high value as a human enterprise. Comparatively, it still provides the greatest promise for solving our problems. In particular, it should provide us with a powerful critique of the mythologies and orthodoxies that reign in every age, the chauvinistic delusions, the systems of narrow moral faith that dominate human behavior and suppress freedom.

Ethical skepticism is not only an epistemological position. It no doubt supposes a number of moral values. It prefers clarity to confusion, truth to illusion. Skepticism can also contribute to a sense of humility and an awareness of the fallible and problematic character of all human efforts. It enables us to appreciate other points of view. It cultivates a willingness to negotiate differences and reach compromises. Ethical skepticism tends to liberate us from vain pretensions.

*PART THREE*
# Humanism and Religion

# 13

# The Case for Naturalistic Humanism

Theistic religion has been widely interpreted as referring to some unseen, transcendent, and divine power controlling human destiny and entitled to worship and obedience. Generally this involves some faith, commitment or belief in the existence of God or of gods.

The issue is clear: How can the theist support his cognitive claim that a divine being exists independently of himself? We have witnessed in the modern world the erosion of the classical religious system and its "eternal truth." Among the conflicts have been those between its cosmology and natural science; between the theistic picture of human nature, with man higher than the beasts but a little lower than the angels, and the Darwinian theory of evolution; between the literal interpretation of the Bible and the higher biblical criticism. Today theism conflicts with criticism by the social, psychological, and behavioral sciences destructive of any privileged status to the religious "soul," or to the special claim of any one religion to be universal. Thus most philosophic naturalists and scientific humanists find that theistic religion has not supported its assertion that God exists and suspect that it will be unable to do so.

## Theism: Unproved

Indeed, skepticism goes further today than in previous ages by showing that the whole theistic question itself verges on meaninglessness; there usually has been little or no clear conception of precisely what was to be demonstrated or proved. In other words, the term "God" appears to be devoid of literal, cognitive, or empirical significance. This does not mean that the symbol or idea is unimportant, morally or emotionally, to people—only that it has not been clearly defined. Thus before we can determine whether and to what extent the claim is true, we must know what we mean. And the analysis of the uses of religious terms in ordinary language, as far as I can tell, has not clarified but only confused the issue with a new form of apologetics. That is why so many contemporary scientific philosophers and logicians would not care to be labelled "atheists," since they do not know exactly

This was published in *The Humanist*, Nov./Dec. 1964.

what they are alleged to be denying; nor "agnostics," since they are not sure that a genuine cognitive question is being propounded. Rather, they are simply skeptics or "ignostics" (that is, ignorant) about the whole matter.

## Religion: Quality in Experience

This analysis does not necessarily mean that all critics of theistic religion are indifferent to religious values. In fact, many take religious values so seriously that they resent the attempt by the theist to preempt the field. Many naturalistic humanists, for example, consider themselves to be religious although they mean something different by "religion" from what the theist means. "Religion" for the humanist refers primarily to a *quality in human experience.* It is centered around man and his concerns. It is, as Tillich suggests, the expression of our "ultimate concern," the basic ideal ends to which a person is committed — the confession of which may call forth a stutter, a smile, or a blush. Thus we have a "religious experience" when we are aware of our basic values and aims.

In what way does this differ from philosophical awareness? Philosophy is cognitive and rational, religion affective and attitudinal. Science describes for us; religion profoundly moves us. A philosophical position is converted into a religious position only when the philosophy is given the strength of passionate devotion and conviction. Religion thus goes beyond thought to stir our irrational natures. Under this definition the communist would be religious in his devotion to the aims of dialectical materialism, as would the Epicurean, the Buddhist, the Taoist in their devotion to other ideals. Here faith does not involve belief in the alleged reality of an unseen being, which is independent of, or contrary to, reason and experience; but it is a conviction that an ideal can be achieved. Religion in this sense is a serious and compelling commitment to a way of life; it gives direction and form to our energies and activities.

There are thus two main characteristics of this humanistic definition of religion: (1) its reference to *fundamental* and *basic* ideals and values, and (2) its reference to *attitudes* and *feelings.* One's values, however, are not held in isolation from one's general cognitive beliefs about the world and one's place within it. Indeed, one's world view, whether naturalistic or theistic, has some effect upon the general attitudes and responses that one takes toward the world in general and other human beings. Yet it is the prescriptiveness and the expressiveness that a system of beliefs may arouse that is the distinctive religious quality of experience. So far as persons are aware of their basic values, and as these have some controlling emotive power in their lives, they may be said to be "religious." When someone becomes concerned attitudinally with his ultimate principles, he is functioning religiously.

## Main Principles of Naturalism

The naturalistic humanist has his own basic ideal values which are related to his view of the world and his place within it. And to the extent that he is religious, he may feel rather deeply about them. But let me state what I take to be the main principles of naturalistic humanism.

First, naturalism is committed to certain methodological principles, primarily scientific and empirical methods, as the most effective way to arrive at reliable knowledge. Thus, to be warranted, a descriptive belief (1) must be experimentally verified; (2) must be logically consistent, internally with itself and externally with our other beliefs; and (3) may be judged convenient in part by its role in inquiry and its relation to the situations in which it arises.

A descriptive belief is considered by the naturalist to be (4) fallible and tentative. It is a hypothesis (5) open to revision, and it must be (6) capable of some public and objectively repeatable tests by a community of inquirers. But this method itself is (7) self-corrective and open to revision should new techniques be discovered. These methodological first principles of naturalism are not articles of faith; they have been gradually elaborated in civilization and have been found to be the most effective means for furthering the aims of inquiry. The empirical method requires that we should be skeptical and suspend judgment wherever there is insufficient evidence; and this involves some skepticism concerning its own first principles.

Second, naturalism provides not only a logic of inquiry, but an account of the generic traits of the world as it is encountered and a reflective commentary on the human scene. Using the empirical method, naturalism rejects any easy bifurcation between nature and supernature. It is dubious of the notion of cosmic teleological purpose and of a transcendental realm lying beyond all rational and empirical interpretation. But the naturalist does not deny that there are aspects of the universe which now (and perhaps in the future) are beyond his investigation; nor does he exclude the transempirical on a priori grounds. He only maintains that any claims to a nonnatural realm must be examined objectively and in the light of the evidence. Nor does the naturalist callously dismiss the reports of religious experience the mystic claims. But he looks upon these reports as events to be explained and interpreted, much the same as other data that are experienced. Such events he finds can be parsimoniously explained by reference to an alleged transcendental reality. In any case, he asks that all claims to knowledge be open to a responsible examination of the grounds under which they are supported; and he does not consider the evidence referred to by the mystic as conclusive.

Third, the naturalist takes man as part of nature, a product of evolution, and capable of being explained scientifically by reference to causal conditions, which operate in other parts of nature as well. This means that there is no break between the human mind or consciousness and the body, no special status to personality or "soul," and no privileged place in the universe for human existence. All eschatological claims to immortality, for example, are held to be an expression of wish fulfillment. Nature, for the naturalist, is indifferent and blind to human purposes and ideals. This does not mean that man does not possess some characteristics not found to the same extent in other species — for example, man's ability to respond to symbols, to build a culture, or to destroy himself. But his symbolic, sociocultural dimensions are, in principle, capable of empirical explanation; at least, no a priori demonstration has been made concerning a limitation to such inquiry.

Most naturalists, however, are not reductionists. While the naturalist maintains that matter, mass and energy, or the laws of physics and chemistry, in some way are basic to and present in all processes, he recognizes the multiplicity and plurality of natural things, their variety and richness. Indeed, the naturalist is reluctant to use the term "nature" in a universal sense; for he is not convinced that nature is a monistic block system, or an interconnected whole. Rather, the naturalist notes there are many different kinds of qualities, properties and relations that things manifest; and he consequently looks to descriptions that allow for the full contextual characteristics of processes. Indeed, there may very well be many different levels in nature, or at least it is convenient to treat the varieties of things on their own levels, as we encounter them, without explaining them away.

Here the naturalist, unlike the classical materialist, maintains that the human being can only be *fully* understood in his own terms. Human experience and history are after all *human* and not to be reduced solely to nonhuman terms. Thus the naturalist takes seriously the diverse qualities encountered in human experience: in art, religion, morality, science, philosophy, and ordinary life. Man is a knowing being, but he is also a passionate being immersed in the immediacy of intense feelings (love, joy, suffering and fear); and he is a dynamic being, entering into the world and changing it. In classical terms, the naturalist wishes to give full play to the "human spirit"; that is, to our developed and civilized natures, moral, aesthetic, and intellectual. The naturalist does not debase man, nor ignore man's higher creative talents. On the contrary, he emphasizes that the highest human excellences are achievable by the full realization of our creative capacities, but he insists that these creative talents are fully describable as natural processes.

## Naturalistic Humanism

The contemporary naturalistic humanist, I believe, accepts the foregoing points of naturalism, but he goes on to emphasize another. This fourth point I shall label *humanism*. The humanist is not primarily committed to a logic of inquiry, nor does he simply describe the world and man's place within it. He recommends a set of ideal values, a way of life. That is, he provides a basic view of the good life. And here a philosophical point of view is translated into a religious position.

Humanism's basic prescriptions concern man and his works. The problem for man is to discover the good life, which is achievable in human terms: as joy, pleasure, happiness, satisfaction of needs, self-realization, fulfillment of powers, productivity, creativity, love, friendship, reason, harmony, and justice. The point is that value is relative to man and to what he finds to be worthwhile. The standard is not to be found outside of human life, but within it. This, I assume, is what Aristotle, Spinoza, Nietzsche, Marx, Bentham, Mill, Freud, Fromm, Santayana, Russell, Dewey, Hook and Sartre (to name some humanistic thinkers) all share in common. Here there is confidence in the power of man to find within himself the sources for the good life, and here is an affirmation that life is worth living. Most naturalists and humanists (such as Dewey) believe that in some sense the methods of empirical inquiry and reason can be applied to human values and that some degree of objectivity is possible. Thus values are not merely capricious or emotive but are given to intelligent criticism and modification.

The naturalistic humanist is an uncompromising critic of established orthodoxies, of theistic and authoritarian religions. For such religions have frequently ignored Jesus' claim that "the kingdom of God is within thee," and they have often suppressed the best human instincts. They have been dishonest concerning man's right to truth; and they have frequently censored and blocked free and responsible intellectual inquiry. The humanist, on the contrary, asks that we, as human beings, face up to the human condition as it is. We should accept the facts that "God is dead" (according to Nietzsche) and that we have no way of knowing that He exists or even whether this is a meaningful question. We should accept the facts that human existence is probably a random occurrence existing between two oblivions, that death is inevitable, and that there is thus a tragic aspect to our lives. A free thinker, too, is capable of stoic resignation.

## Hope for the Living

Yet matters are not hopeless, for with a proper recognition of the human estate, there must also come an awareness of the challenges and possibilities that await us; and there may be a source of genuine confidence and optimism, not despair and cynicism. For while there is death and failure, there is also life and success. And with life come great and bountiful promises: these are the joys of human love and shared experience, the excitement of creativity, the power of reason, the possibility that we as human beings have some control over our destinies. We can, for example, alleviate distress and suffering and help create an equitable society. If we grant that not all human sorrows and evils can be avoided, still the human situation is not totally irremediable; and with some confidence in our powers, particularly of thought and intelligence, we may help build a good life. Scientific intelligence in this regard is a great instrument, though it is not an omnipotent "open sesame" to salvation or certainty.

The theist has not always allowed man to be himself. He has looked outside of nature or human nature, and has created idolatrous religions, worshiping graven images. He has often frustrated and thwarted independent self-assertion. He has thus contributed to the alienation of man from himself and from nature. Man is made to feel himself dependent upon God, a "sinner" who must renounce and suppress his pride. But the more he exalts God, as the Father image, the more he demeans himself. Surely man is dependent upon external forces, and some are beyond his control (such as death), but why worship or submit to them, and why belittle or weaken man? Why exacerbate his guilt complex, and his sense of sin, and why exalt acquiescence? Man needs to be himself (says Fromm). He needs to affirm his personhood, to develop the courage to persist in spite of all the obstacles that would destroy him, indeed to exceed himself by creating a new life *for* himself. The challenge for the free man is to realize his potentialities, and to create new ones, not to cower in masochistic denial, nor to withdraw in fear, anxiety, and trembling, nor to look outside of man for a false help that is not there.

Humanism thus looks to the ennoblement and enrichment of human life, whether in individual terms, as each man satisfies his desires and fulfills his ideals and dreams, or in social terms, where we seek to develop rules and norms of justice (to solve, for example, the arms race, the population explosion, or contribute to the uplifting of underdeveloped areas). Humanism claims that man is rooted in the soil (nature), that it is the flesh (life) that gives him satisfaction, but that it is in social harmony and creative fulfillment (the spirit), that he finds his deepest significance.

"God" for the humanist is only a symbol of man's aspirations, the ideals which stimulate him to devotion and action. Where one takes "God" to be a hidden or transcendental being, he only confuses the issue of life and does not face death. Some humanists (Tillich, for example) are willing to retain the classical symbols of theistic religion, but they wish to demythologize them and reinvigorate them with new meaning appropriate to our age of science and world revolution. They would reinterpret the dramatic symbols of mythological and miraculous revelation in order to arouse concern for man *as man*. "God" thus is not someone who speaks to man from on high, but the word is an expression of man's deepest longings, man speaking to himself.

Other humanists (myself included) are dubious of the attempt to translate all such symbols into naturalistic and humanistic terms and would instead devise new sets of symbols and beliefs appropriate to the present age, symbols better able to dramatize the aspirations of humanity. Sartre has said that there are no absolute values or norms independent of what man chooses. Instead, man is condemned to make man; we alone are responsible for what we are or what we do. Perhaps this is an overstatement of the case for freedom; at least the humanist asks that man begin to shed the chains of illusion that bind him, and assert himself. What man needs is not renunciation but affirmation, nor resignation but confidence, above all, not blind piety and faith but honesty and truth.

The *scientific* humanist, as distinct from others, is cautious and tentative in his judgments, and he is even skeptical about his own naturalism and humanism, recognizing their limitations. He knows that it is difficult to find absolute standards, or categorical imperatives. Yet he suggests that although the human animal finds himself thrust into existence without asking to be put there, he can to some extent define himself and determine who he is and what he shall be. Man can achieve a satisfying and authentic existence here and now. But the first essential for this is that he cease deluding himself about what is and is not in store for him. The humanist recognizes the rich variety, diversity and relativity of value, and the fact that there are alternate paths men may take to achieve the good life. He merely claims that it is *we* who are to choose, whatever we choose, and that we should not shirk our responsibility to so choose, nor escape to a world of dogma and myth.

There are other aspects of humanism—such as a moral commitment to social cooperation, shared experience, and even democracy—which many humanists have strongly supported. But I have not emphasized these, since some humanists might not accept them. Instead I have highlighted what I take to be the central doctrine of humanism: that *value is relative to man.*

# 14

# Functionalism and the Justification of Religion

## I

Are there good reasons and evidence for adherence to a system of religious beliefs and practices? Why do people maintain religious commitments? The justification of religion has always been a troublesome problem, for both the religionist and the philosopher. This problem came to the forefront with the development of modern science.

In the medieval superstructure of Thomas Aquinas, Christianity was wedded to a specific view of the universe and man's place within it. Modern science undermined the foundations of this view. The natural sciences, biological evolution, biblical criticism, comparative studies of religion, and the social sciences all destroyed aspects of the classic religious edifice. Within philosophy, drastic epistemological objections were raised against both cognitive and mystical justifications of religion. The chief controversy in the modern era thus has revolved about the question of the truth or falsity of the claims of religion in comparison with those of science. Theologians attempted to justify religion as a superior form of knowledge by claiming that it supplemented scientific knowledge. Skeptics repeatedly denied this claim on methodological grounds. To many, this controversy still remains central to the problem of religious justification. If pushed to extremes, one is led either to the toleration of apparent contradictions grounded in faith alone or to the blanket dismissal of basic religious tenets.

If religion is interpreted primarily in terms of its truth claims, then an impasse has been reached, and justification of religion is in dire straits. Ever since Kant and, more recently, William James, many philosophers have interpreted religion in another way. Functionalism has emerged as an attempt to go beyond the conflict between religion and science.

In this paper I shall raise two questions: First, what is the meaning of the functional approach to religion? I shall present a modified version, chastened by "implicit truths." Second, does this approach provide an adequate justification? The answer I shall give is that the functional justification is a useful one; still, we must recognize that it provides only a limited solution.

This article was published in *The Journal of Religion* 38, no. 3 (July 1958).

## II

In the functioning view of religion the conflict between religion and science is in one sense irrelevant. If one continues to interpret religion primarily in terms of knowledge or truth, then the problem of reconciliation with scientific claims remains. If, however, one examines the heart of the religious experience—from which religion draws its sustenance—then one gets an entirely different view. The religionist gave the case to the scientist by claiming too much, by taking science (or philosophy) as his model, and by agreeing with the scientist that religion was primarily concerned with literal truth or belief. But to the functionalist the main issue is not what religion says but what it does. Religion is not primarily concerned with fact, but with *value*. From this point of view, the definition, meaning, and justification of religion are not in terms of descriptive beliefs or observances but in terms of the function of such beliefs and observances. For a functional evaluation, then, the real question is: Does religion have a service or work to perform, and, if so, what is it?

Recently, the social sciences have contributed a great deal to answering this question. Indeed, many would contend (contrary to the apprehension of some theologians, who continue to look upon the social sciences as a major critic of religion) that one of the strongest supports for religion now comes from contemporary social science. At least considerable positive empirical evidence to support the functions of religion can be found there. But if we are to appreciate this fact, we must objectively examine human experience.

If we do so, what do we find? Religious experience and the religious response are widespread phenomena. They are nearly universal in occurrence and seem to have existed in almost all cultures. However, because of the wide diversity of religious expression, any analysis and evaluation of the religious per se perhaps should be in terms of the *form* and *function* of the experience and not in terms of the specific descriptive matter or content.

Man is an experiencing being. Experience is dynamic, continuous, ongoing. It is a complex fusion of biological impulse, feeling, motor drive, desire, thought, aspiration. We may distinguish, for purposes of analysis, certain aspects of human response: the aesthetic (the delight in feeling and form), the moral and practical (the sense of obligation in society and the solution of concrete problems), the scientific (the search for predictable knowledge), the philosophic (the quest for meaning and understanding), and, finally, the religious. Each phase of experience is, in one sense, final in itself; yet, in another, it has a function in terms of the wider maintenance and fulfillment of life processes.

What, then, is the religious phase of experience? Religious experience is very complex. It has poetic and moral qualities, and it contains certain general implicit truths and meanings. But it cannot be reduced to any *one* of these elements, as we shall see.

Religious experience has poetic color and aesthetic flavor. It is supported and sustained by art. Religion has been among the chief inspirations for artistic creation. It has expressed the deepest aesthetic impulses, as in paintings and sculptures of the Madonna and Child, as in the Bach Masses, or as in cathedrals of architectural grandeur. But even though the aesthetic response is combined with the religious, religion cannot be reduced to art, as Santayana thought. Religion is not merely poetic creation. Nor is it simply a means of emotive self-expression, as the positivists claim today. It is much more serious and urgent than that—one can take or leave poetry, but one cannot do that very easily with religion.

Religious experience contains moral qualities. Religion has stimulated the sense of obligation and charity. But religion is not primarily a moral code or a set of commandments, as some interpreters of Judaism or Islam claim. Nor is the religious person necessarily endowed with any superior virtue or moral sense. He needs wisdom as much as anyone in resolving concrete problems of choice.

Religious people have been concerned with political issues. But politics, too, is independent of religion in most matters; and the divorce between church and state in the West is well grounded.

Religious experience does claim and possess implicit truth. But religion cannot supplant science. In the area of descriptive knowledge and belief, it can only follow the findings of science. It only usurps its function when it claims to have a special knowledge that will refute what is found to be the case on verifiable grounds.

Moreover, religion does not provide any special philosophical wisdom independent of philosophical methods. Philosophy is concerned with the rational and cognitive analysis of knowledge, experience, language, and existence. As Maritain recognizes, religion can use philosophy or develop it only by the rules of philosophical inquiry. It cannot claim to possess a superior type of philosophical knowledge outside philosophy itself. Religion qua religion is involvement in its subject matter. Philosophy qua philosophy is objective detachment from it as far as possible in order to understand it.

If this is what religion is not, what then is the *unique* character of the religious response? Is it not possible to say simply. Experience differs among individuals. Yet there is a central aspect to religious experience; and many writers have attempted to isolate it. Tillich perhaps best characterizes religious experience when he claims that it is the area of our experience wherein we express "our ultimate concern";[1] or, in the words of Carl Jung, it is the experience characterized by "highest appreciation."[2] Religious experience is the experience of things that we hold to be of fundamental importance and significance. It is, in other words, our experience of final value, our standard of life—the source of all that we find good and noble and worthwhile.

This, I submit, is the underlying character of the religious experience. Any particular religious system attempts to fulfill it. Religious systems are symbolic constructions that attempt to satisfy our ultimate concerns. Religions use poetry, metaphor, parable, myth, liturgy, ritual, and, most important, drama, to do this. Religions attempt to consecrate, sanctify, dedicate, ceremonialize, and celebrate our basic concerns. Religious systems, as Ernst Cassirer noted, play upon the imagination, for it is through imagery that they breathe and function. Jung calls the "collective unconscious" the historical receptacle of such symbols. At least, it is through culture and history that certain religious symbols come to dominate. These powerful religious symbols express similar needs in many human breasts, quicken the pulse beats of many men and women, and flood countless hearts with feeling.

But religious symbols do not only serve as the media through which we express our ultimate concerns; they also express implicit truths. Functionalists frequently overlook this. Hence it is necessary to go beyond simple pragmatism. To be effective, functionalism must be consonant with some of the "realities" of existence. There are at least two main truths that all effective religions seem to illustrate, although some religions no doubt realize them better than others.

1. The religious response is, after all, a response to the demands of the external world. It develops only when men come to realize, in full shock and usually in times of crisis, the flux of existence. The fondest human dreams may come true—but, alas, "vanity of vanities," they rest on quicksand. As the author of Ecclesiastes says: "All go unto one place; all are of the dust; and all turn to dust again."[3] The tragedy of death and transience—so long, that is, as man remains "unclothed," "naked," and "alone"—is the first awesome fact that confronts the sensitive religious consciousness. The existentialists were not the first to discover this fact of nature and life.

2. But, along with this insight, is the recognition that there are powers external to us—whether they are attributed to or called "causal law," "brute force," "demons," "divine personality," or "God." There is a source of our being that we cannot control but one that we can only come to terms with and accept. Some recognition of our dependence upon the tide of events and the limitations of our powers is present in the religious response, and this usually leads to resignation and piety—natural or other.

These implicit truths, devoid of fanciful or mythical frills, I think, all men in essence can accept. They are empirically confirmable by the sciences as descriptive knowledge. They may be abstracted from religious discourse and put into propositional form. Religion, however, does not merely acknowledge the fact of transience and dependence; it *dramatizes* it in a way that science cannot. It portrays the ultimate character of life in nature, as seen "unclothed." The religious response is not merely intellectual; it engages the whole man. Religious utterances are not simply cognitive; they are poetic, emotive, and evocative. They illustrate, render, or present rather than discursively state.

But, clearly, if these two facts are the starting point of the religious insight and response, they are not the end, for religion is not merely negative. It holds forth a positive hope, a way, a free choice. It attempts to "clothe" man. It is here that the ultimate concern is given full meaning. For the religious life also offers a "proposition" (to employ a colloquialism); not a descriptive "proposition" but a prescriptive one. Religion does not state, but *proposes,* an inclusive ideal end to pursue. Religion, claims James A. Pike, is not merely an *ipse dixit,* a "Thus saith the Lord," an external theological doctrine. Rather, it is in the form of a living hypothesis; it pours its faith into its hope.[4] It attempts to "save" man, as far as possible, from the awful facts of naked life. It paints and portrays in eloquent aesthetic terms a basic moral ideal, a goal, a future. It is not merely or chiefly a practical code of day-to-day moral rules, but rather it attempts to give some general direction and meaning to life, to make whole what was previously chaotic and fragmentary. This is its distinctive power.

Each religion, theistic and nontheistic, attempts in its own way to meet and realize our ultimate concerns. For Christianity, the ideal is agape or love, both human and cosmic. "Follow me," says Christ, "I am the way. . . . A new commandment I give you, that ye love one another, as I have loved you."[5] And as Paul says: "If I understand all mysteries and all knowledge, but have not love, I am nothing."[6] Christianity, of course, provides rules of conduct. There is a Christian morality in comparison with other moral codes. Yet the significant and distinctively religious quality of Christianity is the centrality of the ideal of love. For naturalistic humanism the ideal is moral dedication to social cooperation and pooled intelligence.[7]

But one may ask: Since many religions provide ideals, how do we know which ideal is true and which false? At least one type of test can be applied to religious ideals. This is in terms of efficacy. Thus a religious system, incorporating symbols, practices, beliefs, may be tested in part by whether or not it fulfills its functions. A religion is justifiable if it realizes values.

It is important, however, to recognize that there may be harmful results of religion—*dys*functions, as the sociologist calls them. Social scientists, following Marx, Freud, and Sir James Frazer, have overemphasized religion's negative functions. Religion may be authoritarian; it may be the "opiate" of the masses, the defender of the status quo; it may censor art and block free inquiry; it may present superstition, magic, and myth as the literal truth; it may demand blind outward conformity; it may tolerate moral hypocrisy or frustrate human beings; or it may, for some, be the projection of abnormal personality. These things have frequently been the case with religious institutions in the past, as they have been of other institutions as well. They arise, I think, from a misconception of religion's true functions and its consequent usurpation of other functions.

But what are the positive functions that our ultimate concerns fulfill? It is difficult to give a final answer here. By "functions" I do not mean ideal or intended ones but only empirically observable results. Even so, different functions are revealed historically. In certain contexts one may emerge as more significant than another. Yet we can isolate some recurrent latent, and perhaps basic, ones as well.

The principal positive functions of religion seem to be at least twofold: First, religious experience and a religious ideal, in expressing our ultimate concern, may provide some meaning and direction to life. It may integrate, unify, and organize otherwise random impulses, thus contributing to a kind of homeostasis. In this sense, it may save men from despair or meaninglessness. It may render the hopeless hopeful. It may overcome the sense of the tragic, anxiety, alienation, self-estrangement. It may reconcile and reunify our being in inner transformation. In doing so, it may give poise, serenity, self-control, the courage "to be," endurance in adversity, humility in success, dignity in defeat, and strength in moments of weakness. Second, a religious ideal may contribute to the unification of society and culture. It is in society, and through culture in large part, that men realize many of their highest potentialities. Religion may give motive to altruistic moral feelings, so necessary to social life; and it may act as an agent of social control. It may provide the occasion or way for man to share common experiences and needs and celebrate common hopes and joys. These are positive values.

Which *particular* religion best serves these functions that religions in general may perform? This is a matter for detailed empirical observation: Which religion is most effective in fulfilling the need of *homo religiosus*? Which consistently thwarts and which fulfills other significant values? Which has the highest moral excellence, aesthetic beauty, social utility, and ultimate concern? Which is universal and eloquent in its appeal?

## III

There is one question—possibly the basic one for the functional view— that is frequently left unanswered: Will human beings maintain religious commitments, knowing that their *specific* religious beliefs and dogmas are only figurative or symbolic and instrumental or therapeutic?

Functionalism tends to answer in the affirmative. Religion is primarily a way of life. Its justification is closer to that of art than of scientific belief. Thus religions, like works of art, do not have to be justified so much as appreciated. And works of art may be enjoyed, even though they are not literally true.

But critics of functionalism do not think that the analogy with art holds entirely. Since the religious need is more crucial than the aesthetic, religious ideals, they claim, have to be *believed* to be effective.

Functionalism may admit this to a degree. However, it may answer that, to say that we *believe* in something—in the Bill of Rights or the United Nations, for example—does not necessarily mean that it exists but that it is *desirable* and *ought* to be sustained. Thus religious *belief* in some sense is simply confidence in the importance and the attainability of some ideal value. People may have *faith* in it, but it is a normative faith, not a descriptive one.

Yet critics of functionalism do not think this is enough. Nor do they think that a modified functionalism (such as I have suggested), which restricts religion only to "implicit truths," provides sufficient "spiritual" food for man. The Hopi Indian, for example, probably would not continue to propitiate the rain god if he thought himself impotent in causing rain; nor would the Christian believe in Christ without belief in the actuality of the Resurrection. Few men could accept that there are no explicit religious truths and still maintain commitment to a well-defined religious system. Thus we are told that destruction of the specific truth claims of religion means that most existing religions must ultimately lose their vitality and force.

These are serious and telling criticisms brought against functionalism. They restrict the functional theory on its own ground. In view of them, three clarifying inferences must be drawn.

It appears likely that if a person is to persist in practicing a religion, he must maintain some cognitive conviction of the unique truth of its historical assertions and the reality of its ideal. Therefore, our first inference is that the functional view of religion may help theistic believers *reinforce beliefs already present,* but very rarely will it convert the unconverted.

Actually, functionalism is none too happy with existing theistic religions, and it suggests to some a need for religious reconstruction. Accordingly, our second inference is that the functional justification of religion is more applicable to the newer *nontheistic, humanistic,* and *naturalistic religions.* For such religions, there is also a persuasive leap from the descriptive world to a normative ideal. But functionalism is more receptive to these religions because they usually make limited claims about the factual world, and it thinks that their ideals may not be as drastically removed from the realm of probability.

But to many the abandonment of traditional religious forms is held to be unrealistic and utopian. Consequently, our third inference is that the functional justification of religions must be interpreted as intended *for the uncommitted observer* who wishes to survey the religious landscape (theistic and nontheistic) and justify its overall direction. Its appeal is probably limited to the "sophisticated intellectual"[8] who does not seek religious conviction so much as an *explanation* and understanding of why men believe and behave in a religious way.

If the foregoing implications are correct, then from the standpoint of the religious *participant* the modern conflict between science and *theistic* religion (at least) has not been entirely overcome. And we are still confronted with a dilemma: If the older religions continue to give content to their beliefs (to claim the existence of a transcendental God or a special truth of revelation, for instance), then they still may conflict with the scientific-empirical outlook. If they do not make such claims, then they may lose their efficacy and power. In the last analysis, whether a functional view of religion, which limits religion in the way of truth, will satisfy man's religious quest is a subtle psychological question. The recent return to orthodox theisms, however, tend to suggest that for most men and women it will not.

## NOTES

1. Paul Tillich, *Systematic Theology,* vol. 1 (Chicago: University of Chicago Press, 1951).

2. Carl Jung, *Psychology and Religion* (New Haven, Conn.: Yale University Press, 1938).

3. Eccles. 3:20.

4. James A. Pike, *Beyond Anxiety* (New York: Charles Scribner's Sons, 1953).

5. John 13:34.

6. 1 Cor. 12:2.

7. In the functional view, the religious revival now going on may not be so pronounced as it appears on the surface. In the 1930s political programs expressed our ultimate concerns; in the 1940s, war; in the postwar period, theism. The shift undoubtedly has been from nontheistic to theistic; but similar religious qualities, needs, and functions continue to be felt and expressed. There is a difference however. Nontheistic political religions lack the deeper perspective of the human estate, the humility, and the piety that older religions possess. Thus they do not always render or express man's transience and dependence.

8. This fact, of course, is not unique and has prevailed historically with other justifications. Even Aquinas tells us that his proofs for the existence of God are not intended for the mass of men, but for those few who are capable of "rational" demonstration: ". . . disadvantages would result if this [divine] truth were left solely to the inquiry of reason. One is that few men would have knowledge of God. . . . Therefore, it was necessary that definite certainty and pure truth about divine things should be offered to man by the way of faith" (*Summa Contra Gentiles* [London: Burns, Oates & Washbourne, Ltd., 1924], I, 7–9).

# 15

# The Crisis in Humanism

*Victory and Crisis*

Humanism in America is at a critical turning point. It faces an unparalleled opportunity. But whether or not it will respond to the challenge is an open question.

My diagnosis of the present moment is that it is one of both victory and crisis. The victory is that atheistic, agnostic, and skeptical humanism has had some success in its battle against orthodoxy. The crisis is that, radical in yesteryear, secular humanism is now without a clearly defined program.

The warfare between religion and science which Andrew Dixon White[1] depicted, or between religion and philosophy, which has been waged heatedly since the seventeenth century, has shaken the classical religious edifice to its foundations. The idea of a transcendent God or an immortal soul has been subjected to a continual withering critique by scientific logicians and empiricists, so much so that theistic religions have had to modify drastically and reinterpret their key concepts and symbols.

The extent of this victory over theism is apparent to anyone who examines, however cursorily, the history of thought. One by one the props of orthodox religion have been undermined. The so-called classical "proofs" for the existence of God (ontological, cosmological and teleological) have been discredited as unconvincing, inconsistent, and unconfirmed; and the paradoxes of evil and free will remain embarrassingly unresolved for the theist. One by one the argument from miracles and historical revelation, the appeals to mystical intuition, experience, and faith, have been shown to be unreliable on any kind of objective empirical grounds. By the seventeenth century the natural sciences had overthrown the Ptolemaic and teleological cosmologies of the Middle Ages, and by the nineteenth century the Darwinian theory of evolution had dislodged the anthropomorphic and anthropocentric view of man. In the nineteenth century, sociologists pointed out that religious institutions under certain social conditions served as instruments of oppression and often had harmful consequences. Psychoanalysts interpreted religion as pathological, founded on a sense of guilt and a transference

---

This article appeared in *Religious Humanism,* Jan. 1968.

of the father image to cosmic terms. Moreover, comparative studies by linguists, philologists, and anthropologists demonstrated that the alleged uniqueness of biblical claims for divine revelation were unsupported and that the literal interpretation of the Bible falters when submitted to careful criticism. Thus, it was with considerable justice that Nietzsche proclaimed to Western man at the end of the nineteenth century that "God is dead!"

In the twentieth century the advance of scientific humanism has continued, and much of orthodoxy is in retreat from its earlier theology. For example, the developing behavioral sciences have disrupted the dualistic "ghost in the machine" doctrine, providing naturalistic causal explanations for alleged mystical experiences. Within philosophy an even more devastating critique had been leveled by the logical positivists against the idea of a transcendent God. According to the positivists, religious language is unverifiable and nonfalsifiable. Since we cannot in principle find circumstances under which we could confirm its claims, theistic religion is cognitively meaningless and devoid of any literal significance. Modern philosophers who accept this critique are *ignostics* or *igtheists,* that is, they believe that the existence or nonexistence of God is an incomprehensible pseudoquestion. (I believe I first introduced the term "ignostic," but I now prefer the term "igtheist.")

In any case, how surprising for present-day igtheistic humanists to find that "God is dead" is now being proclaimed (some seventy years later) within the churches themselves by liberal Protestants and Jews. Even the Roman Catholic Church is undergoing an agonizing reexamination of its historical prejudices and dogmas that few would have thought possible a few years ago. Moreover, with the general expansion of education and the development of democratic values it is increasingly difficult for a totalitarian church to impose its will, to stifle opposition by sanction and censorship, or to attack individual conscience as "heretical" and "sinful," as it had since the Reformation. Thus we find the Catholic Church, dragged into the twentieth century by the force of events, now proclaiming itself the defender of "true humanism" and "religious liberty."

What a reversal of roles! And what a new religious world the secular humanist now faces. Humanism has intellectually routed its classical adversaries in theology; but a new battle ground has developed in morality and politics; and here humanism faces a new crisis. Many of the churches are no longer the defenders of the status quo; more often than not they have become its chief critic, calling for a radical reconstruction of society. The victory over theological dogma is, of course, never complete, as we have learned from bitter experience: As many times as we think theological error is downed for good (as, for example, during the Enlightenment), it emerges again in a new guise in the next generation. Thus, humanism must keep up its continual criticism of the pretentious mythological truth claims that may arise from the theist. However, for the immediate future secular humanism must shift from simply battling theology to building a constructive morality. In other words, if humanism as an organized movement is to continue to have anything significant to say, then it must shift from mere negative criticism of orthodoxy to a positive reconstruction of moral values.

## Humanistic Religion

It is paradoxical that the devastating critique by logical positivists of the last generation had a telling effect, not only on theists, but on humanists as well. For it led to a kind of skepticism about ethics and trepidation about doing any kind of moral reconstruction. This had a tendency to dry up the development of a vigorous humanistic ethics.

The positivistic critique of religion, even though it was necessary therapy in its day, had gone too far and been too sweeping. Not that it was inaccurate in its diagnosis that religious truth claims were nonsensical; but it did not appreciate fully that religious language has functions and uses beyond the informative one, and especially that it had a moral function. The positivists maintained that, to be meaningful, terms and sentences must designate or refer to something; and since one could not find any referents for God-language, such language was held to be vacuous.

This analysis overlooks the fact, as Ludwig Wittgenstein[2] pointed out, that not all language is referential, and that many terms which have meaning have specialized roles to play in our language. In other words, to understand the meaning of any kind of discourse, whether religious, moral, or aesthetic, one should examine the contexts in which that discourse functions. The meanings of religious terms are discovered by closely attending to their actual uses.

## Varied Conclusions

In the past two decades a great deal of effort (particularly among British philosophers) has gone into the analysis of the complexities of religious language. Out of this analysis have come some interesting conclusions. Some have attempted to use this analysis as a new mode of apologetics for "God" talk. I am thinking, for example, of British writers like John Hicks, Basil Mitchell, I. M. Crombie, Ian T. Ramsey[3] and others who claim that religious discourse has its own special "logic," meaning, and truth. This effort, I think, is bound to fail. The attempt to introduce metaphorical models of religious truth is a misuse of the term "truth" and a misinterpretation of the functions of religious language. I do not doubt for the moment that many or most religious people who use religious language think that they are making truth claims about the universe, whether in asserting that God exists, that the resurrection is a reality, or that the soul is eternal. Some of the truth claims made are indeed meaningful, though frequently false (for example, that a historical figure such as Christ existed). All talk about God as a transcendent being, however, seems to come under the indictment of the verifiability principle. Insofar as theists make assertions about the universe, some verifiability criteria apply.

Others, such as R. B. Braithwaite and Antony Flew,[4] interpret religious language as chiefly noncognitive in nature and function.

### Religious Language

At a bare minimum, and aside from any other roles, religious language seems to display the following characteristics: it is expressive, performatory, moral, and committed. I do not believe that there is, in the nature of things, a special or intrinsic function to religious language but rather several functions in combination.

1. By saying that religious language, symbols, and forms are *expressive,* I mean that they are evocative, that they give vent to our feelings and express our emotions. That is, to say that "God is love" or "Humanity is one" is to express a special emotive response toward man and the universe. Religious beliefs arouse attitudes. Religious symbols, if they are eloquent, stimulate an affective mood. Like poetry, they heighten aesthetic imagination and appreciation. In a sense, they are, like exclamations and ejaculations, currents of feeling and passion; though they are for people most serious and compelling.

2. Religious symbols are *performatory,*[5] that is, they allow us to act, to avow, swear, or promise to do something. They may be ceremonial, dramatizing important events and significant moments in our individual or social lives. Birth, death, marriage, graduation, inauguration are solemn occasions when together we give thanks, share experiences, express remorse, celebrate, "consecrate" or "sanctify" our joys or sorrows. Religious language thus is an instrument of action and deed, in terms of which we pledge allegiance, loyalty, dedication, and devotion.

3. But more importantly, religious language is *moral.* It involves imperatives and commands, as they apply to individuals and societies. "Love thy neighbor" and "Treat all men as equals" are general moral rules which are supposed to provide guidance and direction. They are normative and are based upon values and ideals that we cherish and consider worthwhile.

4. But, still more significantly, religious language seems to engage us in *commitment* to our ideals and values. We have many obligations, responsibilities, and commitments in life. A religious commitment is a fundamental commitment, psychologically and socially, to pursue a way of life or a basic policy. It is a commitment which expresses our deepest concerns and longings, and to which we give our highest affection and devotion. I am talking about our first or most important principles of morality and value, those ideals which we really believe in (democracy, peace, brotherhood, creativity,

love, etc.) and which we would attempt to bring about, if we have sufficient courage and fortitude. Religion beckons us to assume a special kind of posture, and it commits our energies to it.

In the light of this analysis of religious language, we see that it does *not* give us any special knowledge or truth about the universe. Religious sentences may make assertions about the world; but if they do, these are true, if at all, because of their factual or logical grounds, and independently of their alleged "religiosity." Those religious sentences that are effective arouse in us what we may call "religious experiences." Such experiences, however, are at most expressive and moral. Here I am discounting as holdovers from a prescientific age all invocations of "piety" and "awe" before the alleged "mysterious" or "numinous" character of "reality." Religious language no doubt has functioned as mystical and creedal for many believers, but in so functioning it has confused and distorted other elements that are present.

### Moral Commitment

The question is often raised as to how this conception of religion as a moral commitment differs from what we consider ethics or morality to be. Some humanists object to preempting the term "religion" from the theists or using it as applicable to their own moral values. Humanism, they insist, is philosophy or ethics; it is not a religion. I sympathize with this point of view; and indeed find it attractive, if only to reassert that a religion of creed or dogma is mistaken. However, this view of what religion is also plays into the hands of the orthodox theist, who insists that the term "religion" only refers to those systems of belief in which there is some "unseen transcendental and divine power controlling the universe and human destiny." Theists object to the extension of the term "religion" to nontheistic religions. Yet it is well known that restricting the definition of "religion" to belief in God leaves out many important religions, such as Buddhism, where Western notions of a godhead are not present. The theist has tried to impose a narrow definition in order to corner the term "religion."

What is common to all religions is not the content of religious beliefs or their truth claims but their functions. Thus, if we look at the human side of the alleged religious encounter, what we seem to find in virtually all religious experience, as far as I can tell, are expressive and moral components and deep-seated commitment. (No doubt for the atheistic or igtheistic humanist the key question is how to defeat orthodox theism. But this is a question of strategy: One may perhaps argue that theism can be defeated by standing outside and totally rejecting all forms of religion. One may likewise argue that theism can also be defeated from within, by reforming religious beliefs and practices.)

Is humanism to be interpreted only as an ethical and philosophical point of view? The naturalistic or scientific humanist claims that his position is based upon science and reason. He insists that his judgments are grounded upon a considered appraisal of facts as discovered in situations. I am in agreement with naturalistic ethics, for I hold that, in principle at least, value judgments are capable of being objectively grounded. However, although it seems to me that many of our value judgments are based upon empirical evidence, they also involve feelings. So far as they do, humanistic values function religiously. Humanistic religion, as distinct from humanistic philosophy, thus involves: (1) expressive elements; that is, it appeals to the whole man, including his attitudes and emotions, and not simply his reason; (2) social organization, shared experiences, ways and methods of acting out and performing moral principles; and (3) commitments to ideal ends. It is an old adage in ethics, which has roots in Aristotle and Hume, that reason by itself does not move man, but that passions and desires do. Accordingly, an ethical and philosophical humanism based upon objective considerations is translated into a religious humanism when it is supported by feeling, ceremony, and commitment.

This humanistic conception of religion finds some interesting analogies in existentialism. The main point of the post-Kierkegaardian approach to religion is that it cannot be a mere ballet of bloodless philosophical categories; it is not the dogma or creed that is important, but the role of experiences within the individual. I am aghast at much of what Kierkegaard maintains: that "truth is subjectivity," that religion involves a "leap of faith," or is solely "inwardness." But nevertheless I think he is correct in pointing out the role of voluntary commitment and ethical decision in religious experience.

## Humanistic Ethics

Whether one takes humanism as a philosophy or as a religion, all humanists still hold that humanism involves an ethical position. Contemporary secular humanism is in a state of crisis, precisely because it has not fully developed its moral position.

There are at least three notions of humanism. First, when one talks about humanism one may be speaking specifically of humanist organizations and churches. Second, one may be speaking of the vast number of nominal humanists in the United States and throughout the world. Perhaps in this broad sense, humanism is the dominant moral and religious point of view in this scientific age among our intellectual and educated classes, though some may not be aware that they are humanists. Third, one can speak of the humanistic revolution taking place within the orthodox bodies—in liberal Protestant theology, in the Catholic reawakening, and in humanistic Judaism.

The puzzling thing about organized humanism is the fact that it has not developed into an organization of sufficient scope and influence, and that it has attracted only a relatively small number of people. Why has organizational humanism been a failure numerically, having limited growth, whereas humanism in the second and third senses now seems to be building up to a considerable force? In other words, why has the humanist revolution succeeded without the aid of a more strongly organized humanism?

## Moral Goals

The answers are manifold and complex. One of the reasons for the failure of organized humanism to thrive is the fact that humanists, being nonconformists, are nonjoiners; another is the failure to develop effective leaders or attract the best minds to the organization. But it seems to me that the real deficiency at present is the lack of positive direction in terms of viable moral goals. Secular humanism has, for the most part, taken its stance *in opposition to* orthodoxy. This critical function is vital and necessary, but the real need is for humanism to be positive, to provide intelligent direction to our moral life. If humanism is to mean anything, then it must speak to present issues and current needs. If humanism in its religious sense involves moral commitment and if it is to inspire dedication and devotion, then it must have something to offer.

A person who leaves a traditional church in revolt or indifference does not want a warmed-over dish of platitudes, as he often has been served by organized humanism in the United States. If one reads what many humanists write about, one often finds the same old cliches and slogans. I fear that John Dewey would turn over in his grave if he could have heard humanists of the sixties invoking Saint Dewey time and again. Is this vital and dynamic humanism, or is it stale bread and tasteless wine? There is important work to be done by humanist organizations. Humanism should be concerned with moral choice and social change—and not just talk about them.

The most vigorous form of secular humanism in the world today seems to be Marxist humanism, which takes seriously the problems of contemporary man. Marxist humanism rejects theistic hypocrisy and offers direction and hope in the light of man's actual situation on earth. Not that I agree with its ideological dogmatism or the development of such substitute fanatic religions as Stalinism or Maoism. My only point is that here is a thoroughly secular humanism that provides us with alternatives to theism in regard to the problem of men in society.

Interestingly, the traditional churches have heeded the humanist message about the need for religion to be responsive to human needs. More often than not, it is *they* who now emphasize the need to be deeply involved in social problems; it is *they* who are in the forefront of social protest and not the humanists—as can be seen, for example, by the key role that church leaders have played in the moral fight for minority rights.

There are humanists who have claimed that enough liberal organizations exist, fighting for good causes, without humanists adding to them. I seriously challenge this assertion. There are all too few avowedly secular organizations concerned with the clarification and enunciation of humanist moral principles. Who speaks for the humanists when abortion reform or aid to parochial schools comes before legislatures? Frequently it is liberal Protestant or Jewish groups, fearful of Catholic power, who defend the principle of separation of church and state. Humanists constitute a large sector of contemporary society, yet they do not have an effective organization to speak for them on the important issues of the day. But what else is humanism if not a concern for the human condition? Is it not time for humanists to develop a viable organized movement and program to compete with theism on equal ground?

## New Philosophical Approach

We have just passed through a remarkable period in metaethics, a period marked by skepticism and impasse. Beginning with G. E. Moore at the turn of the century and coming down to the emotivists and existentialists of the last decade, there was widespread apprehension that the philosopher must not commit the "naturalistic fallacy" or engage in "persuasive definitions." Although the philosophical minority of naturalistic humanists in this country maintained throughout the twentieth century that it was meaningful and necessary for the philosopher to make value judgments and that some degree of objectivity was possible, there was always foreboding that one's philosophical colleagues were dubious of what was being done. The withdrawal of philosophers from ethics proper to metaethics was rather decisive throughout most of the forties and fifties. It was not the task of philosophers, so we are told, to evaluate or prescribe; that was the business of other men. It was the task of the philosopher only to analyze how men used language in order to uncover the implicit structure of moral language. Fortunately, we have come out of this extreme kind of ethical subjectivism on both sides of the Atlantic. Analytic philosophers heir to logical positivism now maintain with naturalistic humanists that *there is,* after all, a kind of "logic" of moral judgments, and some reasons for choices may be said to be "good" reasons. Accordingly, philosophers once again can frame moral judgments and be concerned with concrete moral issues, provided, of course, that they are cautious and careful.

Surely there are a number of significant moral problems we now face and to which ethical humanism should turn. There is, first of all, the fact that so many of the younger generation find that the liberal intellectuals have failed them and that they all too often defend the establishment and tolerate hypocrisy. Many liberals are stunned to find that so many of their programs have become realities. From critics of the system they have been converted to its defenders.

They have been lulled into lethargy. Liberalism of the thirties lingered in the sixties and moved apprehensively into the seventies and eighties.

## Failure of Liberals

Liberals for years talked about the need for sexual emancipation, and all of a sudden it is upon us. There seem few frontiers to conquer since premarital and extramarital intercourse, adultery, divorce, and homosexuality are widely accepted.

The black revolution has reached a critical juncture: militant blacks are attacking liberals, humanists, Unitarians, and Jews. But who stood beside them through all of those early years of civil-rights struggle? And when the liberals preach moderation and reason, they are identified with racists.

What has happened to our dream of world government? The United Nations, once the bright hope of mankind, now evokes despair. We talked of conquering disease by means of medical technology, and in its wake we are presented with the frightening prospect of overpopulation and an increase of poverty in the underdeveloped countries.

Self-determinism, freedom and independence of nations against aggression once seemed like fine moral principles. Once the foe of colonialism, we are now considered its chief defender. And most ominously, the sword of nuclear destruction still hangs overhead, poised at any moment ready to fall, with no method as yet discovered for controlling nuclear armaments.

Modern life has brought us unheard-of prosperity. Yet our cities and countryside are polluted with foul air and dirty streams, and the sheer quantity of production erodes the quality of life. There are so many good things that we have achieved; yet for every problem solved, ten more seem to appear. All too often the well-meaning humanist is bewildered as the twentieth century passes him by. The old moral slogans and formulas no longer seem appropriate to the present age; violence and hate, conflict and hopelessness seem to result.

If scientific and naturalistic humanism in the United States has meant anything, it has meant a commitment to critical intelligence, and it has meant a willingness to inquire and to develop fresh creative solutions for the challenges and problems that vex us. It has meant the willingness to reconstruct our moral principles in the light of new conditions.

Orthodox theism has always looked outside man for salvation and help. And it still carries with it vestiges of an outmoded supernatural morality, as in the blind opposition of the Roman Catholic Church to contraception and abortion, in the face of the population explosion.

Humanism claims to be based upon a realistic appraisal of the universe and man's place within it. It claims to be able to view the human condition with clarity and honesty, devoid of illusion or myth. Humanism has as its central concern man, not God; humanity, not mystery. Humanism is at a critical juncture in its history, and time is running out. The present situation calls for new vision and courage. It calls for humanism to enlist the aid of all sincere men to help solve the frightful problems that the rapidly changing world now faces. It calls for the creation of a new and intelligent morality, which is truly responsive to the present condition of human civilization. Unless organized humanism can help meet these new challenges, it will, I fear, be supplanted by something else. The test of humanism in the last analysis and by its own terms is not how it accords with theory, but how it works out in practice.

## NOTES

1. Andrew Dixon White, *The History of the Warfare of Science with Theology in Christendom* (New York: D. Appleton and Co., 1896).

2. See especially Ludwig Wittgenstein, *Philosophical Investigations* (New York: The Macmillan Co., 1953).

3. See John Hicks, *Faith and the Philosopher* (Ithaca, N.Y.: Cornell University Press, 1957); Basil Mitchell, ed. *Faith and Logic* (Boston: Beacon Press, 1957); Ian T. Ramsey, *Models and Mystery* (London: Oxford University Press, 1964).

4. R. B. Braithwaite, *An Empiricist's View of the Nature of Religious Belief* (Cambridge, England: Cambridge University Press, 1955); Antony Flew, "Theology and Falsification," *New Essays in Philosophical Theology*, ed. Antony Flew and Aladair MacIntyre (New York: The Macmillan Co., 1955).

5. See John Austin, "Performative Utterances," *Philosophical Papers* (London: Oxford University Press, 1961).

# 16

# Toward a Catholic/Humanist Dialogue

## Crisis Humanology

The question "Will mankind prevail?" is not an idle speculation; it has the highest practical import. For mankind may have only a few more decades to solve its problems, which are building up with ominous rapidity. Mankind now possesses the technology to destroy itself—unless, that is, man is able to redirect by means of rational control the blind forces now threatening his existence, to seize his own destiny and become his own master.

The urgent problem that we face today is not the death of God, a crisis theology, but the possibility of the death of man, a *crisis humanology*. This possibility is so real that we must put aside any ideological, religious, metaphysical, or political differences we may have had as humanists, Catholics, Marxists, and so on, and turn our attention to their solution. For we are first and foremost members of the same species, and our concern must precede any ideological, national, racial, or religious commitments, narrow loyalties, or parochial allegiances. In other words, we no longer can afford the luxury of subtle metaphysical controversies but must face the concrete problems now confronting the human species. To flee from them, or even to minimize them, would be flagrant moral irresponsibility. The point is, we are *all* responsible for what will happen and no person can renounce his obligation to do what he can to save mankind.

I

The twentieth century is preeminently the age of technology. It is the century in which scientific humanism has finally emerged as the dominant force in human civilization. It is the epoch in which man has learned that he can tame nature but also that he can be destroyed or dehumanized by the instruments of liberation he has invented. Technology can be either an inspiration for further creative progress—the Promethean unfolding of the highest human aspirations—or a monster ready and able to devour its Frankenstein creator.

To relate this point directly to the Catholic/Humanist dialogue: It should now be apparent that it is scientific humanism that has prevailed in

This essay is from *A Catholic/Humanist Dialogue*, ed. Paul Kurtz and Albert Dondegere (London: Pemberton Books, 1972).

the contemporary world, not orthodox theism. The world we now face is to a considerable extent a result of the new science and its impact on civilization. Humanist thinking now strongly influences the intellectual and educated classes of the world and as education continues to spread, so predictably will the humanist outlook. Scientific humanism has transformed the planet earth—often in spite of intransigent opposition from the church. Accordingly, scientific humanism must take a large measure of responsibility for what has happened to the world, both the gains and the losses. In the historic battle between humanist freethinkers and the church, it is the humanists who emphasized the benefits that might accrue to mankind from the use of scientific method, in understanding nature and in applying technology to the solution of human problems; and it was the church that was skeptical about these claims.

In intellectual terms the first major victory for the scientific outlook occurre ' with the Copernican revolution; the Galilean-Newtonian world view overthrew the classical Aristotelian-Thomistic conception of the universe, in which the earth was at the center. The second major shock to the theological view came with the Darwinian revolution, which dethroned a teleological theory of man, supplanted it with evolutionary hypotheses, and naturalized man's origins in biology. Third, and more recently, the behavioristic revolution destroyed the notion of a privileged homunculized "soul" and showed that natural causal explanations could be applied fully to the study of man. Thus the successive scientific revolutions have undermined any defensive efforts by the church to show that anything was "unknowable," "irreducible," "mysterious," or "beyond understanding" by science. Science is a method of inquiry, a way of dealing with nature, not a body of fixed knowledge. If any conclusion is to be drawn from the great controversies of the last four centuries, it is that all obstacles placed in the way of the scientific advance have been overturned by the success of the controlled use of scientific method. Appeals to "metaphysical mystery" or "faith," "free will," an "inner mind" or "soul," or "historical contingency" or "indeterminism" have not been able to demonstrate on a priori grounds that there were aspects of nature that were basically unintelligible or beyond science. Rather, we now know that what can or cannot be known is an open question to be determined by the course of inquiry and the ingenuity of scientific investigation. Rather than delimiting investigative research beforehand, the strategy is to leave it open for future inquiry and discovery. And thus, a great drama and intellectual adventure has been unfolding, as scientists have introduced hypotheses and theories to describe and explain how and why phenomena occur the way they do and as they have verified their findings by means of powerful mathematical tools and experimental tests. Thus science has made possible the continued introduction of novel and unexpected dimensions of explanation and understanding, not only of the physical-chemical world and of biological matter but of man himself, his psychological behavior and social and cultural institutions.

Theoretical explanations, however, do not in themselves enable us to modify or control nature; only applied knowledge does. As Francis Bacon foresaw, the great advantage that modern science has over Greek science is its power of prediction and the fact that scientific hypotheses can be used to develop technology; it is scientific technology that has opened up and transformed nature. It sparked the industrial revolution, the green revolution, the medical-biological revolution, the electronic and computer revolution, and man's leap into space. Scientific principles are no longer abstract theories but instruments by which conceptual thought and imagination are implemented in action. If classical man sought to make the universe intelligible to his reason, modern man has sought to master nature and use it for his own purposes.

## II

If we examine the progress of science, we find that the balance sheet has both pluses and minuses. The gains to mankind are truly astounding. These are due to several revolutions in technology. I will mention only three.

*The Machine Revolution.* The invention of machines has greatly reduced the necessity for physical labor—whether human or animal. Man has invented machine tools for extracting natural resources and for manufacturing goods for distribution and consumption. Man can now control and remake his environment to fit his needs. He has discovered new forms of energy— steam, fossil-fuel, and nuclear—to do his work. The technological revolution has provided man with the power to travel at unheard-of speeds. For the first time in human history all barriers to communication have broken down, and the instantaneous transmission of ideas, sounds, and pictures by means of electronic devices is a reality throughout the globe. In addition, a new electronic-computer technology has enormously increased man's ability to think, to make symbolic connections with great precision, and to transform his life by automation. A machine technology thus can banish drudgery from human civilization.

*The Green or Agricultural Revolution.* This has increased man's ability to produce foodstuffs by means of concentrated fertilizers, new forms of cross-breeding, and machine technology. In previous epochs, the bulk of mankind devoted most of its time to hunting, foraging, and growing food. Today only a small part of an industrial society needs to be tied to the land. And for the first time man knows how to produce enough food to get rid of hunger.

*The Revolution in Medical Technology.* This has banished the terrible diseases and plagues, premature death and suffering that were the scourge of life. The discovery of antibiotics, the use of new techniques of surgery, organ transplants, sanitary measures, and nutrition have increased the life expectancy of mankind and helped reduce pain.

There are still large areas that need improvement and there are great problems to be solved. The underdeveloped countries of the world need to achieve the ability that the developed countries have of utilizing technology to eliminate poverty, disease, and illiteracy. All of these things are now within the power of man. Problems with him since the dawn of human history are for the first time now capable of solution. All of this means that large sections of the human race can enjoy unparalleled affluence and prosperity, maximize literacy and cultural enrichment, and have the leisure time to pursue the arts and sciences and appreciate the good life.

The scientific humanist affirms that it is possible for mankind to spread the goods of science over the entire globe for the betterment of all men and also to open up new doors for adventure in the future. As space travel beckons, the human race may be able to inhabit the solar system and beyond, guiding the course of human evolution, and creating by means of biological engineering the kind of human race suitable for life in outer space. Science can improve memory, expand intellectual capacities, and prolong life expectancy immeasurably. We can build a utopian civilization that is breathtaking in promise, far beyond what men have dreamed about in the past, even outstripping what was considered to be science fiction only a few short years ago.

## III

Yet, as mankind stands at the dawn of a new tomorrow, he is threatened; for scientific technology has brought in its wake new dangers and perils. It is clear that scientific technology can be used for good or ill. A Nazi or a commissar, a democrat or a Christian, can turn the discoveries of science to his own purposes. Thus, scientific technology may be either functional or dysfunctional. Indeed, man faces the real possibility of becoming an extinct species. Nuclear or chemical-biological weaponry has given him the capacity to destroy the entire race and, indeed, most forms of life on earth. Agricultural and medical achievements have reduced poverty and disease but have also increased population at an incredible rate. The lowered death rate and the higher birth rate have thus threatened the human species, and a population cloud overhangs the future of mankind. Thus if men are not exterminated by an explosive war, they may be inundated by an explosion in biological reproduction, so that if present trends continue unchecked some six to seven billion humans are expected by the year 2000, and perhaps some ten billion by 2020!

Another peril to the future of mankind is the destruction of the ecology. Man's technology has polluted the waterways, poisoned the atmosphere, misused and wasted natural resources. In addition, man has been increasingly dehumanized and depersonalized by the conditions of modern technological life. Uprooted in a relatively short period of time from the natural environment he occupied for millions of years, he is hurled into an artificial, urbanized context; his natural biological needs and drives, which have served him throughout history, are often redirected and thwarted by the new technological milieu that he has created; and he often feels alone, alienated, lost.

Man faces a crisis unprecedented in human history. Having discovered the key to a rich and bountiful life, he finds in the very process of his emancipation new forms of enslavement and destruction. The crisis man faces is that he does not know how to use what he has discovered. Once the discoveries are out—like the genie in Aladdin's lamp—he doesn't know how to control them.

## IV

The crisis man faces is primarily a crisis in morality. It concerns the use, direction and control of knowledge. Man cannot retreat into ignorance; he can only step ahead to new knowledge. The real option he faces is whether he is ready for a fourth revolution, intellectual and technological—a moral revolution. Can he remake and reorder his ethical priorities? Can he alter moral prejudices inherited from the infancy of mankind? Can he thoroughly adapt to the new world he has made and reconstruct a set of values appropriate to it?

For the scientific humanist the great question is whether man can extend the method of scientific intelligence—fused with compassion—to make moral decisions. Men are still held back by vestiges of racism, chauvinism, nationalism, class antagonism, religious bigotry, and prejudice; for their value systems were often formed in isolation. Based on older cultural institutions—perhaps appropriate to their times—they are no longer relevant to the current urgencies. Hence, we need to experiment with new forms of morality.

Paradoxically, at the same time that scientific progress has assured the highest rate of development, new forms of religious idolatry emerge: Marxism, Leninism, Stalinism, Maoism are new faiths, rooted in scientific materialism, yet passionate in intensity. They are replacing the older theistic religions, though they often lack wisdom or maturity. With the breakdown of old faiths, new fanaticisms appear, "rational" enough to attract some intellectuals and the young, yet imbued with violent and irrational intolerance.

The overriding issue is this: Can man face the world for what it is? Can he (as Paul Tillich asks) develop the courage to be? Can he apply his ingenuity and intelligence to refashion a new set of ideals and norms appropriate to the present epoch? Is he capable of moral reconstruction?

What is clear is that he cannot afford the luxury of delay. For issues press in on him, and the terrible problems he faces will not wait.

To the scientific humanist the option is clear. We should not retreat from scientific intelligence, but extend its range. Reason, we all recognize, is not perfect. There are many problems that defy solution. Often we can choose only the lesser of many evils, and often we are unable to predict all the consequences of our actions. Rational men, committed to objective canons of inquiry, may indeed disagree about what is fitting in a given context. Moreover, man must be considered as a whole being, with emotional needs and desires as well as reason.

All of this demonstrates the dramatic character of the human condition in history, the facts of contingency and possibility. Yet for the scientific humanist, the rational intelligence, always learning from experience and correcting judgments in the light of the consequences of practice is, in the last analysis, the best instrument we have. The posture we should assume is not one of fear and trembling before the awesome problems we encounter, but rather one of courage and determination. For man, of all the creatures on this planet, is *audacious*, standing up, fashioning tools, crossing the oceans, soaring in the heavens. Man has made and can continue to make his mark on nature. As a toolmaker he has the power to create a Garden of Eden; what still resists him is the knowledge of good and evil. But until he eats of the fruit of the tree of moral wisdom, he can go no further.

Thus, the central need at the present moment in human history is for moral reconstruction. But alas, at the present juncture one of the key obstacles to this pressing need is the church. The church stood against the Copernican, Darwinian, and behavioral revolutions. Will it continue to resist the moral revolution?

The church has had a long career. It has eloquently grasped the need for the basic human moral virtues of love and sympathy, kindness and charity, benevolence and altruism. But, regretfully, it has enshrined other moral values, now archaic, seeking to sanctify them with religious authority. Some forces within the church have a humanist awareness of what is now at stake and wish to meet the awesome challenges we face. Yet others cling to the old customs and past dogmas and attempt to resist what will in the end be irresistible. The church at one time opposed the new science; it now knows that it can no longer do so. At one time the church opposed democracy and allied itself with reactionary forces and the status quo. Churchmen now recognize that they no longer can do so. For centuries they opposed humanism but now are apparently cognizant of the futility of such opposition; they are willing to enter into dialogue with humanists and even to claim their own form of humanism. Will the church not now participate in a new moral revolution, one designed solely for the survival and benefit of mankind?

## V

There are certain overriding problems of social morality that must be solved if the human race is to survive. We live in a common world, which all men of goodwill must work cooperatively to improve. In some respects the church—at least in the eyes of the scientific humanist—is the chief foe of reform. In other respects it is not, and need not be. What are some of the crucial problems that demand solution?

The most pressing area in which the church resists change concerns the need for a worldwide policy of population control. Implicit in this is the need to create a new kind of sexual morality. The dangers of runaway population growth is no doubt a familiar litany, but the demographic tide is real; should present trends continue, at some point life will become intolerable. The problem is exacerbated primarily by scientific advance. A lowered death rate and increased food supply have made population leap ahead. Yet scientific technology cannot now be blamed, for it has also given us methods for limiting population: birth control, voluntary sterilization, safe abortion. Human suffering will increase where there are unwanted children and inadequate resources to care for them. Yet the church, heir to a repressive morality in which sex is considered to exist for reproduction and not for psychological satisfaction or pleasure, abhors tampering with the processes of "natural law." Birth control, sterilization, and abortion are considered "wicked" and "sinful." But the point is that man intervenes to transplant organs, correct birth defects, install pacemakers in hearts to regulate rhythm, etc. Why is it any less "natural" to regulate sexual reproduction? All of the above, it is said, improve natural functions and do not impede them. Tranquillizer drugs administered by psychiatrists to alleviate anxiety and tension suppress or restrict natural functions. Should they not on the same grounds be proscribed? Surely not.

Sexual education for adolescents and adults is necessary, if we are to check population growth, if we are to avert famine, avoid ecological destruction, and preserve the quality of life. Some theologians have said that science will discover a way to avoid destruction—perhaps by shooting procreating humans out into space to populate the universe. Perhaps. Yet refusing to allow a new morality consonant with present scientific probabilities to restrict population growth is irresponsible. What is at stake is not the quantity of life, but the quality of life, which can be enhanced by intelligent family planning and population control.

Closely related to the need for a new sexual morality is the changing character of the family. Monogamous relations are sometimes difficult to sustain throughout a long life. Thus plural forms of marriage relationships and a more just and humane attitude toward divorce are called for, as well as a recognition that homosexual relationships need not be wicked or bestial but may involve a measure of enriched experience. Repression is the cauldron in which psychological neuroses and pathology are brewed. Man needs to develop a positive view of sexuality: that it is good and noble, not evil and corrupt. This is no place to start an extended discussion of the new sexual revolution brought about by the expansion of science and education. It is enough to emphasize that reconstructed attitudes toward sexuality should be developed.

In other areas the church is not necessarily an obstacle to progress. But it is important that it exert its tremendous power and influence to see that certain goals are realized. An otherworldly concern often deflects attention from the need for social reconstruction.

There is the continued need for economic development, especially of the underdeveloped areas of the globe. We need to overcome the disparity that exists between the have and have-not nations. It is necessary that mankind develop planning and allocation of natural resources on a worldwide basis. Future generations cannot be hostage to our misuse of limited resources. There are different economic systems in different areas of the world that seem best adapted to expand the forces of production, provide for their equitable distribution, and overcome economic injustice and exploitation. We should not oppose socialist systems or mixed economic systems which — in harmony with democratic values — seek to meet the needs of the people. I am saying that we should not be committed to either capitalist or socialist ideology; we should be receptive to the possibility of using different economic systems in different parts of the world.

There is the need to break down narrow political loyalties and allegiances, to transcend nationalism, especially where it is self-interested and destructive. Nation-states that contribute to the arms race and are willing to resort to violent warfare to achieve their own national aims are immoral. With the end of nationalism, we also need an end to all forms of religious bigotry and racial or ethnic separatism.

Thus, it is clear that the great demand for mankind today is to create a world society in which a system of world order and the rule of law can evolve, a system in which peace and justice can prevail. This means that for the first time some system of world government is not only possible but required. Mankind needs to develop a system that will provide for security and protection against war, allow for rational economic growth and development, and promote a sensible population policy. Only by building a world community can happiness and the common good for humanity as a whole be attained. This should be our chief interest as humanists.

Of course, if any of this is to be achieved, then it is essential that pluralistic toleration reign. We cannot remake the world in our image. While we are building community, we need to respect diverse interests and needs and forego compelling others to accept our practices and beliefs.

Although men have dreamed of the brotherhood of mankind and of one world, it is now for the first time made possible by means of technology. For the technological revolution has broken down false barriers and frontiers between isolated cultures.

The highest moral obligation of man as he faces the future is to see that a world community can develop, but it can occur only if we are stirred by a moral vision and if we are willing to make sacrifices to bring it about.

## VI

From the standpoint of the scientific humanist, continuous dialogue among Roman Catholics, secular humanists, and others is long overdue. A church comprising hundreds of millions of people must take seriously, and be taken seriously by, the millions of humanists in today's world.

The church cannot resist or oppose the power of the technological scientific revolution, nor can it resist efforts to update morality in terms of our expanded knowledge of nature and man. The church cannot bear the burden of further obstruction or delay, for human history has reached a critical moment. Will a new church emerge based upon science, not contrary to it, with a new morality that speaks to the desperate needs of present-day humanity? This is perhaps no place for me to give advice, but I am convinced that unless Catholicism adopts a "human face," it may become faceless in time and perish. I realize that Roman Catholics believe that the church is timeless, but the same claim has been made for other moribund institutions of the past.

The scientific humanist is working hard to develop a new morality appropriate to the age in which we live and consonant with scientific discovery. The humanist has faith in man and confidence in the powers of human intelligence and fortitude. Some liberal Catholics admit that they could accept the ethical and social principles of humanism, which are designed to create a better life for men and which consider human beings to be free and autonomous. But they insist that they still believe in God—and they ask whether this means that they are not humanists in the full sense.

The scientific humanist thinks that God-belief is profoundly mistaken and that there is not sufficient evidence for or meaning to the claim that "God exists." Yet so long as the believer does not attempt to impose his belief on others, to censor free thought, stand in the way of scientific advance, or limit genuine moral and social reconstruction, we would have no objection to his belief. But then, for us, the final meaning of religion is its role in praxis, or conduct. If on pragmatic grounds Catholicism expressed a full and genuine concern for man, then its "transcendent hope," which for humanists is an illusion, might have little real effect upon human experience or social life. If it makes no practical difference in concrete practice then it would have little, if any, independent meaning.

Humanists are not unaware of the tragic character of human existence and the paradoxes of human life. We possess the potentialities for happiness and joy, as well as for sorrow, failure, and death. For humanists, life as we now know it is finite. Religion is a form of poetry or metaphor in a material world: "a lyric cry in the midst of business," says the Catholic-humanist George Santayana. It expresses the pathos and poignancy of life. But religion cannot stand opposed to the deeper stirrings and affirmations of human life or it will be overwhelmed.

Insofar as Christianity dramatizes the existential paradox of man facing death yet affirming life, it expresses a poetic truth about the human condition. But this should not be allowed to turn man from life—in the hope of eternity—when all he faces is nothingness.

For the scientific humanist, we humans enter the world with a loud yell as infants, and we should leave it not with a whimper or a bang, but perhaps with a chuckle. Given dependence upon intelligence and the willingness to use our powers to solve our problems, human beings can still be saved *in this life,* and we can discover and create a rich and meaningful existence. If we are to be saved, however, it is only by using our own resources, by believing in *man,* not depending upon faith or mystery. Nevertheless, since we live in the same world, Catholics and humanists have to work together, whether or not we agree that belief in God is a truth or an illusion.

# 17

# Humanism: The Meaning Function

**M**any humanists claim that the present age is the "age of humanism." They have pointed to the growth of modern science and technology, the increase in education and learning, and the development of new standards of value related to contemporary conditions as evidence for the progress of the humanist outlook. It is true that a steady line of humanist thought can be traced from the classical civilizations of Greece and Rome, through the Renaissance and the Enlightenment, to the modern world. Moreover, on the contemporary scene the ideals of reason, freedom, and democracy have come to fruition, and millions have been emancipated from traditional superstitions and dogmas.

Yet, paradoxically, while humanist ideals have flourished, at the same time the ancient myths persist. At times, humanism seems only a slender reed, ready to be overwhelmed anew by apostles of dogmatic intolerance. Indeed, the humanist is doubly perplexed, for whenever humanists appear to have vanquished the orthodox religions by pointing out their fallacies and foibles, inconsistencies and contradictions, they reemerge with renewed strength in the next generation. This process is dramatically evident today; witness the persistence of liberal Protestant fundamentalism, Roman Catholic orthodoxy, nationalistic Judaism, and the fanatical sects of Islam.

If the humanistic outlook is a strong trend in modern culture, why do not more people identify with it? Why do there seem to be so few adherents willing to stand up and be counted?

Humanists recently have been undergoing critical self-scrutiny in an effort to explain what they deem a lack of success. Some have sought to politicize humanism by identifying it with social reform or political programs, believing that if it is not humanitarian in impulse, it is nothing. Unfortunately, in so doing they alienate all who do not share this political outlook. Some humanists have even deceived themselves into thinking the humanist cause victorious. Most contemporaries, they say, appreciate the contribution of science and hold secular values, rejecting the simpleminded, literal faith of their forefathers. This *may* have been true a decade ago. It is much less true today, when Bible-thumping preachers sing hosannas

---

This was published in *Religious Humanism,* Spring 1980.

to the Lord and recruit countless born-again Christians, Roman Catholics virtually adore the pope as a Christ figure, and fanatic Shia Muslims parade the streets of Iran in rituals of self-flagellation.

These traditional religions have not escaped devastating critical analysis by philosophers and scientists. In the eighteenth century, Hume's *Dialogue Concerning Critical Religion* provided a refutation of theism. Thomas Paine's *Age of Reason* pointed out the inconsistencies of the Bible. And a long line of eminent thinkers, including Mill, Marx, Schopenhauer, Freud, Sartre, Dewey, and Russell, have defended atheism against religion. Still, billions of adherents are enlisted in God's cause. Why do so many cling so persistently to traditional religion? Will religious belief always remain strong? Is humanism or rationalism destined forever to be a minority position? Miraculous revelation, the Bible, and the Koran have been questioned by critics. Yet belief persists, and, however irrational, the word of many different prophets is taken as the authentic word of God. Even in parts of the West where traditional Judeo-Christian sects are rejected they are all too often supplanted by new, more bizarre ones like Krishna Consciousness and the Unification Church. There is an almost inherent need to believe something transcendent, miraculous, mysterious: the bigger the lie, the more incredible the promise, the more likely are there to be devout believers.

Surely, rationalists and humanists have not lacked the power of brilliant intellect and wit to lampoon and debunk the myths. Yet if for one generation religion is dormant, in the next new life is breathed into it; it again becomes a potent force. And the conflict between religion and science or between religion and philosophy is renewed.

The reason should be apparent. Although the illustrious critics of theism—atheists, agnostics, skeptics, rationalists, humanists—have presented powerful negative commentaries, they have neglected to develop a *positive* alternative. For men do not live by intellect alone, but hunger for passion, romance, and the meaning of life. They are burdened by trials and tribulations, tragic dilemmas and failures, the knowledge that eventually death vanquishes us all.

Religion, however impervious to logic, has a deep source. It dramatizes the vital turning points of life and celebrates the rites of passage: birth (baptism), puberty (confirmation), marriage (wedding ceremony), death (funeral ceremony). Simply to reject the deeply entrenched faith of our fathers, institutionalized by the church and sanctified by custom and tradition, rich in heritage and ethnicity, is not enough unless and until one makes the attempt to provide new symbols of meaning and purpose.

Thus, nontheisms of whatever variety may seek to enlighten the converted and attempt to set them on a new path. But they will not succeed simply by destroying the old faiths and symbols, for new ones, perhaps more appealing, will replace them. It is necessary to substitute moral equivalents. It is necessary to answer the key questions we have always asked:

Where did we come from? Where are we going? Can life be meaningful? Is it bearable? How do we face adversity and death? Where do we get the courage to be and become? These are all deeply felt, existential questions, not idle speculative exercises. Almost everyone asks them at some point in life. And theism, whatever its defects, at least attempts to cope with them.

Indeed, if there is a failure of humanism as an *ism* it is precisely at this point. As a competitor of the churches it offers almost nothing imaginative or eloquent; it has not heeded the meaning function of religious symbols and ideals. Overwhelmed by the brilliance and clarity of its thought, it has been unwilling or unable to see past the spectacles on its own nose. In the scientific universe, it has eschewed metaphysical conjuring. But it has also ignored the root questions about the meaning of life. And for this reason, believers have rejected its "message" as they would cold and stale porridge.

If humanism is to succeed and not be banal, it should not be identified with specific social programs or platforms. Christians and Jews can be Republicans or Democrats, Laborites, Liberals or Conservatives. Why not humanists and unbelievers? Humanism should not be wedded to a specific ideology—although humanists surely need to have political convictions and to work cooperatively with others to create a better society. But not at the price of the deeper function of the humanist outlook. It is, distinctively, an alternative to theism. It says that while there are mysteries about the universe and man's place within it, the option is not piety and dependence on an unseen Being—that is sheer illusion—but affirmation and independence of human powers and the cultivation of intelligence and excellence. Humanism will not succeed in attracting human beings to its fold in this generation and those to come nor will it enlist commitment beyond intellectual conviction unless it pays heed to the meaning function that all the great religions seek to perform. Humanism, too, must address itself to this issue as its primary, if not sole, mission: *human life has meaning in its own terms.* There is no need to look outside it for success or salvation. Life is pregnant with opportunities and possibilities. But whether these are tapped depends upon what we do. We are responsible for our destiny. No god will save us; we must save ourselves. Life can be a wonderful adventure. But we must individually and collectively develop the courage to solve our problems and create a humane world here, without delusions about worlds beyond. We can do so only if we develop self-reliance, cultivate critical intelligence, and build a truly humanistic ethic.

# 18

# The Meaning of Life

*Ethics Minus God*

Does life have genuine meaning for one who rejects supernatural mythology (or Marxist ideology)? Can one realize a significant life if he abandons faith in immortality or providence? Is life tragic because it is finite? Since death surely awaits everyone, is life therefore absurd? (In answer, religious Marxism seeks to invest the cosmic void with historical purpose: Mankind is larger than any one individual and provides the individual with a beloved cause.) Faced with this existential dilemma, man cries out, "Why live?" Can we be happy? Is there a basis for moral conduct? What can we do if God is dead, if there is no immortal soul, if there is no purpose immanent in nature?

It is important that we focus on the so-called problem of the meaning of life as it is posed by the theist. (The humanist at least shares with the Marxist the assumption that life is worth living.) In answer to the theist, we may say that the existential question, as framed by him, is mistaken. We should not grant the religious believer the validity of his challenge. Instead we should ask whether life is really meaningful for *him*. Does he not deceive himself by posing the theological-existential paradox and by assuming that only a "broader" purpose can save him? Is it not the theist who squanders life? In what sense would life be worthwhile if God existed, if the universe had a divine purpose—and given the existence of "evil"?

The conception of an omnipotent God connotes the correlative notion of helpless creatures. "Man's chief end," admonishes the Scottish shorter catechism, "is to glorify God and enjoy him for ever and ever." What kind of life can be said to be significant if we are totally dependent upon this God for our existence and sustenance? The relationship of creator to created is analogous to that of master to slave. The religious picture of the universe is akin to a model prison, wherein inmates are beholden to the warden for their daily bread and their highest duty is to praise and supplicate him for life. The immortality myth warns that if we do not pledge allegiance to His will, we shall suffer damnation. Is not the life of an independent free man to be preferred to one of eternal bondage?

---

This was published in *The Humanist*, Jan./Feb. 1975.

No, replies the believer to this skeptical question. God promises eternal salvation, not oppression, for the elect. But upon what condition? As Bertrand Russell has said, to sing hymns in praise of Him and hold hands throughout all eternity would be sheer boredom. What of the lusts of the body, the joys of the flesh, the excitement and turmoil of pleasure and passion—will these be vanquished in the immortal life? For the free man, Hell could not be worse.

The religious believer insists that man is free; for he is created in God's image, capable of choosing between good and evil. The rub, however, is that only if he chooses to obey his master will he be rewarded with immortal life. But the problem of evil turns this eternal drama into divine comedy: God entrusted me with the power and freedom of choice, yet He will punish me if I stray from Him. Why did He not program me during the act of creation, so that I could not avoid knowing Him and following His guidelines. Since it is He who created me, why does He condemn me for satisfying my natural inclinations, which He implanted in me? Why does God permit suffering and pain, torment and tragedy, disease and strife, war and plunder, conflict and chaos? In order to test us, responds the theist. But why the necessity of the trial, with so much apparent vindictiveness? To punish us for the sins we have committed. If this is the case, why punish the innocent? Why cut down the seeming paragons of virtue, the valiant and the noble? For the sins they have committed but may be unaware of? Why visit pain and torment upon infants and children—as in cancer or accident? Are they paying for the sins of their parents? If so, is this not a morality of collective guilt? One who believes in reincarnation may attempt to rescue the case by insisting on a prior existence. Possibly children are made to pay for the sins they have committed in an earlier life, though as an ill child writhes and cries out, he does not remember those prior existences—as a Caligula or a Hitler—for which he now suffers.

The rationalization continues: Perhaps evil is due to man's omission, not God's commission. Man should discover a cure for cancer, for example, or learn to stop floods. But if God is all-powerful, why doesn't He intervene? There is no natural evil, say some theists, attempting to resolve the problem; the only evil is "moral evil," they assert, the evil of man, not God. But the inescapable inference is that God permits evil. Why does He not stamp it out? Why should not God be merciful and loving rather than legalistic and moralistic? Is He, as Hume suggests, like us: limited in power? Then why worship another finite being?

Some theists insist that evil may be only an illusion and that from a larger perspective what appears to be evil may turn out in the end to be good. In the total divine plan, pain and suffering need not be bad. Why is not the converse true? From this point of view, what appears to be good may also be only an illusion, and everything in the end irredeemably evil.

Thus the believer has woven a fanciful fabric by mythological imagination in order to soothe his fear of death and to comfort those who share his anxiety. His is an ad hoc rationalization professing to settle his doubts; but it is ridden with loopholes more puzzling than the universe we encounter in everyday life.

Believers finally concede that there are things — from the Book of Job down to the present — beyond human understanding; these include the paradox of free will versus determinism and the problem of evil. Unable to resolve the contradictions, they end up with simple confessions of faith.

Should we not rather deal with life as we find it — full of sorrow, death, pain, and failure, but also pregnant with possibilities?

But, insists the believer, man cannot be happy if he knows that he is going to die and that the universe possesses no larger purpose. What is happiness? Does it require acquiescence to another, dependence on a greater being, religious faith and devotion, credulity and piety? Why is religious masochism a form of bliss? It may release us from torment and anxiety, but it involves flight from the full realization of our powers. Not only, therefore, does religious theism fail to give life meaning, but it also fails as a source of happiness. More often than not it has exaggerated the pathology of fear, the anxiety of punishment, the dread of death and the unknown.

The believer is tormented by his overextended sense of sin and guilt, torn by a struggle between natural biological impulses and repressive divine commandments. Can a religious believer who submits to a doctrine of sin be truly happy? For the humanist the great folly is to squander his life, to miss what it affords. The cemeteries are filled with corpses who bartered their souls in anticipation of promises that were never fulfilled.

But can one really be "moral," remonstrates the theist, without religious belief? Are we capable of developing "moral virtues" and a sense of responsibility without a belief in God as a presupposition of morality?

The answers in part depend upon what is meant by the term "moral." Morality for the believer requires the existence of a faith, a pious appreciation of God's redemptive power. This entails the "virtues" of acquiescence and obedience, as well as the suppression of natural biological desires, including appreciation of sexuality — and even some degree of self-hate. Humanists, however, deny that most of the so-called moral virtues of traditional theism are either moral or virtuous. The highest virtues lie in man's existing for himself; self-interest, self-respect, pride, some element of self-centeredness are essential components of morality, which in the last analysis focuses on happiness. This being the case, it is possible to be "moral" without belief in God.

But, asks the theist, if God is dead, is not *everything* permissible? Would not man be rapacious and misuse his fellow creatures? How, without God, can we guarantee charity and justice? The brotherhood of man presupposes a divine conception of individual dignity based upon the fatherhood of God. To abandon this postulate of the moral life would be to reduce men to hunter and prey and open the way to every form of barbarism.

Basically, these are empirical questions. There is no logical connection between the fatherhood of God and the brotherhood of man. A hierarchical church has defended an unequal society with strict social class and privilege. Moral sympathy is not dependent upon theistic belief. The crusades and the Inquisition, the massacre of the Huguenots, the Muslim-Hindu slaughter in modern times, Catholic-Protestant battles, as in Northern Ireland, are among the cruelties perpetrated by theists. Moreover, belief in God often deflects a concern for one's fellowmen to supernatural goals; faith supersedes charity. If one's interest is the afterlife, then there is a temptation for some — though not all — to render unto Caesar the things that are Caesar's. Churches have had little difficulty in suppressing progress and revolution. Franco and Salazar were true believers, as have been powerful men in authoritarian regimes in South Africa, Greece, Portugal, and Pakistan.

Religious devotion is no guarantee of moral devotion. Rather, there is good evidence that moral concern is autonomous and rooted in independent phenomenological experience. The history of mankind demonstrates that atheists, agnostics, and skeptics have been as moved by moral consideration for others as have believers. Marx, Engels, Russell, Mill, Dewey, and Sartre had deep and abiding moral interest in the good of mankind and did not depend upon religious faith to bolster their morality. On the contrary, they demonstrated that morality grounded in human experience and reason is a far more reliable guide to conduct.

## Is Life Worth Living?

There are other sources of despair. I have in mind the "existential plight" caused by life's exasperating and sometimes tragic difficulties, failures, and conflicts. There are moments when everything seems pointless; we wish to abandon all our commitments; we may even contemplate suicide in profound crises of self-doubt and frustration. We may ask: Why beat one's head against a stone wall? What's the use?

At some point in life many of us have suspended desires, interests, and ideals, brought about by the death of a loved one, a cherished friend or relative, intense personal suffering, a disease, defeat of one's country, failure, deception uncovered, injustice perpetrated. The young burdened with the choice of a career, the middle-aged facing divorce or financial ruin, the old enduring pangs of loneliness — all know moments of desperation.

Yet in spite of adversities and frustrations, the humanist maintains as his first principle that life is worth living, at least that it can be found to have worth. Can one demonstrate why the principle ought to prevail? Why express the courage to be? Why not die? Why life instead of death? If we are all going to die one day, why defer the inevitable?

One cannot "prove" that life ought to exist, or that a universe with sentient beings is a better place than one without them. The universe is neutral, indifferent to man's existential yearnings. But we instinctively discover life, experience its throb, its excitement, its attraction. Life is here to be lived, enjoyed, suffered, and endured.

We must therefore rely on ourselves and distinguish two major, though distinct, questions. The first is epistemological and the second, psychological. Epistemologically, we may ask, can we "demonstrate" the basic principle of humanist morality, that is, that life is worthwhile? As his first principle, the theist adopts belief in a divine order beyond empirical confirmation or proof, which is in the last analysis a leap of faith. Does the first principle of humanism rest on the same footing? My answer is no. For life is found; it is encountered; it is real. It needs no proof of its existence, as does an unknown and unseen divinity. The question is not: Does life exist? This is known as intimately and forcefully as anything in our universe of experience. The question rather is normative: *Ought* life to exist? This first principle does not make a descriptive claim; it is prescriptive and directive.

There are different kinds of first principles. They are not all of the same logical order, nor do they function in the same way. There are first principles that assert truth claims about the universe: for example, the assertions that God exists, that determinism is real, and that the dialectic is operative in history. All of these principles have to be judged by the requirements of evidence and logic. Those that cannot provide sufficient grounds of support fail. A normative principle, as distinct from a descriptive assertion, is a guide for future conduct. It does not talk about the world in descriptive or explanatory terms. It lays down recommendations for us to follow, values to uphold, ideals to live by.

It is no doubt true that the epistemological principles of deductive logic, which provide for clarity in inference and thought, and of inductive science, which apply to the criteria for weighing evidential claims, function in one sense prescriptively; for they provide guidelines for clarity and truth. In the last analysis they are justified pragmatically: Do they assist in the course of inquiry? But still these are not truth claims of the same order as the God claim; for they are not attributing properties to the world. (If the theist were willing to abandon any descriptive claims about the universe, then "God exists" would be a normative principle, indicating moral imperatives for man. Such an ethical interpretation of theism would not suffer the objections that classical transcendental supernaturalism has. The major issue then would be the status of its moral principles, and whether they are viable.)

Theistic descriptive claims are bad answers to bad questions, such as: Why in the universe at large should organic matter exist? This makes no more sense than asking why things exist in the inanimate world. "Why ought there to be anything at all in the universe?" is a meaningless question, though no doubt for the religious consciousness a poignant one. The demand for an explanation of "being in general" or for an answer to the "riddle of the universe" is inevitably elusive, because there is no such thing as "being in general." There are a multiplicity of beings that may be said to exist—objects, organisms, persons. These entities are encountered in experience and may be submitted to analysis since they have discernible properties. The question *why* they exist with the properties they have, may be accounted for scientifically; they may be explained in causal terms, as having evolved in nature and as conditioned by natural laws. To ask *"why* being in general?" is both fruitless and pointless. To posit God as the alleged ground of being does not advance inquiry. We can always ask why He exists. There are limits to genuine explanation, and certain kinds of questions and answers are beyond the range of intelligibility. The universe *is,* in a distributive way; that is, there are particular things. These we may encounter in experience. Similarly, the question "Why should there be life in general?" can only be treated empirically. Any response would be in terms of known physical, chemical, and biological principles. Life came into being in our solar system when certain physical-chemical conditions were present.

The question sometimes raised in moments of existential despair is "Why should I exist?" or in recent decades, because of the threat of nuclear holocaust, "Why should the human race exist?" or still further, in consideration of ecological destruction, "Why should life on earth exist?" We have no guarantee, of course, that any form of life will persist. Indeed, there is some probability that life on our planet may, in the distant future, become extinct; this applies to the human race as well, unless by ingenuity and daring man can populate other portions of the universe. There is no a priori guarantee of eternal survival.

Whether or not the race of man continues indefinitely, however, an individual cannot live forever. Thus the question "why" applies here most appropriately. "Why ought I to live?" "Can I prove that my life is better than my death?" ask the nihilist and skeptic in a mood of despondency. The answer should be apparent by now. One cannot prove that he ought to; all such proofs are deductive. From certain assumed premises, inferences follow. But what is at issue is precisely the premise that life itself is worthwhile; life is the origin of all our knowledge and truth. Nor does "proof" mean empirical certainty based upon verification, for in the range of experience there are no certainties. In a strict sense, that life is worthwhile is not amenable to a descriptive confirmation; it is not capable of being tested as other hypotheses are. Rather, it is a normative postulate, on the basis of which I live.

There is, then, a second question—not the epistemological demand for proof of life's value—but the quest for psychological stimulus and motivational appeal. What is at issue here is whether we can find within life's experience its own reward. Many persons in times of desperation and defeat lose the desire for life and cry in the darkness for assurance that they ought to continue. Can we provide the sustenance they seek? Surely not, as I have said, by means of any logical or empirical proof. For these persons the will-to-live has its source deep within their psycho-biological nature. If it is absent, what can we say? Does this mean that the value of life is merely irrational preference and quixotic caprice? No—there is more than that. We can give reasons and point to overlooked facts and consequences in seeking to persuade a desperate person not to commit suicide. We can try to arouse an affirmative attitude, hoping that the person will find *some* redeeming features remaining in life, by considering the possibilities: The beauty of dawn and sunset, the pleasures of eating and making love, friends and music and poetry.

Life must have some attractions, and stimulate some interests. But what if it does not? What if the pain and sorrow are too great? For some people life may not be worth living in every context and at any price. In some situations, a sensible person may conclude that death with dignity is the only recourse. An incurable cancer accompanied by great suffering, being a burden to the family, a betrayal of incalculable wretchedness, the defeat of a person's most important aims, the death of a loved one, a life of slavery and tyranny—these things may for some be too crushing and overwhelming to endure. The point is, it is not simply biological existence that we seek; modern medicine keeps many people alive. It is the *fullness of life* that we want; if that is completely absent, a heroic exit may be one's only recourse. I may conclude that I would rather die on my feet as a free man, than on my knees as a slave or on my back as an invalid without interest or passion.

The humanist need not answer the theist or existentialist by justifying the view that life is *always* worth living, that people must be motivated to believe this when they cannot. We can make no universal claim. What we can say is that most human beings, in normal conditions, find life worthwhile. But, I reiterate, it is not simply life at all costs that men and women seek, but the good life, with significant experience and satisfaction.

It is nonetheless true that for the humanist the cardinal "sin" is death; survival is our highest obligation. Self-defense against injury or death is a necessary precondition; we tend naturally to wish to preserve ourselves. The continuance of life remains an imperative rooted within our basic animal nature. If life seems empty it is usually because our basic needs are unsatisfied and our most important desires frustrated. When misfortune befalls a person and sadness is his companion, he may still respond that though daily life may seem insurmountable and though his spirit  may appear suffocated by events, still he ought not to give in; he ought to fight to survive.

Why? Again—one cannot "prove" this normative principle to everyone's satisfaction. Living beings tend instinctively to maintain themselves and to reproduce their own kind. This is the primordial fact of life; it is precognitive and prerational and it is beyond ultimate justification. It is a brute fact of our contingent natures; it is an instinctive desire to live.

## The Fullness of Life

There is, as I have already indicated, another vital normative principle, concomitant with the will-to-live; that is, that we seek, not simply to live, but *to live well.* What we want is a full life in which there is satisfaction, achievement, significance.

What is the good life? What constitutes fullness of being? What is significant satisfaction? Philosophers such as Plato, Aristotle, Spinoza, Bentham, and Mill have reflected upon the nature of the good life, as have prophets, poets, theologians, judges, psychiatrists — experts and plain men alike. Philosophers in the twentieth century generally have cautiously eschewed the question because they have been fearful of committing the so-called naturalistic fallacy; that is, in assuming their value judgments to lie in the nature of things — which they do not. Granted the analytic pitfalls, it is still important that we re-pose the question, for the nature of the good life is a perennial concern in every culture and every epoch. Even if there is danger that we are merely engaging in "persuasive definitions" of "good" and "bad," it is important that in every period some efforts be made to redefine the excellences of the good life. Even if the moral life is not to be resolved by metaphysics, logic, or science alone, there are degrees of rationality, and our principles can be informed by analysis.

Thus we may ask, what are the characteristics of a life well-lived, at least for contemporary man? As I have said, what most men seek is not simply life or bare existence, but the good life, what philosophers have usually called "happiness." What precisely happiness is, however, is open to dispute. It is not an ideal Platonic quality resident in the essence of man or in the universe at large; it is concrete, empirical, and situational in form and content. It is a concept relative to individuals, their unique needs and interests, and to the cultures in which they function. As such, happiness is in constant need of reformulation. Nor is it elusive or unattainable, as the theist believes; it is fully achievable if the proper conditions are present. Historically, there has been confusion about whether happiness refers to *eudaemonia,* health and well-being, to peace and contentment, or to pleasure and enjoyment. I wish to use the term in a somewhat different way to designate a state or *fullness of being* — a life in which qualities of satisfaction and excellence are present. What, at least in outline, would such a life entail?

### Pleasure

The hedonist is correct when he says that a full life should contain enjoyment or excitement. It is difficult to achieve a full life if there is excessive pain or suffering, particularly over long periods of time. To live a full life, one must be able to enjoy a wide range of interests and experiences: delicious food, good drink, sexual love, adventure, achievement, friends, intellectual and aesthetic pleasures, the joys of nature and physical exercise; and one's experiences must be marked by a reasonable degree of tranquility and a minimum of protracted anxiety. It is a mistake, however, to identify pleasure totally with the full life, as hedonists have done. For one may have hedonistic thrills, yet be miserable; one may pursue pleasure and suffer a mundane, narrow existence. The complete sensualist or opium eater may undergo intense pleasurable excitement, but be in a state of melancholy, grief, or boredom. Although moderate amounts of pleasure would appear to be a necessary condition of the good life, pleasure is not a sufficient condition for the fullness of being; the hedonist may be the unhappiest of men.

There are, of course, many varieties of hedonism. There are, for example, voluptuary hedonists, who flit from one sensation to the next in an intense quest for physical pleasures. But the voluptuary rarely finds life satisfying. Did Don Juan, Casanova, or Alcibiades lead full lives? Does the alcoholic, glutton, or addict? The search for new thrills and the focus on the immediately usually mask an underlying insecurity and instability; they are often signs of immaturity and irresponsibility. Children scream and demand instant gratification; adults learn from experience that it is often wiser to defer gratification. The voluptuary's appetites for touch and taste constitute a vital aspect of the good life, but surely not the be-all or end-all of human existence.

Recognizing that such a life may lead to anxiety and pain, some hedonists, such as Epicurus, have preached the quiet pleasures, advocating retreat from the cares of the world in order to achieve a neutral state of *ataraxia*. They seek peace of soul and emancipation from tension. Quiet hedonism has often meant withdrawal from the adventure of life, a limiting of experience, a narrowness rather than a fullness of life. A glass of wine, a piece of cheese, and a quiet garden constitute a closed universe. Aesthetic hedonists, such as Walter Pater, have emphasized the cultivation of taste, especially the joys to be gained from works of art. But this model is in the end precious, appropriate for a leisure class rather than for doers. Other hedonists focus on intellectual, spiritual, or religious pleasures. Still others, such as utilitarians, emphasize the moral pleasures of altruistic dedication—pleasures that require development by means of education, and compete with the physical pleasures of food, drink, sex. It is often asked: Which pleasures are "higher" on the scale of values and which are "lower"? Many moralists consider the biological pleasures demeaning, and the aesthetic, intellectual, moral, and spiritual pleasures superior.

Hedonists have located an enduring truth about the human condition: without some pleasure life would not be worth living. But they make a cardinal mistake in isolating pleasure from the process of living. Pleasure is intermingled with life activity and different kinds of experience; what we seek to attain in a full life is a vigorous mood receptive to varieties of enjoyment, as Lucretius and Goethe recognized. Aristotle observed that pleasure is part and parcel of the good life, helping to complete and bring it to fruition, but that the person who seeks it preeminently will probably never find it. Pleasure must accompany and qualify certain fundamental life activities. Nor are pleasures to be measured quantitatively by any hedonist calculus, as

Mill noted, but judged qualitatively. The pleasures of a developed human being have an appeal that infantile hedonists are unable to appreciate.

To come back to our earlier question: Which pleasures ought we to prefer? The basic biological pleasures, or the developed pleasures of an educated and sophisticated being? Efforts by moralists to prove that the so-called "higher" pleasures have a claim and quality intrinsically superior to the "lower" pleasures seem to me to fail. A librarian who can appreciate good books, fine music, and art but not enjoy sex is not necessarily leading a fuller life than the bucolic maiden who cannot read or write but who enjoys the thrills of sexual delight. Though I must grant that the person who knows only physical pleasures but has never cultivated his sensibilities is limited in his range of appreciation. But it is an exaggeration to maintain, as Mill does, that educated people who have tasted both the so-called higher and lower pleasures invariably prefer the former. If it comes to a choice between an orgasm or a sonata, most people who are honest would opt for the former. But it is not really a question of one or the other; in a full life we want both. To ask, which ultimately we should prefer—an embrace or a moral deed, a steak or a symphony, a martini or a poem—is senseless; we want them all.

### Satisfaction of Our Basic Needs

To realize the fullness of life requires some satisfaction of basic needs. Without it we are prey to malaise; there are certain norms of health that must be satisfied. The wisest of men have recognized that health is the most precious of possessions, more important than riches or fame. Contingent upon our biological and sociocultural nature are needs or lacks that we must reduce or satisfy if we are to achieve organic and psychic health.

Our basic needs are of two dimensions: *biogenic,* that is, they have biological and psychological origins and roots; and *sociogenic,* that is, they are made manifest in and are given content through society and culture.

1. The primary need of the organism is of course to survive. Threats in the environment must be overcome; injury must be avoided. Natural biological mechanisms of self-protection have evolved, fairly simple in some species but complicated in the human species—a built-in set of structures that operate constantly to preserve the integrity of the organism. Fear of death is the deepest of human forebodings; it is from this primal source, as I have argued, that religions are fed. Fear has roots deep within our somatic nature. It assumes profound psychological and sociological dimensions in civilization. Where the rule of the jungle prevails, any form of peaceful life is impossible. Civilization is possible only because it affords security and protection for individuals. Life need not be dangerous and brief; it may be enjoyable and long, but only if the social environment guarantees this.

2. A concomitant requirement is the need of the organism to maintain itself and function biologically by achieving homeostasis. The simplest

requirements are oxygen, water, food, shelter. As the human ingests materials from his environment in order to survive, the struggle for self-preservation is dependent upon finding that which will make life possible. The organism tends naturally toward a state of equilibrium; any rupture in it stimulates counteractivity to restore the state of organic harmony. Social institutions come into being to serve basic biological needs; the economic structure of society, methods of production and distribution, make available a range of goods necessary for survival.

3. Related to these needs are those of growth: egg and sperm, fertilization and fetus, to infant, child, and adult. At different periods of life different needs and capacities emerge. Each state of life has its dimensions and expectations: enthusiasm in childhood, impetuosity and idealism in youth, the perspective of maturity, and the virtues of wisdom or accomplishment in old age.

4. Reproduction is essential to the species. Nature rewards those who engage in the act of copulation, necessary for sexual reproduction, by intense pleasure. Our whole being yearns to love and be loved, to hold and be held, to fondle, embrace, penetrate or be penetrated, to be one with another. The celibate faces a void, which he may try to fill but never can. The world is denuded for those who suffer sexual famine, and no degree of sublimation or substitution can make up for it. Although sexuality instinctively serves a reproductive function, it exerts a more powerful claim upon us and plays a vital role in psychosomatic health.

Many philosophers who have written about happiness have overlooked sexual satisfaction. Happiness is not primarily, as the Greeks thought, a matter of cognitive reason; it requires deep-seated emotional satisfaction and psychic adjustment. Freud has made us aware that we ignore sexuality at our peril. Unhappiness, neurosis, and pathology are bred in sexual frustration and repression.

5. The need to discharge surplus energy is another organic requirement. We see it more graphically in children and animals, as they romp and play games, but it is also present in adults. We need to relax and wind down. Amusement and entertainment, which release us from built-up anxieties and tensions, are expressive experiences that give a special quality to life. Are these only frills? No, for organisms spill out overabundant reserves; and expressive play is one way by which they do so. Surplus energy is also released by physical exercise and work; we feel vital after exercise, a walk, or a swim; it is an expressive need which appears to be related to the tendency to reach levels of homeostasis and equilibrium. Reservoirs of energy need to be released for healthy functioning.

The biogenic needs apply not only to all forms of human life but to animal life as well.

But man does not live as an isolated individual. The family, tribe, clan— small and large forms of society—help to satisfy our needs and fulfill our interests. Our sociogenic needs help us to realize our biological needs and allow them to develop a primacy of their own, but the mere satisfaction of biological needs is not enough for civilized man. The fullness of life — its variety and quality — is always related to the cultural context in which we exist, and whether or not we flourish depends upon the materials of culture with which we work.

Each of our primary needs is transformed and extended by culture. Food and drink are necessary for survival, but their refinements — infinitely various recipes, subtleties of preparation, cultivation of wines, sophisticated settings, appropriate circumstances — all are social inventions conditioned by our culture; and so our needs are eventually transformed by complexity. The same principle characterizes the relation of sex to society. As a necessity of survival, its nature is transfigured by the considerations of love, by passion, by its significance in the changing mores of marriage and divorce, by its practice in deviant forms, by its exploitation as commerce — all expressive of evolving cultural concepts.

Thus biology and culture converge upon us. Both chance and causality make us what we are. The challenge for each man, though he is culture-bound and time-bound, is to make what he can of his life, to savor his finite moment in history. There are as many models of excellence as there are individuals.

We can never go back. As cultural change takes place rapidly, we need always to remake what we are, to live authentically while we can. Given all our differences, there are general sociogenic, as there are biogenic, needs that apply to all men and women. It is useful to try to spell them out. Though they are no doubt limited by our culture — other cultures and other times may reject them — they are nevertheless pertinent to us and perhaps to most peoples and cultures.

6. If literature and art, psychology and religion, and indeed all experience, teach us anything, it is the power of love in human life. There is no doubt about its central importance. No one can live entirely alone, without the affection of others and without being able to reciprocate.

Love has two primordial roots: one, in the dependency of the young, in the mutual need and affection that develops out of the parents' care of the child, and the other in orgasmic sexual arousal and attraction. But there are of course other dimensions and levels, all revealing how dependent we are upon others; and our very self-image is defined by the responses of others to us, as we define theirs. Among the finest and most enduring moments of life are those that we share with others. It is not enough that we receive love or appreciation, we need also to give it. To want only to be loved is infantile, possessive, hardly conducive to growth. To genuinely want the loved one to flower, to be interested in the interests of the other — this is the perfection of human love: in the parent willing to allow the child to become what he will, following his own vision of truth and value; and similarly in the man or woman who, in regard for the loved one, wishes him or her to be a full individual. Reciprocal love is not necessary for survival, nor even for sexual enjoyment, but its presence is always a sign of a full life. Unless one develops mutual relationships and thus experiences the joys of life, whether with a beloved, a parent, a child, a friend or colleague, one's heart tends to close, one's roots become dry.

7. Another precondition for a good life, and related to love, is the ability to develop a generalized sense of community, to broaden horizons, to belong. Many today are alienated because they have discovered no goals they can share with their fellow humans. In the long history of mankind, the extended family or the tribe, the village or town, have been able to nourish this need. No man who is an island finds life fully significant. During the feudal period each man had his station and his duties, which, though unjust to those at the bottom of the social hierarchy, tended to give a sense of psychological security, some identity. Post-modern man tends to be rootless; he rarely has a beloved community with which he can identify. Unable to participate in common goals, he feels outside.

Belonging to some community has in the past assured interaction on various levels. A small group in which there was face-to-face encounter was the bedrock of the human relationship. However, as society changes and population increases, as small units coalesce and are absorbed by larger ones, men tend to broaden their sense of community and allegiance. One's community may include his state or nation, religion or culture; eventually it may refer to the brotherhood of man. Religion at its finest has attempted to inculcate a more universal commitment to that moral point of view which treats all men as equal in dignity and value.

8. There is an important element in the quest for well-being that religious and philosophical theories have often underestimated—the need for self-affirmation, the need to love one's self. This is as important for our sanity as love of others. I do not speak of those who, puffed up with pride, self-centered, or selfish, need to be restrained for the sake of society, but of those who have too low an estimation of their talent and worth and therefore little self-respect. Indeed, they are often victimized by self-hate, though it is hidden from consciousness, and assumes different forms in self-deprecation, perfectionism, timorousness, excessive caution, or extreme forms of asceticism. A form of self-pride that is balanced and temperate, as Aristotle noted, is important for our well-being, for a healthy reaction to daily challenges. Every human being has something to contribute, but he cannot do so if he finds little value in his own individuality.

9. This leads to a vital element: creative actualization. Individuals need more than to satisfy their basic needs; they need to bring into fruition their potentialities. This means that there should be a striving to develop. Unless this effort is made, the fullness of life will not be realized. The ideal of creative self-actualization is essential to the concept of happiness that I am

delineating. It is actualization of my basic species needs, those that I share with other men, but it is also individualized; it expresses my unique and personal idiosyncrasies and talents. The injunction is to be myself, not what others would have me be. I must express my own nature in all its variety, and create something new.

This is an activist model of life; it calls upon us to expend energy, to realize what we can be—not what we are; nature is in a process of unfolding. There is no complete, static human essence or nature that defines me and that I merely need to uncover and fulfill. Rather, I am constantly being made and remade in dynamic processes of growth and discovery.

I have certain native capacities but, largely unstructured, they can take various forms. The direction I choose depends upon the cultural context in which I act as well as upon my native abilities. To act is to bring something new into existence. The goal is creativity, the spring of life.

The full life in the last analysis is not one of quiet contentment, but the active display of my powers and of their development and expansion. The creative life involves exploration and curiosity, discovery and ingenuity, the delight in uncovering and introducing novelty. This life is one of forward thrust; the achievement motive dominates. To venture, to experiment— these are the delights of the ongoing spirit, which untap and express hidden powers and implicit capacities, and formulate or create new ones. It is natural to regret a wasted life—a child prodigy who fizzles out, a unique talent that lies fallow, a great person who is reduced by burdens—and to applaud a creative person, whatever his endeavor or area of excellence.

To succeed is not merely to attain one's ends; rather it is to exceed them. The model I am presenting is contrary to the historically idealized quest for a state of eternal bliss. It proposes enjoyment achieved by full participation in life, not necessarily as defined by society, but as found in an individual's search. Perhaps this exuberant approach is an expression of cultural bias, even of individual taste. Other civilizations have emphasized the value of meditation and spiritual exercise. Is the incessant quest for achievement simply self-serving ambition? And is this not possibly self-defeating? Do we not in the process often lose the capacity to appreciate the immediacies of experience? Not as I conceive it. This creative model exults in the present moment. It does not necessarily involve a quest for public approval; creative individuals frequently must move against the times. The achievement motive refers to ambition in more personal terms: our wish to excel by our own vision of what life can afford. The spirit of contemplation, like that of celibacy and the priestly mood, if overemphasized, may express fear, even neurosis, a withdrawal from the challenges of life. I do not deprecate contemplation as part of my nature, a source of intellectual joy and peace. What I am criticizing is the notion that the contemplative life is to be pursued to the exclusion of all else, and that it is the highest form of sainthood. My model of the true "saint" is Promethean man, the creative doer. The counterculture properly points to the false values of the competitive society. The option we face, however, does not make it necessary to withdraw from the strenuous mood; for we can use it to our own ends.

### Audacity, Freedom, and Reason

The ability to live a creative life involves audacity, a defining characteristic of man and a key to his greatness. The audacious life is a life of risk-taking. The nobility of man is not simply that he can develop the courage to be, but to become.

There are the fearful and the weak—people of little imagination and daring—who warn that this or that is absolutely unattainable and cannot be done. But the advance of civilization is sparked by the decision not to accept the cliches of one's age, not to be penned in by nature or caged by history. Man as a Promethean figure is venturesome and bold. These are the virtues of the true heroes and geniuses of history, who have given us new ideas and inventions, new departures in truth and beauty; they are nonconformists with independent spirits.

All human beings have some capacity to be self-activated, provided they are willing to recognize their freedom and seize it, and not to become mired in limitations. I am not, by this, asserting that determinism is false. We are determined by antecedent conditions, but organic life expresses a form of teleonomic causality. There is no contradiction in affirming that we are both free and conditioned, autonomous and determined. Determinism is not a metaphysical generalization about the universe; it is simply a rule governing scientific inquiry; it presupposes that if we inquire, we will most likely discover the causal conditions under which we act. It need not deny that human life is self-affirming nor that we can create goals and strive to attain them.

The free person is autonomous because he is unwilling to forfeit his existence to external events, but resolves to control them himself. He acts freely insofar as he can, recognizing not only the constraints within a situation, but also the potentialities. Man *is* possibility, an open and dynamic system where alternatives are discovered and created. We are what we will and we can become what we dream. Not all of our dreams can come true—only a madman believes that they can—yet some can, if they are acted upon by reason and experience and applied to the realities of nature.

Though each of us is unique, we are all faced with a similar challenge to create our own future; our lives are the sum of the projects to which we commit ourselves. A full life involves artistic vision and creation. The person with a career he enjoys and finds rewarding is the most fortunate of humans, especially if he can blend labor and action, work and play, and can turn his work into a fulfilling outpouring of himself, an expression and an adventure. Our lifework should not be measured only in relation to job or career, for there are many significant sources of creativity: building one's house, becoming involved in a cause, acting in a play, traveling—these are some forms of enterprise in which a personality can express itself in excellence. The full life is psychologically abundant, bursting at the seams, capable of exulting in consummatory experiences.

This does not mean that life does not have its defeats and failures. Our best-laid plans often fail. Our loved ones die. We are aware of the breakdown of means, the tragic conflicts of ends, the abandonment of plans, the moments of despair. Unless these events are completely overwhelming, a rational person can take them in his stride. The creative person is capable of some measure of stoic wisdom.

Human freedom, however, is most complete when our actions are determined by rational means. Can one who is irrational be happy? Does happiness basically involve emotional satisfaction? Philosophers have thought that reason was the essential key to the good life. They have no doubt overestimated the rational life and underestimated the deeper forces in our somatic and unconscious behavior. Human beings may achieve contentment without developing their full rational faculties; they may lead enjoyable lives and even be capable of some degree of creativity. Yet one who doesn't develop his rational ability is deprived. Like the virgin who suffers sexual starvation, such a person is incapable of full functioning. Reason expresses and has become for most humans a crucial biosocial need rooted in our cultural history, necessary if we are to develop fully as individuals.

How and why? In a negative sense, because it is the method of overcoming deception. Human beings, as we have seen, are all too prone to credulousness, to seize upon false idols. Without reflection, we become prey to quackery, whereas reason uses logical analysis and evidence to debunk falsehood and expose fraud. As such, it is an instrument of liberation and emancipation, a source of freedom from illusion.

In a positive sense, rational impulse provides us with both science and ethics. Reflective experience has a double role: in developing an awareness and understanding of the external world and in formulating the values by which we live. In the practical life reason cannot exist independently of our passionate nature. The union of thought and feeling is essential to happiness. Reason that is divorced from its biological roots becomes abstract and oppressive. Cognition that is fused with affection and desire in lived experience expresses the whole person. In the final analysis, it is critical intelligence that best enables us to define and develop our moral principles; and although reason alone is never sufficient for the fullness of life, it is a necessary condition for its attainment.

# 19

# Two Views of Death

## I

Secular humanism and theism differ on the basic metaphysical questions: What is the ultimate nature of the universe? Is there a divine purpose to reality? What is the place of man in the scheme of things? Does human life have some ultimate purpose or meaning? One issue that especially divides secular humanism and theism is the immortality of the soul. Theists believe that a person's soul survives the death of the physical body and retains its personal identity; they relate man's highest moral obligations and religious duties to this article of faith. Humanists reject the thesis that the soul is separable from the body or that life persists in some form after the death of the body, on the grounds that there is insufficient evidence to support it. They maintain that we should seek to create an authentic life here and now without worrying about the "blessing of immortality."

The humanist critique of the immortality thesis is threefold: (1) the concepts of "soul" and "immortality" are ambiguous, often unintelligible; (2) there is no evidence to support claims of immortality; and (3) the so-called ethical case for immortality—the view that life or morality would have no ultimate meaning without eternal salvation—is self-contradictory. I shall address myself to all three points but concentrate especially on the third one because of its profound implications in the practical world.

## II

The first objection to immortality—one that is very popular today—is logical; that is, there is no clear meaning of the term "soul." Classical philosophers from Aristotle to Hume and Kant have raised serious doubts about the idea of a substantial "soul" separable from the body. Many contemporary philosophers have raised more fundamental questions. John Dewey and the behaviorists, for example, rejected "mentalism" and the existence of a mind-body dualism as empirically unwarranted. In recent years, Gilbert Ryle, Antony Flew, Peter Geach, and other linguistic philosophers have found the concept of "soul" logically unintelligible. Ryle thinks that we do not make any sense when we talk about "the ghost in the machine," and he indicts Descartes and all who had a dualistic or Platonic view for committing a category mistake. The human being is an integrated unity; what we call the "soul" or the "mind" is simply a functional aspect of the physical organism interacting in an environment. If this is the case, it is difficult to know what it means to say that something called the "soul" survives the dissolution of the body. The notions of a "disembodied self," "astral projection," or "non-material soul" are based upon abstractions and reification and are a puzzling misuse of language.

Hume pointed out the problem of personal identity. One may ask: Is there an independent, substantial soul or self underlying my particular experiences? If my body no longer exists after my death, and if I survive it, will I remember my past self? Will I continue to have feelings in my limbs, genitalia, stomach, etc., after they are gone? How can I have memory if I have no brain to store experiences? Will it be I who survives or only a pale shadow? Antony Flew asks: Can I witness my own funeral? As my corpse lies in its coffin, can I, lurking in limbo, view it? Does it make any sense to say that I can see if I do not have any eyes to receive impressions or a nervous system to record them?

Thus many contemporary philosophers point out all sorts of linguistic confusions over what it means to say that an alleged "soul" survives the body. The basic issue for them does not involve the factual claim as to whether the soul exists so much as it involves the logical puzzle about the definition of the concept itself.

This being the case, perhaps the only meaning that can be given to immortality is to say with St. Paul (Rom. 6:5; 1 Cor. 15:42-58) that at some point in the future there will be a physical resurrection of the body, including the soul. This would avoid the issue of whether the soul is separable from the body, and we would merely need to say that some divine being will in the future ensure the survival of the whole human being.

### III

To agree with St. Paul avoids the meaning muddle, perhaps, but it raises still more serious questions: What is the evidence for the claim that I can survive my death in some form, whether as a separated soul or as a being resurrected in one piece? For, in truth, the claim is being made that people who die come back at some time immediately after death in some form or another, or that in some remote future they will be resurrected in some new guise.

Many cultures and individuals have believed that something survives the physical death of the body; some have thought it to be part of the world soul, others to involve personal identity. Yet, as far as I can tell, we have been unable, in the entire history of the race, to find sufficient evidence for these assertions. Here I am asking for objectively confirmable evidence. I am talking not about hearsay, old wives' tales, unsubstantiated reports by the uninformed or the credulous but about hard data. What would constitute a test: the ability of the dead to communicate with or influence the living and to have some observable effects in this world? Or for us to die, return to life, remember our disjointed state, and recount it to others?

I do not find the so-called data of physical research convincing. The history of such paranormal research thus far has failed to prove the hypothesis of discarnate survival. There have been inexhaustible efforts to communicate with departed spirits—for example, by using mediums in seances. But these have been discredited. There are also numerous accounts of apparitions, ghosts, and poltergeists. Should these be taken as veridical or are they more likely products of subjective imagination and hallucination? Of late, efforts have been made to use new technologies in order to communicate with the dead—as in recordings of "voices from the dead." But this is also extremely unreliable; and it seems likely that some tape recorders function as receivers and that what is being picked up are background noises rather than the voices of ghosts.

Recent research on the "hour of death" (Karlis Osis and Erlendur Haraldsson) do not describe persons about to enter the pearly gates so much as their psychological states as death approaches. Nor do recollections of patients whose heart and lungs have stopped and have been resuscitated prove that there is "life after life." (Raymond Moody, Michael Sabom, etc.). An alternative naturalistic hypothesis is that resuscitated patients do not undergo brain death; what they are describing are near-death experiences, and the attendant psychological defense mechanisms as individuals confront their imminent demise. In many respects these phenomenological states are similar to other forms of "out of body" experiences that are quite common (as in hypnagogic or hypnapompic sleep); they are also similar to drug-induced hallucinations. One might claim that we cannot *decisively* confirm the existence of an afterlife *until* we die and find out. But if so, we ought to suspend judgment until then—though it would seem to me that the preponderance of evidence about human and animal death as a biochemical process points to the high improbability of discarnate survival.

Of course, some things do survive death in one form or another. Although the physical body decomposes, the skeleton can, under proper conditions, be preserved for thousands of years. It may even be that, just as urine is expelled from the bladder at death, some discharged energy remains— hovers, haunts, or whatever else—for a period of time until the body is fully decomposed. But whether this discharged energy has personal consciousness or identifiable experiences is another matter. We would have to submit this to careful scientific measurement, but it has never been done.

A further question about survival concerns the time scale. Suppose energy patterns do survive for a brief time, say ten minutes or a few years, at most a few centuries (like the alleged ghosts haunting English castles until they are released). But the claim for eternal survival is virtually unverifiable. How would we go about proving that something that survives death (a soul or something else) will never become extinct? In any case, it would be difficult for us to date any souls which we might discover—even if we should manage to discover an incorporeal-like carbon 14 technique for dating surviving souls. If we were to uncover a very old soul, it would not necessarily be eternal. It would have had a beginning (unless one believed in reincarnation and prior existence) and most likely would not have preceded the origin of the human species in time. But, more importantly, we would have no guarantee that it would continue into the infinite future, unless by eternity we mean beyond the categories of time altogether. Such claims would at best be in the form of postulates or conjectures, not proofs. Thus the immortality thesis needs to be tested. It never has been.

It is of course apparent that belief in immortality transcends the categories of science. Of this we are reminded by immortalists. Belief in immortality is coherent only in terms of a larger metaphysical-theological system. The immortality thesis is part of a theist's general picture of the universe (which humanists also reject). But the point is that not only can the immortality thesis not be made intelligible but also it has not been independently confirmed by a sufficient body of evidential data.

Thus, in the last analysis, belief in immortality is an article of faith, an inference from a broader view of a divine universe, an item of revealed— not philosophical or scientific—truth. It involves faith that a divine being will in some way enable us to survive death so that we can exist throughout eternity and that the divine being will resurrect the physical body and soul at some point in the future and reinstitute personal identity and memory, even though there may have been a lapse of several thousand years during which worms have picked clean our brains, marrow, and flesh.

It is paradoxical that the doctrine of immortality is not peripheral to belief in the existence of God and that it cannot be deduced from it. On the contrary, belief in immortality is itself, in my judgment, central to belief in God and perhaps is even its chief psychological support. What I mean is that the doctrine of immortality is not so much a descriptive claim about an alleged reality as a normative ideal that is postulated to satisfy an apparent psychological hunger. Indeed, the God-idea takes on meaning dramatically because man faces death, and God is introduced, along with immortality, as a solution to the problem of death. This is the existential-psychological argument for immortality, which many earlier humanists such as William James and Santayana defended. It involves at least three factors: (1) a response to the problem of death, an attempt to explain away death and overcome it; (2) some moral direction and focus for what otherwise seems to be a random and purposeless universe; and (3) psychological sustenance and support, giving courage and consolation to the bereaved and fearful, helping individuals overcome anxiety, forlornness, loneliness, and alienation.

In this ethically pragmatic sense, the doctrine of immortality is interpreted as providing normative guidance rather than making a descriptive truth claim about the world. To say that one believes in immortality as an ideal is not the same as saying that immortality of the soul necessarily exists in a literal sense.

## IV

The secular humanist critique of the ethical argument for immortality is equally decisive. The humanist considers the doctrine of immortality to be basically morbid. It grows out of both fear of death and fascination with it. The immortalist is fixated on death, yet he endeavors to deny its awesome reality. A humanist views this as a failure to face the finality of death and an inability to see life for what it really is. This attitude has all the hallmarks of pathology, for one is out of touch with cognitive reality. It is an immature and unhealthy attitude, a form of wish fulfillment. It exacerbates an illusion in order to soothe the heart aching over the loss of a loved one or avoid accepting one's own impending end. Death is a source of profound dread. There is an unwillingness to let go. One hopes for an opening to another life in which all one's unfulfilled aspirations are realized. The primitive mind, not possessed of science, invested death and dying with mystery and awe. Death was unfathomable — the source of brutal suffering. The eschatological myth enables one to transcend the pain.

This mood of denial expresses a basic lack of courage to persist in the face of adversity in *this* life. Immortality is a symbol of agony before an unyielding universe and of hope for future deliverance. It is the tenacious refusal to confront the brute finitude of existence, the contingent and precarious, often tragic, character of human life. Those who believe in immortality trust that somehow someone will help them out of their misery, however long they have to wait; that this vale of tears can be overcome; and that in the end, despite present suffering, they will have a reunion with departed loved ones. Belief in immortality offers therapeutic solace; and in the past history of mankind, when disease was so prevalent and life so brief for the mass of people, it seems to have made some sense. Life was often "nasty, brutish, and short," and three score and ten was not the norm but the exception. Thus, the immortality myth functioned as a tranquilizer. Today, other attitudes dominate. Armed with modern medicine and technology, we can combat death in other ways. We attempt to prolong life and to make it abundant and enjoyable as far as we can — that is, until the dying process sets in, at which point many are willing to hasten its onslaught if there is great pain and to accept the inevitable with stoic resignation.

Existential courage is a key humanist virtue. So essential is courage that Kierkegaard and Tillich have recognized that without it life becomes difficult and unendurable. For the humanist, it is not enough to muster the courage to be—merely to survive in the face of adversity; he must cultivate the courage to become. In other words, the problem for each of us is to remake our lives constantly in spite of all the forces of nature and society that seek to overwhelm us.

In the eyes of the humanist, the immortalist has forsaken full moral responsibility, since he is unwilling to take destiny—as far as he can—into his own hands. Of course, there *are* limits on human achievement and independence. We need to make a distinction between the things within our power and those beyond it, as the Stoics recognized; but with those within our power we are challenged to make the most of life, to re-create and redefine it, to extend the parameters of human power.

Freedom of human choice and action is pivotal. The humanist is not content with simply discovering and accepting the universe for what it is, in an act of piety; he seeks to change it. Nor is the task of life merely to discover what our nature is (whether God-given or not) and to realize it; rather, it is to exceed our nature. Thus man invents culture. We are post-Prometheans, stealing fire and the arts of civilization from the gods, continually tempting and recasting our fate.

The humanist levels a key objection against those who cling to the doctrine of immortality: it undermines ethics. A person is unable to be fully responsible for himself and others, creative, independent, resourceful, free, if he believes that morality has its source outside man. The reflective, deliberative, probing moral conscience is too vital to be deferred to the transcendent. We are responsible for what we are, and out of compassion for other human beings and a desire to see that justice be done, we can achieve the good life here and now if we work hard enough to bring it about. It is not fear of damnation, or hope of salvation, that moves us to seek a better world for ourselves and our fellow humans, but a genuine moral concern without regard for reward or punishment. Morality is autonomous.

The humanist thinks that the theistic believer has committed a grievous mistake: he has wasted much of his life. Life is short, yet it is rich with possibilities, to be lived fully with gusto and exuberance. Those who are morbid, fearful, timid, unwilling to seize destiny are unable to experience fully the bountiful joys of life.

All too often those who believe in immortality are full of foreboding, laden with excessive guilt and a sense of sin. All too often the pleasures of the body, sex, and love are repressed, and a variety of opportunities for creative enjoyment denied. Such individuals have bartered their souls for a future life; but if the promissory note is unfulfilled—as I think it is—then this means that they have lost important values in life. In retrospect their lives seem barren; they have missed many chances, failed to do what they really wanted. They could not seize their opportunities because of deep-seated fear and trembling.

Many theists believe that without immortality life would have no meaning. How puzzling and contradictory to argue thus. It is a confession of their limitations as persons. For the humanist contends that it is precisely the doctrine of immortality that impoverishes meaning. If you believe in immortality, then nothing counts here. It is all preparation; life is but a waiting-room for transcendent eternity. But life per se has no meaning except what we choose to invest it with. All it presents are opportunities, which we may choose to capitalize upon or let pass by. The humanist maintains that life is full of plans and dreams, hopes and aspirations, joy and sorrow, tragedy and achievement. It is too beautiful to be squandered in idle wishing for a tomorrow that may never come.

# V

One question often raised is: Even if immortality is unintelligible or unproven, can we live without illusions? Perhaps we all have our illusions, for it seems that as soon as we outlive one myth another appears to beguile us. The Marxist utopian vision, for example, seems to be replacing theism in various parts of the world. But is this inevitable? Perhaps illusion is the result of a tendency toward gullibility engrained in human nature. (For the humanist, this is the doctrine of "original sin.") But some illusions are perhaps less false and harmful than others.

Humanists no doubt have their own illusions. The belief that we can solve life's major problems by the use of intelligence and achieve a good life of happiness may very well be one of them. Yet some illusions become irrelevant to human interests and social needs. The immortality myth, as powerful as it was during an era of poverty and disease, is no longer relevant to human concerns.

Does belief in immortality actually satisfy a psychological need? I doubt it. I have found that people without belief in immortality often fear death much less—are able to face it with greater equanimity—than those holding such a belief. These unbelieving individuals are able to develop confidence in their capacities, independent moral conscience, and a commitment to social justice or species welfare on this planet. Such individuals need not be without "transcendent" ideals, ideals larger than they. They believe in contributing to a better world and are deeply concerned about the future of humankind; and they have a sense of obligation to that ideal that is as powerful as any the immortalist possesses.

Secular humanists may indeed believe in "immortality" *in a metaphorical sense*: we are devoted to the good works that will outlast us. But we strive to accomplish them, not because we will be rewarded or punished in a future life but in order to contribute to a better future for our children's children's children, even though we may never live to see it. We need nothing beyond that motive to sustain our moral dedication. Secular humanism does not need a doctrine of immortality to give life meaning or to provide morality with a foundation. Both meaning and morality grow out of lived experience; commitment to the good life, as we define it, can be as powerful a stimulus to life as the traditional immortalist doctrine.

# 20

# The Future of the Humanist Movement

I

Humanism is a major force in the United States and the world, according to our critics, who claim that we dominate the schools and universities, the media, literature, the sciences and arts, the courts and other
institutions of modern society. Certainly humanist ideas and values have
had a powerful and continuing impact on the modern world. Yet those of us
who have been involved in the organized humanist movement are dismayed
to hear of the influence our critics attribute to us. We are perplexed by our
*failure* to build viable humanist organizations, despite our alleged "success."

Indeed, some believe this is a time for deep soul-searching and hard decisions. The truth is that humanist associations are weak institutions. I am
referring principally to humanist organizations in North America: the
American Humanist Association, American Ethical Union, Fellowship of
Religious Humanists, Society for Humanistic Judaism, Council for Democratic and Secular Humanism, and the Canadian Humanist Association.
My analysis, I believe, also applies to most other humanist organizations
worldwide. They have pitifully small budgets, woefully small memberships
and relatively low circulations of their publications. The average local
church in almost any city has more members and resources than any of the
major humanist groups, yet they claim to be a national movement. And so
it is natural to ask: What can they do to increase their effectiveness?

I think we should recognize that humanist organizations are not the epi-
tome of humanism; indeed, at times I think they have betrayed its ideals.
We sometimes exaggerate their importance. These groups are certainly not
coextensive with humanism as a movement. Humanism is broader in scope
and will continue long after they are gone. There are many humanistic personalities, organizations, and publications in the world — perhaps hundreds —
who do not call themselves "humanist." Humanism, in this broad sense, is
one of the deepest currents of thought and feeling in the world. It will not be
easily swept aside. Nevertheless, historical trends are not predetermined,
and humanist ideas and values may be overwhelmed by forces of unreason

---

This appeared in *Free Inquiry*, Fall 1983.

and intolerance. This happened in the fourth century when Hellenic and Roman civilization was subverted by an obscure mystery cult (Christianity) from Asia. It may happen again. If it does we may have to re-create humanism. Meanwhile we must treasure, defend, and expand it wherever we can.

By every comparative standard, we have failed in our mission. There are two questions to be answered: Why have we failed? What should we do about it?

From a perspective of intimate involvement in the humanist movement and in the spirit of constructive and responsible criticism, I propose to make an in-depth analysis and raise some basic questions about the future of organized humanism, at least in North America.

## II

Why has humanism failed to develop strong and viable organizations? In my view, they have never been sufficiently clear about their goals and to whom they were addressing their message. They have also lacked a clear strategy of growth or development. There are various reasons for this. First, the organized humanist movement has failed because it *lacks an inspiring message* of sufficient clarity and drama to command public attention. The humanist message has been couched in a way that has made it seem boring and redundant. To many younger men and women it sounded outworn, outdated, based on nostalgic hunger for spiritual pablum inappropriate to the deeper needs of contemporary society. Second, organized humanism *lacks charismatic leadership* of sufficient skill and dedication. Third, each of these organizations have mistakenly *sought to become another denomination or sect* competing with other denominations and sects, when it should have become a broadbased educational movement. These are reasons why the movement has not been able to build or sustain an institution strong or viable enough to function effectively.

Other factors are pertinent, and I shall enumerate them briefly and without discussion. Although the following seem to be less important, they may prevent us from coming to terms with the main difficulties:

- The humanist membership is dominated by individuals who lack sufficient natural stature or impact.
- It has not been able to develop a mass base of support independent of a small power elite with its own financial supporters.
- It tends to attract dissident anomics — often cantankerous individuals — from other movements.
- It often bickers itself to exhaustion by petty internal squabbles.
- It has at times become narrowly political and strident, identified with only one part of the political spectrum.
- It has been infiltrated by its opponents, whose aim is to keep it off balance and destabilize it.

• It has been badly mismanaged and has lacked efficient business procedures.

It is obvious that I do not include the lack of finances as the main problem. I do not deny, of course, that sound financing is important; although money may be the root of all evil, it is not necessarily the secret of virtue or success.

If we have no viable ideas to communicate or a charismatic leadership with a motivating message to do so, we cannot hope to attract financial support to promulgate humanism. To blame the failure of our growth on the lack of money is irresponsible, a self-deceiving extenuation. We in the humanist movement have no one to blame for our failure but ourselves.

## III

The first question to be asked is: What is it that we want the humanist movement to accomplish?

In looking at contemporary humanism, many humanists often compare it with religious institutions and churches around us that may wax and wane but never disappear. Humanism, some say, should be a strong alternative to them and should attract adherents as the others have. I question the premise that humanism will ever become or should become another religion. Is membership in a humanist organization analogous to membership in a church? I think not. Let me explain why.

But first, let us focus on three religions and the charismatic individuals that helped (at least indirectly) to found them: Judaism and Moses, Christianity and Jesus, Islam and Mohammed.

*Judaism* is one of the oldest religions; it has survived for more than three thousand years. Moses, its alleged founder, was a tongue-tied savior, who led the children of Israel out of Egypt to the promised land. He communicated with God on Mt. Sinai and proclaimed his message with all of the authority of divine sanction: the Hebrews were God's "chosen people" and had to follow His law obediently. There were seven million Jews in the Roman Empire at the time of Christ; there are twelve million today. They have suffered persecution at the hands of the Gentiles, and tens of millions of Jews over the centuries converted or intermarried, became Christians or pagans. Yet a hard core has survived the destruction of the Temple, A.D. 70, the period of the Diaspora, and the Holocaust of World War II.

What is the Jewish religion? It involves (1) a *message* of divine power and the promise of a Messiah to restore the children of Israel to the homeland; (2) *charismatic figures* (Moses and the prophets) to interpret it; (3) *institutions,* a strict legal code (circumcision, dietary laws, the Talmud, etc.), synagogues, and a rabbinate.

At least two other ingredients were essential to its long survival and provided continuity: (1) *ethnicity*—strong prohibitions against intermarriage (though it constantly occurred) and (2) *a common cultural heritage,* including the Hebrew language, understood only by Jews. Anti-Semitism, in my judgment, has its roots in part in the Old Testament and the synagogue, both of which advanced the view that the Jews were the exclusive "chosen people." This could only engender hatred. But it also helped solidify the resistant inner core, leading to a ghetto mentality that fostered survival.

*Christianity,* unlike Judaism, intended its message to be universal. Whether Jesus existed is still open to dispute; but assuming that he did, he was either mad (his relatives believed he was) or a magician. The ancient Jews and pagans thought that he was a fraud, that his father was Panthera, a Roman soldier, that he performed magical tricks like others of his day, and that he did not die on the cross but was spirited out of his tomb by his disciples, and that he then fled in fear. It was Paul of Tarsus who converted the simple moral message of the Sermon on the Mount into a mystery religion, by making Jesus the Christ, the mediator between God and suffering humanity, and promising eternal life to those who accepted the new faith. One didn't have to be circumcised, abstain from pork, or follow the Mosaic laws. The mythology of Christianity was far more wondrous than that of the Old Testament prophets, and it promised more to all human souls—the poor, the sick, the enslaved, as well as the wealthy—who were converted and thereby "saved."

Today there are about one billion Christians, nominal or genuine. (1) They have accepted the dramatic and incredible *message* of a dead and risen deity, a God who took on human form and can save all who believe in Him. (2) Christianity involves a central *charismatic figure,* Jesus, a man of great appeal; and it attracted charismatic disciples and martyrs, Paul, Peter, and a host of saints, who gladly sacrificed everything to bring the gospel to the world. (3) From the early years there developed *church communities* (quite unlike humanist chapters or ethical societies) and rules and dogmas that were eventually codified by the Council of Nicaea in the fourth century. The church developed as an institution, with a priesthood and political leadership. (4) Although Christianity is missionary in its initial impulse (unlike Judaism), once it is accepted in a territory or by a people, it also has *ethnic roots,* and one is born into a particular denomination or sect. One's children are Irish or Polish or Italian Catholics, German Lutherans, English Anglicans, Southern Baptists, etc. (5) A *common cultural and linguistic heritage* preserves the religious faith that is woven almost without question into the social fabric and becomes part of a person's being.

It is interesting how the basic Christian message has had a charismatic appeal in generation after generation; new sects and denominations are still being founded. In the nineteenth century, the Seventh-Day Adventists (following Ellen G. White) were founded; there are now over 600,000 members. The Mormon Church of Jesus Christ of the Latter Day Saints, founded by Joseph Smith, now has over five million members. And Mary Baker Eddy's Christian Science church is still growing. Today there is Reverend Moon of the Unification Church and Reverend Armstrong of the Worldwide Church of God.

A similar analysis may be applied to *Islam*. Like Christianity (1) it has a *message* from God as revealed in the Koran; (2) it has a *charismatic founder,* Mohammed; (3) it has established *institutions* of mosques and clergy and strict rules that regulate conduct; (4) it has an *ethnic basis*—non-Western, Arab, black, or Asian; and (5) it has a rich *cultural heritage*. The point is that once a religion—in the case of Islam conquering by the sword at first—is implanted, it becomes the way of life of a people and grows by osmosis and heritage. Eventually it becomes intertwined with nationality and even with race.

For a classical type of religion to grow, at least four rules seem vital. (1) One should try to convert the heathen; both Christianity and Islam did that. (2) One must insist that those who are in the fold bring up their children in the faith. (3) One cannot permit marriage outside the faith. (4) One must stamp out dissent and excommunicate heretics. These implicit rules, especially the last three, have been more or less utilized and explain the persistence of the major religions, which generally have dominated an ethnic or geographic domain. The problem for classical religions in the modern world is that with mobility, rapid communication, and the growth of secularism, there are pluralistic sets of competing religions, so that it becomes difficult for the established religions to enforce their hegemony.

As humanists, surely we do not wish to develop according to the model of the classical religions. Though these religions have provided a social structure, a moral framework, and psychological comfort for their adherents, humanism is not and should not be a denomination or sect competing with others. We reject the notion of *ethnic* identification; we have none. We are committed to a universal ideal. We do not have an exclusive cultural heritage but consider ourselves part of world culture. We are opposed to and have not built churches and accredited clergy, although Ethical Culture societies and Unitarian Universalist churches have done so. We are ethically pluralistic. We do not enforce strict rules of conduct or require a creed or dogma. More important, we do not pretend to have an "inspiring message" nor do we claim a charismatic leader.

Our model is not Moses, Jesus, or Mohammed, but Socrates. And for many secular humanists in the twentieth century, there is also Karl Marx—but Marx the fighter for human freedom, not the mummified god of Moscow, Peking, and Havana. I mention these two individuals because they express humanist ideals and values; they provide sharply contrasting models, however, for fulfilling humanism. Socrates, like Jesus, was martyred, dying at the hands of the Athenians. He never founded a church but instead inspired a literature of philosophy and ethics, beginning with Plato, who was so enamored of Socrates that he dedicated his Dialogues to him and founded the first great university, the Academy. Socrates was a curious figure. He was condemned by what amounted to an "Un-Athenian Affairs Committee" for "making the better appear the worse," "denying the gods of Athens," and "corrupting youth." As a result he was forced by the Athenian democratic party to drink the hemlock. Was he a charismatic figure? Plato thought so, but his contemporary, Aristophanes, did not; in the comedy *The Clouds* he depicted Socrates as an uncouth figure and a buffoon. Morever, Socrates had no clear message. Although he believed that we ought to practice virtue, said he was inspired by the legendary priestess Diotima, and had intimations of immortality, he never claimed divine revelation. Indeed, he insisted, in Plato's *Euthyphro,* that ethics was independent of the traditional religious pieties. He was committed to inquiry. He did not know what truth, beauty, or goodness were. He was the wisest of men, he said, because he knew how ignorant he was. Yet although Socrates talked about absolute ideas and even a utopian society in which justice prevailed, it was his devotion to the life of the mind that became his lasting contribution. Plato's pupil Aristotle went on to found the Lyceum, and his successors ever since have fulfilled the basic principle of humanism: a commitment to free inquiry and rationalism.

A large city in the United States has several hundred churches and synagogues, but may have only a few colleges or universities, an art, history, or science museum, or a planetarium. These, in a sense, are the legacy of Socrates. There is no cult that reveres his name, yet Western civilization (in spite of its indelible Judeo-Christian influences) can draw on the heritage of the Socratic quest for truth. Perhaps that is why the disciples of the Socratic mission have failed to build institutions, for we are dealing with the realm of ideas. It is the difference between philosophy and science on the one hand (which are committed to the open mind and open society) and religion on the other (which, in its original Latin sense, means "to be bound" to a set of beliefs and practices). Religion, when given sufficient political power, shows a marked preference for the closed society.

Karl Marx, for a large part of the world, has been the most influential humanist of the twentieth century, even though his followers have taken a different approach. Marx was a disciple of the Enlightenment. He, too, rejected traditional religion and was committed to reason. But he thought that in order to bring humanism into reality, we need to go *beyond* atheism, to build a "classless society." This could best be accomplished, he believed, by revolutionary means. He argued that mankind needs to destroy class oppression and thus liberate human potentialities. Both Socrates and Marx pictured an ideal utopia, but the followers of Marx, inspired by his *millennial message,* became Marxists and were resolved to put it into practice. In my view, most forms of Marxism have betrayed Marx and the ideals of humanism. Implicit in Marx's writings, I submit, are antihumanistic elements;

for instance, the dialectical process is at work, leading to the allegedly inevitable achievement of socialism. In this view the ultimately beneficent laws of history take the place of providence.

I am not talking about democratic socialists, who wish to use Marx's dialectic only as a method of analysis or a guide, and who (despite Marx's jeers about justice) have been influenced by Marx's indictment of the injustices of capitalist society. Rather, I am thinking of the committed communist idealogue, who has developed a new religion, albeit a secular one. For these disciples Marxism has its *charismatic figures.* However, it was not Marx the person, a poor scholar supported by the surplus value his wealthy friend Engels sweated out of the proletariat of Manchester, a man who spent a good part of his life in the library of the British Museum, was afflicted with boils, and, unlike Job, had a fairly nasty temper. I am referring rather to political-ideological figures such as Lenin, Mao, Castro, and Ho Chi Minh, who led national revolutions. Following Leninism-Stalinism, there rapidly developed a strict structure and code, *bureaucratic commissars* replaced priests, and the party replaced Mother Church as the infallible source of truth. Moreover, obedience to party authority became the ultimate moral code and the test of loyalty; and heretics who dissented could be liquidated. In the place of ethnicity emerged new bonds, those of *class identity* and nationality. It was national liberation from colonial oppression, particularly in the third world, that became the wellspring of communist devotion.

Humanists must reject this kind of ideology, for it has abandoned freedom and democracy, a central principle of humanism. Willing to use any means (even terror) to achieve its ends, totalitarian regimes have emerged as terrible as any the world has seen. Would Christ be a Christian or Marx a Marxist if they could return? Marx disclaimed being a Marxist at one point. Both inspired — in spite of themselves — dogmatic religions in their names. Humanists surely do not wish to follow that direction. In regard to Marxism, a new *egalitarian world culture,* burdened with Marxist symbols, is beginning to emerge virtually everywhere except in the United States. This may swamp democratic culture and, like Christianity, eventually dominate world culture. Only time will tell whether it will succeed. Interestingly, Marxism has enlisted vast numbers of ordinary people, intellectuals, and students under its banner, not where it already rules but only where it is promised. Once it is implemented, however, disillusionment sets in.

## IV

I beg your indulgence for the preceding analysis, but it was essential to my questions: What is the humanist message? What do we wish to accomplish?

I interpret the message of contemporary humanism as having four major components: (1) it is a method of inquiry; (2) it presents a scientific world view ("cosmic humanism"); (3) it offers a set of moral values to provide meaning and direction for life; and (4) it provides a rich storehouse of artistic, poetic, and literary forms of expression.

Our first principle is a commitment to free inquiry. That is, we maintain that our beliefs should be grounded as far as possible upon rational methods of inquiry, not faith, mysticism, revelation, authority, or custom. This entails a commitment to evidence as the test of truth claims, and it means that we wish to extend the methods of scientific inquiry. Although rationalism has its roots in Greek philosophy, it came to fruition with the development of modern science in the sixteenth and seventeenth centuries and the ensuing Copernican, Darwinian, and behavioral revolutions. Concomitant with the use of critical intelligence is the need to cultivate skepticism about beliefs that transcend experience. That is why we are dubious about claims of divine revelation or transcendent deity, though we are always open to new discoveries. To be committed to science does not mean that we ignore art, poetry, morality, passion, or other aspects of human experience, which we seek to cultivate and enjoy. Moreover, it means that we will seek to apply reason, science, and technology to the solution of social and moral problems.

Humanism is also committed to a scientific view of nature. This world view is constantly changing and expanding. Basically, it is the model of astronomy and physics: the universe is probably fifteen billion years old and life has evolved over an extended period of time. Social institutions can also be explained by this historical process. Thus naturalistic evolutionary hypotheses compete with a theistic view of the universe. As far as we can tell, man does not have a privileged place in the scheme of things, nor is immortality promised.

A challenge for humanism is to compete with traditional religion in the sphere of the imagination. I believe that within the sciences there are tremendous opportunities for exciting the imagination. The sense of mystery and awe that we develop from studying astronomy can be far more breathtaking than religious piety. The possibility that life—indeed, perhaps even intelligent life—exists in outer space is among the most exciting possibilities of our times. We live in the age of space travel when, using scientific technology, our satellites can escape our solar system and explore the universe. That is why it seems to me that we need to defend a *cosmic humanism,* not an earthbound humanism. The tremendous growth of interest in the paranormal, UFOlogy, and science fiction points to the emergence of new cosmic religions. However untested their claims, we must admit that they are inspired by the vast splendor of the boundless universe. Carl Sagan, Isaac Asimov, and George Abell are secular humanists, members of the Committee for the Scientific Investigation of Claims of the Paranormal, but they are also interested in possible interplanetary communication. Here is the great new frontier for a humanist adventure in ideas.

Humanism is also an ethical philosophy. Indeed, many people consider this aspect crucial to its message: we offer an alternative sense of the meaning of life. "No deity will save us," says *Humanist Manifesto II,* "we must save ourselves." We are responsible for our own destinies on this planet, as individuals, as a society, and as a species. This is the great battle in America today with our fundamentalist critics. We believe that their moral codes are archaic insofar as they are based upon theological foundations.

What are our humanist values and principles? There is a long list, but I shall mention only thirteen here, without elaboration. Ethical humanism involves:

• a commitment to free inquiry and the open mind;
• a belief in the courage to live without fear or trembling;
• a confidence in the power of human creativeness, inventiveness, achievement;
• constant efforts to improve the human condition, mitigate suffering, and eliminate disease, conflict, war, and cruelty;
• respect for the rights of others;
• dedication to the preciousness and dignity of the individual, his or her creativity and growth;
• cultivation of happiness and the full life;
• emphasis on love, shared experience, human joy;
• tolerance of other points of view and styles of life;
• social justice and humanitarian help;
• a universal focus transcending national, ethnic, sexual, and racial barriers—the ideal of a world community;
• an emphasis on compromise and negotiation of differences;
• belief in a free, open, pluralistic, and democratic society.

Humanist morality is not fixed or final. Although the ethical humanist draws upon the collective wisdom of experience and there is a body of tested moral principles, he is nonetheless willing to develop morality. He should always be willing to use intelligence to revise principles and values in the light of altered conditions and to bring into being new forms of morality.

Humanism not only has an intellectual and moral component; it can also arouse the deepest forms of aesthetic appreciation. If the theist seeks to render his visions and aspirations in aesthetic symbols and metaphors—magnificent cathedrals and mosques, music and literature, sculpture and painting—so too can the humanist artist express in art form his deepest insights and values. The heroic art of classical Greece and Rome—its architectural and sculptural splendor, the power of its literature and philosophy—can still inspire us today, as can great Renaissance cities like Florence and Venice and great artists and authors such as Leonardo and Michelangelo, Shakespeare and Montaigne. Much of modern art, the novel, drama, poetry, music—from Beethoven and Picasso to Frank Lloyd Wright and Hemingway—also expresses humanist values and outlook. Some products of modern industry and technology likewise exemplify the highest ranges of human creativity, as Promethean men have sought to tame nature to suit human interests and needs and fulfill human aspirations. Thus, the fine and the practical arts are eloquent witnesses to the highest forms of creative aesthetic expression, and they constantly provide us with instruction and inspiration.

Now, if we examine the preceding statement of the humanist point of view, it seems to me there are three points we need to make clear. First, it is vital that we offer strong negative criticism of false religions and ideologies. All the great religions have grown by attacking those about them. As secular humanists, we need to defend skepticism, nontheism, agnosticism, atheism; and we need to question the false doctrines found in Judaism, Christianity, Islam, and Marxist ideology, as well as the newer cults of unreason. Moreover, we need to guard against the intrusion of religion into our secular institutions. Second, we need to enunciate the positive thrust of humanism. That is why humanism is more than atheism, for humanism is committed to an alternative set of ethical values. We are not simply negative naysayers; we have a constructive, alternative perspective full of meaning and significance. Third, we should not clothe our message solely in rational terms but must make it eloquent and dramatic, appealing to the whole person, including his emotions, and expressing both the tragic and humorous elements of the human condition. This means we are committed to the expansion of the creative dimensions of humanism.

## V

The vital and practical questions I now wish to raise are: (1) To whom should we direct our message? (2) Do we have charismatic leaders to enunciate it? (3) How shall we deliver it?

Clearly, we are interested in the widest possible dissemination of the humanist outlook to the general public throughout the world. However, we face several obstacles. Gullibility is very deep in human nature. Our message has been somewhat esoteric. At the very least it presupposes some degree of sophistication and education. Although people demand certainties, we only offer them probabilities. When they seek absolutes, we say that they should examine situations and be aware of possible exceptions. When they hunger for easy solutions, we point to complexities. They thirst for spiritual bread and wine, and we serve them skeptical doubts. Is it possible to develop in the wider population an appreciation of the methods of critical intelligence, the open mind, the suspension of belief, and skepticism? Can we, along with this, arouse joy in choosing how to live and an aesthetic appreciation for the humanist stance? Because humanists are skeptical, it doesn't mean that we do not have strong beliefs and commitment. Is it possible to cultivate a sense of tolerance and the willingness to negotiate differences in values? If it is hard enough keeping our values alive among humanists, how can we possibly spread them widely? I believe that we can and must.

However, our first task, indeed our primary task in my judgment, is not salvation but education; that is how we differ from Judaism, Christianity, Islam, and Marxist ideology. We are not interested in converting souls or gaining disciples, but we do wish to transform lives by keeping alive the free play of intellectual interest, the exploration of values, and aesthetic appreciation. That is what we mean by creative growth and why we are interested in the realization of human potentialities.

I submit that a humanist organization is not and should not be a religious organization and should not attempt to compete at that level. We don't have a "Thus saith the Humanist!" dogma or creed. We are not concerned with indoctrination, but with inquiry; not with blind faith, but evidence; not with unquestioned trust, but with wide ranges of knowledge. We are secular (not religious) humanists because we believe that it is possible to lead the good life without need of deity or clergy. Many of us believe that religious institutions that grew up before or with science are no longer necessary for humanity. We believe in morality and the possibility of a genuine ethic relative to human needs, not divine dictate.

As a first task, I submit that our main focus should be the educated public. The battle for humanist ideals still has to be waged on the intellectual level, involving theologians, politicians, educators, scientists, and poets in dialogue and debate. We can expect progress, for upwards of 50 percent of the population goes on to institutions of higher learning in the United States. Hence, much of the spadework has been done. The principles of humanism that I have defended are now already being widely espoused in society and are accepted—however inconsistently—by wide sectors of the public. Moreover, innumerable institutions that further these humanist ideals exist. The most important are our schools—primary and secondary, private and public—and our colleges and universities. The latter in particular are secular institutions that keep alive the basic themes of modern humanism: the quest for truth, free inquiry, the scientific outlook, the exploration of values, and aesthetic creativity. There are three million schoolteachers and half a million college and university faculty. Moreover, the millions of scientists, professionals, lawyers, and doctors are concerned with many or most of the ideas and values we espouse. What is Harvard University, the Smithsonian Institution, California Institute of Technology, the American Civil Liberties Union, the Philadelphia Symphony Orchestra, the American Museum of Natural History? Our society is rich in humanist institutions performing all the functions we wish to fulfill.

What then can *we* do, inasmuch as the humanist revolution—modernism—is well under way? We can deal with those areas of the modern humanist outlook that are not being properly addressed: (1) the defense of the rational method wherever it is under attack; (2) promotion of the scientific-naturalistic outlook; (3) strengthening of the humanist ethical stance as an alternative to the cults of unreason, the ideologies of despair, the churches of dogma; and (4) a cultivation of humanist artistic expression. In other words, our present mission, as I see it, is to keep alive free thought, criticize theological and ideological nonsense, and present the meaning of life from a humanist perspective. Our message has been watered down, distorted, and deflected. Instead of dealing with the deeper truths of the human condition as an alternative to messianic theology and ideology, we have become bogged down in trivia and banality; we have become fixated on the political battles and slogans of the day, rather than the more profound issues.

If I could present a scenario for a future humanistic society, perhaps every city would have a "Humanist Center for the Meaning of Life" to supplement the other schools. I am not talking about humanist chapters or ethical societies, which have failed to gain support, but creative centers for renewal, creative opportunities to explore naturalistic ideals. Existing alongside art galleries and symphonies, these centers would be places for creative dialogue and stimulus. But I am going to put that scenario aside; there is too much else to do before we go that far. Since the task is so great, it seems to me that we must move on to another urgent scenario, one that is achievable.

Humanist organizations, I suggest, should be at this stage leadership organizations, generating new ideas, keeping alive alternative possibilities, stimulating provocative discussion. Our primary audience at first should be educators, movers of public opinion and the media, professionals, doctors, psychiatrists, lawyers, scientists, ministers, and theologians. If we cannot convince them of our position, at least perhaps we can influence them to moderate, liberalize, and humanize their beliefs and make them tolerant of dissenters. Many in the humanist movement have agreed with this aim. Unfortunately, we have never succeeded in achieving it because of the caliber of our membership and leadership. Our basic problem is that we have an uninspiring message and we lack the leadership to enunciate a new one. The trouble with humanism as it is currently organized is that it is too often an intellectual and moral embarrassment, particularly for the most sophisticated and educated part of our society, and for that reason it lacks support. It fluctuates between two extremes, strident noise or warmed-over porridge, neither of which will inspire the educated world. To put it bluntly, I'm afraid we turn off more than we attract.

However, those who are dedicated to humanist ideals should not give up. We have an urgent role to play in society, especially in light of the massive attacks on humanism now coming from many quarters. This is a time to move ahead, not retreat into a humanism of nostalgia. All humanists who share the conviction that our most important task is *educational*— at least at this stage of our development—need to work together to fulfill that noble aim. The humanist movement can still attract new support, but this will require a shift in emphasis.

This analysis, I should add, applies to the existing humanist groups. Although the American Humanist Association has only 3,500 members after forty years of effort, other groups have not done any better. The American Ethical Union has only 3,500 members after a hundred years, the Society for Humanistic Judaism 4,000 adherents, and the Fellowship of Religious Humanists 300 — and these figures may be on the generous side. Within the Unitarian Church, which is declining in members, humanism is beleaguered and is losing its influence.

My suggestions would not necessarily mean supplanting existing humanist organizations. Rather they should move in a new direction, away from the model of a church to that of an educational institution. Our eventual goal is to reach the broader public — students and men and women from all walks of life — but we must first address ourselves to their educators.

I have not suggested practical methods to implement our educational goals; that is the task of another analysis. I have merely suggested that the building of societies, chapters, churches, or temples — on the model of existing religious institutions — is a wrong direction; if we are to have any lasting effect on the larger issues of the day or the public imagination, we need to alter both our strategy and our ends. We need to be clear about what it is we wish to achieve and why. To think that we can found a new religion to compete with the ancient or ideological religions of the day is to betray and contradict humanist ideals. Let us turn our attention in a positive direction, one in which we can succeed.

# 21

# Will Humanism Replace Theism?

I

H umanists have been committed to the proposition that human beings are capable of rationality and ought to use their critical intelligence to understand nature and solve human problems. This has been a defining characteristic of humanism from its origin in Greek and Roman thought, through the Renaissance, to the emergence of modern science in the present day. Humanists have also expressed the hope, especially since the Enlightenment, that with the growth of science and the extension of education to the average person, with the decline of poverty and disease, and with the improvement in standards of living, humankind could be liberated from irrational, superstitious fears that have been the bane of human existence.

The modern world has witnessed three encouraging humanistic developments. First, there has been an enormous expansion of the sciences. The scientific revolution has dazzled us with its achievements. Astronomy, physics, and the natural sciences have increased our knowledge and control over nature and made possible technological innovations for the benefit of the human species. The theory of evolution has radically altered our conception of how the universe operates, and the development of the social and behavioral sciences has expanded our understanding of human behavior. Second, educational opportunities have been significantly extended so that now education is considered the right of all individuals—even though many still are deprived of educational opportunities. A larger percentage of people, especially in affluent countries, now receives higher education. New communications technology makes information available to human beings in all corners of the globe, leaving few pockets of isolation. Third, we have the potential for the first time in history of becoming a truly global community; our chauvinistic beliefs and values are open to comparative critical scrutiny, and we can find a genuine basis for some common goals.

At the end of the nineteenth century many intellectuals believed that, given these scientific and educational developments and the emergence of a world community, the dominance of ancient religions would disappear.

---

This was published in *National Forum*, Spring, 1983.

What our primitive forebears attributed to hidden occult forces or acts of God could now be explained in natural causal terms. Scientific humanists believed that we could make a leap beyond illusion into a world where reason and humanity would prevail. Given these convictions, it is now dismaying to find that the forces of unreason are still strong. Ancient religions still persist in all parts of the world—Christianity, Islam, Judaism, Hinduism, Buddhism—and we have witnessed a growth rather than a decline in the most literalist forms of religious dogmatism. Today we see an Islamic revival in the Middle East and even in China, the persistence of Hinduism in India, the growth of Protestant fundamentalism, and so on.

In certain parts of the world the more liberal and humane religions are losing ground, as the most doctrinaire and militant forms gain adherents. In the United States, for example, advocates of scientific creationism denounce the theory of evolution and demand equal time in the schools. Even in such an advanced scientific and technological society as the United States, some 67 percent of the population believe in life after death, 53 percent believe there is a hell, and 71 percent a heaven (George Gallup, Jr., *Adventures in Immortality* [New York: McGraw-Hill, 1982]). Recent polls indicate that 79 percent believe that the Bible is the literal or inspired word of God and 76 percent believe that both creationism and evolution should be taught in the public schools (Princeton Religious Research Center, *Religion in America* and *Emerging Trends,* 1982). Other polls indicate that many people believe that God created Adam and Eve and that angels and devils exist.

To compound the problem, recent decades have seen the proliferation of new cults of unreason. There has been a renewed interest in astrology and horoscopes. On the subcontinent of Asia the overwhelming number of people apparently believe in astrology. In Western Europe and North America a substantial and growing minority of devotees read their horoscopes or have them cast. There is no evidence to support popular astrology; yet there are tens of thousands of professional astrologers offering quasi-religious advice. They far outnumber professional astronomers. There has been an enormous increase in devil cults and the rite of exorcism. Belief in psychic phenomena also continues to grow as so-called psychic seers and gurus are everywhere hailed for their magical powers. There is widespread belief in clairvoyance, telepathy, precognition, levitation, psychokinesis, astral projection, faith healing, psychic surgery, poltergeists, and apparitions.

Whether or not the existence of extrasensory perception is supported by the experimental evidence is an important issue for parapsychological research. We need to have an open mind about such inquiries. What I deplore are the untested religious extrapolations that have erupted in the wake of such claims.

Another event of considerable religious significance is a development in UFOlogy—the view that extraterrestrial, perhaps semidivine, beings from outer space (of suprahuman intelligence and power) have visited the earth in the past in flaming chariots or come now in spaceships. It is possible, perhaps even probable, that some type of life exists in other parts of the universe, and perhaps intelligent life has evolved in other galaxies. But, although extraterrestrial beings *may* have visited us or *may* now be visiting us, the evidence for this hypothesis is still totally unverified. UFOs have replaced the angels, witches, and demons of previous eras. Added to this are new religious cults like Scientology and the Unification Church, and claims of anomalies like the Loch Ness monster, Bigfoot, and the notorious Bermuda Triangle. Advocates of the paranormal today either invoke the occult or invent new pseudosciences in order to transcend experience and nature and to postulate new, hidden, and deeper realities of mystery and imagination.

## II

No doubt there has been an increase in atheistic, agnostic, and humanist thought in the twentieth century. But these skeptics of the supernatural represent only a minority of the population. Theistic and magical religious beliefs persist. I should point out that there is no guarantee that secularism is a source of rationality or of humanistic ethics. The world has seen brutal secular ideologies in the twentieth century. For example, fascism marked a retreat from reason, drawing upon a racist pseudoscience. Similarly, some forms of totalitarian and Stalinist Marxism have created state ideologies similar in function to traditional religions and have betrayed humanist ideals. This is a pity, since Marxism is considered by many intellectuals to be the most important intellectual movement of our day and the chief secular alternative to traditional theism.

We may ask: Can a secular humanism based upon reason and devoted to humane values ever prevail? My own research in the past decade has shaken my confidence that magical thinking will easily disappear and that secular humanism will take its place. There are many reasons for this. For one, theistic religion is not simply a question of belief. Although there are periods of upheaval in which old religions die and new ones emerge and are spread by conversion, most individuals are born into a religious tradition. One's religion is more a question of ethnicity and kinship, of blood and nationality than one of conscious choice. Religions persist especially where there are strong traditions governing intermarriage and the rearing of children. We are today living through a period where many of the traditional religions are being challenged. Individuals are wrenched from locality and ethnicity; many experience a mixing of many influences. Thus there is a greater possibility of free choice of religion. Moreover, wide sectors of the population have had the benefit of comparative history, scientific knowledge, and philosophical skepticism. Why is it that evangelical, literalist, and fundamentalist religions seem to be multiplying, rather than the liberal and humanistic ones? Why do bizarre cults of unreason thrive? Why is it that new folk religions fixated on the paranormal seem to be making headway?

What is so dismaying on the current scene is the fact that even the strangest of beliefs will find dedicated supporters. Why do people accept beliefs for which there is little or no evidence, or evidence to the contrary?

One reason is that there is an information overload, and it is difficult for people to evaluate the plethora of conflicting claims. Moreover, there is a real need to develop critical intelligence, skepticism about unproved claims, and appreciation for the standards of objective thinking. Another reason is that all too few people have heard the skeptical case against theistic religion and the paranormal. The public has not had the benefit of the opposing scientific data. Skeptical debunking has not had equal time with probelief propaganda. No doubt many people prefer the positive to the negative. This applies both to traditional religious beliefs and to the newer paranormal cults.

Regarding traditional religion, we are confronted today with a situation of imbalance. Millions of people are exposed to exhortations about the Bible, the Koran, and other allegedly sacred texts. Fundamentalist preachers and missionaries claim that these teachings are literally true, divinely inspired, and the ultimate source of human salvation. In the West at least, there is a rich tradition of biblical scholarship, which includes studies in comparative religion, folklore, archeology, and literary analysis. These disciplines have scrutinized the claims of the Bible (whether interpreted literally or metaphorically), and the methods used to compile the biblical record have been laid bare. The Bible, in the last analysis, is a human document, a product of an ancient, prescientific people. It is full of contradictions and inconsistencies, and its world view is confuted by modern science and philosophy. Whether Jesus ever existed or whether the claims to miracles and revelation so appealing to the primitive mind can be sustained by scientific scrutiny has been intensely debated. Rudolf Bultmann and others have attempted to demythologize the Bible. Unfortunately, although these criticisms have appeared in serious philosophical and theological journals, the public is largely unaware of them.

The powerful rational analysis of religion that developed from the eighteenth century through the first decades of the twentieth has been dissipated by various forms of neo-orthodoxy. They reintroduced religious and metaphysical principles by ambiguous language and asserted that men and women can live adequate lives only if they immerse their uncertainties in ancient myths, symbols, and rituals. This new obscurantism is perpetuated by theological scholars who seldom have their views scrutinized or challenged. The public is thus led to believe that the claims of religion are more genuine than is the case. Powerfully entrenched religious institutions are fearful of such dissent, and heretics have long discovered how dangerous it is to advocate nonconformist beliefs.

Similar considerations apply to the paranormal. The public should be exposed to negative claims about astrology, psychic phenomena, UFOlogy, and so on. But this happens all too rarely, since the media constantly present as true a whole series of unfounded paranormal claims.

The question can be raised: If people were to receive such criticism, would they abandon their unverified religious and paranormal beliefs? We would hope so, but this may not be the case. Two rather disturbing studies published recently by the journal of the Committee for the Scientific Investigation of Claims of the Paranormal have jarred my confidence that this will easily happen, at least not without a massive educational program—and even that may not be sufficient.

Is traditional religious belief declining? With the growth of education and science, one would expect this to be the case. Western Europe, for example, shows a marked decline in formal religious identification. Unbelief is widespread in Great Britain. In the United States, studies indicate that 68 percent of the population identify with religious bodies (Princeton Religious Research Center, *Religion in America,* 1982, p. 100). What happens to those who are not affiliated? Do they become freethinkers? Are they imbued with the scientific spirit and humanistic ideals? In a recent study, sociologists William Bainbridge and Rodney Stark of the University of Washington in Seattle show that those who claim to believe in the newer cults of the paranormal and the occult come from the religiously unaffiliated. Seventy-three percent of those with no religious affiliation, for example, agree that some Eastern practices, such as Yoga, Zen, and Transcendental Meditation are probably of great value. This is much higher than for ordinary religious believers. And this group also scores higher on the whole in belief in ESP, UFOs, Tarot readings, seances, and psychic healing. According to the latest figures, some 35 percent of American adults claim to be "born again" or identify with fundamentalist Christianity. This group is more resistant to paranormal and occult claims, no doubt because of strong church strictures against such beliefs. Nevertheless, the conclusion to be drawn is that those who break away from traditional religious organizations are especially sympathetic to the claims of the paranormal and the occult. Far from being resistant to superstition, they tend to adopt new ones (William Sims Bainbridge and Rodney Stark, "Superstitions: Old and New," *Skeptical Inquirer,* Summer 1980).

A second series of studies, by psychologists Barry Singer and Victor Benassi at California State University, Long Beach, provide unexpected results. Singer and Benassi introduced students in various psychology classes to a person (named Craig) dressed in a long purple robe and sporting a medallion, who performed so-called "psychic" feats. He bent a metal rod seemingly by psychokinesis. Blindfolded, he demonstrated the ability to read numbers on a concealed note pad. He was able to transfer ashes from the back of a person's hand to his palm. These acts seem to contradict ordinary experience and our notions of causality, but they were simple magic tricks that any good magician can perform. In some of the classes, the professors did not tell the students anything about the performer other than to say that he claimed to have psychic powers, though they were not convinced personally. In other classes, they told the students that the performer was a magician and that he would present a magic act. They were surprised to find that in both the "psychic" and "magic" classes about two-thirds of the students clearly believed that the performer was a psychic.

Only a few students seemed to believe the instructor's description of Craig as a magician in the two classes where he was introduced as such. Psychic belief was not only prevalent; it was strong and loaded with emotion. A number of students covered their papers with exorcism terms and exhortations against the Devil. In the psychic condition, 18 percent of the students explicitly expressed fright and emotional disturbance. Most expressed awe and amazement. We were present at two of Craig's performances and witnessed some extreme behavior. By the time Craig was halfway through the "bending" chant, the class was in an excited state. Students sat rigidly in their chairs, eyes glazed and mouths open, chanting together. When the rod bent, they gasped and murmured. After class was dismissed, they typically sat still in their chairs, staring vacantly or shaking their heads, or rushed excitedly up to Craig, asking him how they could develop such powers. We felt we were observing an extraordinarily powerful behavioral effect. If Craig had asked the students at the end of his performance to tear off their clothes, throw him money, and start a new cult, we believe some would have responded enthusiastically.

Obviously, something was going on here that we didn't understand. Further, many students were experiencing serious emotional disturbance as a result of what we had done. Although in retrospect we might have known better, we did not imagine that having someone dress in a choir robe and do elementary-school magic tricks would produce such fright. (Barry Singer and Victor Benassi, "Fooling Some of the People All of the Time," *Skeptical Inquirer*, Winter 1980-81, pp. 19-20.)

Singer and Benassi were so intrigued that they continued the experiments by bringing the magician to other classes. This time they changed their introduction to make it clear that they were presenting a magician and that he was doing tricks. This description did succeed in reducing psychic beliefs slightly, but never below 50 percent. Thus the most salient result of the tests, they said, was their inability to reduce psychic beliefs more than slightly even though there were strong and clear explanations that trickery and magic were taking place. Singer and Benassi have concluded that people will stubbornly maintain a belief about someone's psychic powers no matter what evidence is presented to them. I should point out that at no time did the magician himself say that he was a psychic or make a psychic claim. The Singer and Benassi tests have since been replicated by others at UCLA and Ohio State University with similar results. In my own classes at the State University of New York at Buffalo, I find that upwards of 80 percent of the students accept various forms of magic as true paranormal events. Singer and Benassi conclude: "We believe that our results, as bizarre as they may

be, are of wide generality and that the psychological processes we have ten-
tatively identified as being involved in supporting psychic beliefs are present
and active in the general population." It may be that the students in these
classes were not exposed long enough to criticisms of psychic magic. Their
attitudes are so deep-seated, perhaps because of the uncontested religious
culture, that they need extensive treatment and redirection. Nevertheless,
the results are disturbing because they demonstrate how difficult it is to
develop a secular and scientific outlook.

## III

What light does this research shed on the subject of this paper? The question is important because we are focused not on traditional religions but on
the formation of new beliefs, where we have control groups in a sense. This
leads to a number of questions I shall address briefly.

First, is gullibility or self-deception deeply embedded in human nature?
Is there an inborn tendency to accept beliefs without evidence? Are there
limits to scientific objectivity? Does the will to believe enter in? How effective can education be in developing rationality and skepticism? Why do
some scientists who are competent in their own fields often discard their
objective attitudes in other areas?

Second, how deep-seated is magical thinking? Is there an enduring fascination with the unknown (which incidentally motivates much of science as
well as religion)? Does the lure of the mysterious entice human interest? Is
man an imaginative animal, forever hankering after the transcendental? For
many, the traditional miracles and revelations surrounding Moses, Jesus, and
Mohammed have been supplemented or replaced by intelligent semidivine
creatures from UFOs who have ESP and other psychic powers. Science fiction has, for them, become Holy Writ and seems to perform functions similar
to those of traditional theistic religions. Does the humanism of the future
need to be dressed in prophetic garb and infused with myth and drama in
order for it to succeed? What about the role of charismatic figures in
transforming morality and awakening commitment and dedication? Perhaps
Marxism, as a secular alternative to classical theism, has succeeded in attracting mass support because its messianic, millennial, and utopian vision has
come to the forefront. And so we may ask: Will secular humanism, in order
to be viable, need a new mythology, and will this betray its very nature?

Third, traditional religions seem to perform positive functions that are
independent of their cognitive belief-systems. They appeal to deep needs. If
traditional religions decline, along with the psychological security and
sociological moorings they offer, does this not imply that alternative support systems must emerge to replace them—the family (in one form or
another), ethnic identity, a community to belong to, some celebration of the
rites of passage (birth, puberty, marriage, and death)? Many humanistic

organizations have attempted to offer such alternatives, but without great success. Is it because they are basically intellectual in content and lack a powerful emotional appeal? Is it because their messages do not emphasize the mystery and drama of reality and the human condition?

Fourth, on a deeper level, one may then ask, will a secular humanism ever succeed in satisfying man's existential quest? Perhaps this is the most troublesome issue. Humanism focuses on the development of self-reliant individuals willing to accept the responsibility for their own destiny, capable of freedom, autonomy, rationality, and willing to live with uncertainty and ambiguity. But it may be that this is a moral ideal appropriate to only a limited number of individuals. It demands courage and fortitude, will and perseverance. But some people are weak and timid, fearful of life and its challenges and especially weighed down by its burdens. The humanist is a person alive with a sense of the opportunities that life presents; he expresses the strenuous mood. He does not wish simply to fulfill human nature, but to exceed it in a creative display of his powers. But the average man or woman, in many cases, seeks solace and peace, tranquillity and quietude. Thus there may be an escape not only from reason but from freedom as well (as Erich Fromm has pointed out).

Daniel Bell in a controversial essay, "The Return of the Sacred" (*The Winding Passage* [Cambridge, Mass.: ABT Books, 1980]), argues that the sacred can never be dispensed with entirely. This is so, he says (agreeing with Kierkegaard) because of the tragic dimensions of human life. How will a secular morality deal with existential despair, the awesome reality of human finitude and death? Bell thinks that the secular city, which we seek to construct and improve, ultimately provides a limited vision. Lurking in the background is always the quest for eternity as a solution to our existential predicament. He maintains that the traditional forms of religion, though they are not literally true, provide some consolation for the weeping soul. He thinks that tradition gives firmer moorings for our longings and some psychic stability in an otherwise transient sea. It may be that the fascination with the paranormal, the speculative leaps to the edges of the universe and to the possibilities of other dimensions of reality are feeding this desire for there to be something more.

Now I do not have a simple answer to many of the questions I have been raising. Humanists do not have a central place for the tragic, and surely not the morbid or exaggerated one. We look upon life as a joyous scene; problems are to be solved, not moaned about. Although we strive to fulfill life and avoid death, we recognize that at some point we must accept death as a natural act. Perhaps for some of us life has been too good and we owe the universe some suffering. It may be a question of glands; perhaps it is biochemical or genetic. Or it may be that different personality types are looking at the universe through different lenses. Nevertheless, there are countless numbers of individuals who crave "something more" in the universe.

Unable to face death and nonbeing for themselves or their loved ones, they create fantasy worlds of magical wish-fulfillment. Will they continue to need to do so in the future? These are all problems for further empirical research, not philosophical speculation.

A number of questions need answering: (1) Why do human beings believe the way they do? What is the role of cognition in the formation of both beliefs and values? (2) Why does fascination with magical thinking persist in this age of science? Is it simply because the skeptical view has not been heard, or does it have its roots in some natural psychological hunger? (3) To what extent are *all* individuals capable of autonomous choice, self-reliance, and independence? If all are not, is the humanist adventure accordingly a limited option? I hope that psychologists and behavioral scientists can help resolve these questions. We need to know more about human nature, its limits and possibilities. Until we have such knowledge, we should be wary of venturing predictions about whether a secular humanist world is possible and what forms it might take. The present worldwide growth of paranormal and fundamentalist beliefs may only be a throwback to a prescientific mode of thinking. Perhaps it is the last gasp of a dying culture, to be replaced by a scientific and secular moral order. Or could it be the harbinger of a future civilization based on a new myth?

My own guess is that both cultures will continue to exist side by side. We have no guarantee that a thoroughly secular and scientific morality will make appreciable and lasting headway. Perhaps the most we can do is to provide criticism of the excesses of religious fanaticism and offer meaningful humanistic alternatives for those who seek them. Perhaps the most we can hope for is that we may liberalize intolerant moralities and develop mutual respect and tolerance as moral principles necessary in a pluralistic world. In any case, we should not give up struggling for a humanist world, nor should we lessen our commitment to the ideals of reason and humanist morality. It is important, however, that we recognize the arduous and long-term character of this task.

# 22

# Humanism and Critical Intelligence

## I

The prevalence of irrational beliefs and superstitions in modern culture is a cause for concern to humanists. In surveying the current state of belief in the world, we find that large numbers of people are willing to believe in many things, however outrageous, without evidence or proof. Indeed, one can usually find some group somewhere in the modern world passionately devoted to patent falsehoods. We need only look at the religious landscape to note the persistence of ancient orthodoxies based upon blind faith. Christianity, Hinduism, Islam, Judaism, and Buddhism remain with us in spite of devastating critiques of their foundations by philosophers and scientists. No sooner does one generation make progress by debunking the old myths than the next seeks to reendow them with meaning or it invents new kinds of foolishness. Even in those societies where traditional religions appear to be in decline, new *isms* appear in their wake.

A case in point is the state of belief in Western society today. Concomitant with the growth of fundamentalist religious sects, there has emerged a new set of bizarre cults. Some of them have been resurrected from the past, some of them are new absurdities; occultism and spiritualism abound. Gurus, many of them imported from Asia, flourish; their disciples find inspiration in astrology, exorcism, Krishna Consciousness, transcendental meditation, or Zen, to name only a few. As part of this revival, interest in the paranormal has attracted otherwise sophisticated people, who seem willing to outdo each other in their acceptance of nonsense: from astral projection and reincarnation, to levitation, poltergeists, precognition, psychokinesis, and psychic healing. New cults have become fashionable, some of them based on science fiction: belief in UFOs, lost continents, Bermuda triangles, or chariots of the gods. In addition to that—and far more dangerous in the twentieth century—many of the orthodox religions have been supplanted by virulent forms of militant ideology, such as fascism and Stalinism. These demand emotional commitment from true believers and lead to the abandonment of

An address delivered to the All-India Conference of the Radical Humanist Association, Ahmedabad, Nov. 1975, this was published in *The Radical Humanist,* Feb. 1976.

independence of thought. They set ethnic cultures, nations, and races against each other and divide human loyalties. Their authoritarian intolerance of those with whom they disagree and their conviction that they have a monopoly on absolute truth become new dogmas enshrined and enforced by the state.

## II

All of this is especially appalling to humanists; for humanism, if nothing else, is dubious about excesses in religious faith. We can talk about two aspects of humanism: its negative criticisms and its positive dimensions.

The first point I wish to make is that *skepticism* is essential to the humanistic outlook. The key epistemological principle is clear: one is not justified in affirming a truth claim unless one can support it by evidence or reason. It is not enough to be inwardly convinced about one's beliefs. They must at some point be objectively validated by other impartial investigators. A belief is not warranted just because it is "subjectively true." If it is true, then it is because it has been confirmed by a community of inquirers. To validly believe that something is true is to relate one's beliefs to a rational justification; it is to make a claim about the world, independent of one's wishes.

The specific criterion for testing a belief depends upon the subject matter under consideration. Yet there are certain general criteria we should take into account. First, we need to examine the *evidence*. Here I am referring to observation of facts or data that are repeatable by independent observers and that can be examined experimentally in test cases. This is, of course, the empiricist or experimentalist criterion. A belief is true if and only if it has been confirmed, directly or indirectly, by reference to observable evidence.

Second, a belief can be validated by supporting *reasons*. Here there are logical considerations that are relevant. A belief is related to a set of other beliefs that has been established by previous inquiries. This criterion is that of logical consistency. A belief is invalid within a framework, if it contradicts other well-grounded beliefs that are held.

Third, we evaluate our beliefs in part by their observed *consequences* in practice and by their effects upon conduct. This is the utilitarian or pragmatic criterion: a belief is judged as useful or not by reference to its function and its value. One cannot claim that a belief is true simply because it has utility; independent evidence and rational considerations are essential. Nevertheless, reference to the results of a belief in action, particularly about normative beliefs, is important.

The foregoing criteria are familiar in logic and the philosophy of science. It is the hypothetical-deductive method of testing hypotheses that I am talking about. In my view the scientific method is coterminous with common sense; it is not some esoteric art available only to the initiated. Science employs the same methods of critical intelligence that the ordinary man uses in everyday life in formulating beliefs about his practical world; and these are the methods one has to use to some extent if one is to live and function, to make plans and choices. To deviate from objective thinking is to be out of touch with cognitive reality; we cannot avoid using it if we are to deal with the concrete problems we encounter in the world. The controlled use of scientific method, where applied, has had enormous success in the past three centuries, contributing to the advancement in knowledge and technology and improving the standard of living, health, happiness, and welfare of human beings. India and Western civilization had relatively the same level of technology before the sixteenth century. The great leap forward in the West occurred primarily because of the development of the sciences as instruments of human progress.

A puzzling paradox is that many people abandon the use of their practical intelligence when they enter the fields of religion or ethics; caution is often thrown to the winds when they flirt with the so-called realm of the transcendental.

Moreover, there is today, particularly in the affluent societies, a disturbing disillusionment with science and technology. Science is blamed for ecological destruction, the depletion of natural resources, the dangers of nuclear destruction, or the abuses of technology. This attack is unfair as applied to science across the board. For science is primarily a *method of knowing,* whereas technology is the practical application of scientific principles to the real world. Technology more often than not is controlled by political, military, or economic leaders, not the scientist. Those neoromantics who condemn technology overlook its great boon to humankind in medicine, agriculture, education, industry, and other fields. The problem perhaps is that it has not been extended far enough nor its uses judged by critical intelligence.

In any case we are talking primarily about the scientific method. Humanism, like science, is committed to the use of critical intelligence in appraising beliefs, and insists that they be based upon evidential grounds. As a corollary to this is the further criterion: *where we do not have sufficient evidence, we ought, wherever possible, to suspend judgment.* In addition, beliefs should be considered tentative hypotheses, based on degrees of probability. They should not be considered absolute or final. The principle of fallibilism (as Charles Peirce pointed out), to which we ought to be committed, considers our beliefs to be fallible; they are not to be construed as infallibly certain. We should be willing to revise them if need be in the light of new evidence and new theories.

Humanists have generally been skeptics in the area of religious belief, for they have not found the traditional beliefs in God, divinity, or the transcendental to be intelligible. Nor have they found sufficient evidence for the claim that God exists.

Religion is more an institutionalized form of culture than it is a doctrine of statable beliefs. It is deeply embedded in a society as a way of life. Individuals are born into a religion and accept it on the basis of custom. The mode of justification usually appealed to to support commitment, is that of authority (long-standing traditions and conventions) or of faith (that the convictions of our forefathers embodied in ancient documents—the Bible, Koran, Bhagavad-Gita—are true).

But the historic religions do not stand the test of critical scrutiny. Christianity, for example, based upon the alleged miraculous revelation of a dead and risen Jesus fails all of the tests of confirmation, and goes contrary to everything that we know about natural causality. Islam, rooted in the Koran, is dependent upon a questionable *petitio principii*: Mohammed is the true prophet of Allah because Mohammed says he is. Millions of the faithful continue to believe in these religions, in spite of the fact that they violate the most fundamental canons of objectivity.

The humanist, of course, does not foreclose a priori any examination of claims about the transcendental. Even though we tend to be atheists or agnostics, we are committed to free and open inquiry. We cannot refuse to engage in research, particularly into paranormal phenomena. But we have the right to ask that it be conducted responsibly and carefully and that the evidence not be outstripped by sheer conjecture nor the conclusions based upon faith or the will-to-believe.

## III

One may ask: Why are people willing to allow their fancies to exceed the evidence? Why does irrationality persist in human cultures? There no doubt are significant sociological and historical explanations that can be given for this, and in some societies mysticism and subjectivism are especially rampant. But there are also profound psychological factors that are operative, and this may say something about the peculiar nature of the human species.

There seems to be a *perverse tendency in the human animal toward gullibility*—that is, a psychological readiness to accept untested beliefs, to be gulled or dulled into assent. This tendency seems to be so deeply ingrained in our nature that few are without it entirely. There is the temptation to swallow what others offer us as the gospel truth. I am not talking simply of stupidity and ignorance so much as uncritical naivete about some matters.

Unfortunately, there are some individuals who specialize in deceiving people. They are the purveyors of false gods and empty services, the perpetrators of fraud and distortion. There are no doubt sincere believers who delude themselves, who believe in something without adequate evidence, and who seek to convert others to their misconceptions. The motive here is not so much conscious fraud as it is self-deception. The curious thing is that if a psychotic repeats himself often enough, in time many will come to believe him. Moreover, if a lie is big enough, people are more apt to believe it. People would rather believe a liar who promises them wondrous things than a nay-saying debunker; the heretic always risks being burned at the stake, especially after the new mythology becomes institutionalized as official doctrine. The best antidote for gullibility is a strong dose of skepticism! Yet some people find it bitter medicine.

The gullible person uncritically accepts as true what he is fed, and he goes on and seeks to base his deeds upon it. He infuses undigested falsehood into his life style; it becomes his "faith," salvation, and guide. Thus the committed Christian believes that Jesus is the Son of God and that to believe in him is to achieve immortal life; his whole existence is built around the myth. It permeates his very being, his moral values, and social attitudes. Some of the gullibles today reject orthodox religion, yet they are willing to follow every fad and fashion that emerges on the horizon. For example, belief in astrology, a long-standing tradition in Asia, has come back in force in the West, after having been buried by science. In the year 1900 encyclopedias referred to astrology as a historical superstition no longer held in the modern world. Yet today there are once again millions of people who seek to guide their destiny by reading their horoscopes (the positions of the planets at the moment and place of birth). Astrology persists after 4,000 years, in spite of overwhelming scientific evidence against it. Why is this so?

There is I think still another tendency in human nature that feeds gullibility—*the fascination with mystery and drama.* Life for many persons is humdrum and boring. Daily existence is often a burden, the same work, family, or friends day in and day out. Overcome by ennui and the tyranny of trivia, they may seek escape by the use of drugs or alcohol, by dulling or suppressing their consciousness. Release into nothingness is their goal. Another method of diversion is the quest for hedonistic pleasures and thrills. Still another is the role of the imagination. The arts of literature and drama give free play to the creative imagination, as does religion. It often is difficult for many individuals to distinguish fiction from reality, truth from falsity. The new arts of the media, especially television and the cinema, appeal to our sense of mystery. Frankenstein and Dracula become as *real* as anything else. The cults of unreason and the paranormal attract and fascinate. They enable us to skirt the boundaries of the unknown. For the ordinary person, there is this world—which is often a source of boredom and anxiety, pain and suffering—and the possibility of escape to another. And so he looks elsewhere for another universe and another reality.

There is thus a search which is fundamental to our being: *the quest for meaning.* The human mind has a genuine desire to plumb the depths of the unspoken, to find deeper significance and truth, to reach out to another realm of existence. Life for many is without meaning, especially for the poor, the sick, the forsaken, those who have failed, or have little hope. The imagination offers a way of salvation from the trials and tribulations encountered in this life. Thus the God-idea, reincarnation, and immortality offer solace to individuals in the face of tragedy and death and the existence of evil in the world. For ideological religions the means of salvation is the utopian vision of the perfect society of peace and justice in the future. The soul cries out for something more, far beyond, deeper, more lasting and perfect than our contingent and transient world of experience.

Accordingly, the persistence of emotional faiths may be explained in part by something within our nature: gullibility, the lure of mystery, the quest for meaning. People will take the least shred of evidence and construct a religious system. They will pervert their logic and abandon their senses, all for the promised land. Some will gladly barter their freedom to the most authoritarian of systems in order to achieve comfort and security. Religions promise solace; they seek to invest the solitary individual, who often feels estranged and alone, with an important role in the universe. God, atman, the ultimate reality, the heavens have a place set aside for each and everyone who is part of the total system. Religions thus offer soothing balm for the pain of living. They transcend evidence and reason, for they speak to a passionate hunger that has its roots within the very depths of our being.

## IV

Now humanism, if it is to gain acceptance, must deal with these psychological-existential considerations. It must provide a constructive alternative to religious mythologies.

The first part of the humanist program, as I have indicated, is to provide criticism. Our rational faculties need to be used to debunk beliefs that are unfounded or false. Skepticism or the suspension of judgment is a responsible part of the task. Our fund of reliable knowledge about nature and life can grow, but only if it is based on careful methods of inquiry.

The critical development of knowledge is the primary task of *education*. The most vital institutions in society are not necessarily political or economic—important as these are—but those charged with the educative process, knowledge and learning. The starting point for education is, of course, the schools, from primary and secondary to higher education. It is not enough, however, for educational institutions to simply inform young people of the facts or to disseminate a body of knowledge. Education of that sort may be nothing more than rote learning or indoctrination. Rather, a key purpose of education should be to develop within individuals the use of *critical intelligence*. It is not enough to get people to memorize a subject matter, amass facts, pass examinations, master a specialty or profession, or even to be trained as citizens in society. If we do that and nothing more, we have not educated fully; a central task is to cultivate the ability to test beliefs, evaluate hypotheses, appraise arguments. It is to develop an attitude of objectivity and impartiality. Given the tremendous information explosion today, individuals are bombarded on all sides by competing claims to truth. What is vital is that individuals develop some understanding of the effective criteria for judging these claims. I refer here not only to our ability to examine claims of knowledge about the world but also to our ability to develop skills in appraising value judgments and ethical principles. The goal of education should be to develop reflective persons, skeptical yet receptive to new ideas, always willing to examine new departures in thought, yet insisting that they be tested before they are accepted.

This is the basic philosophy of progressive education as enunciated by John Dewey, America's leading humanist philosopher of the twentieth century. If we humanists have any primary mission, it should be to reconstruct education—to train teachers how to think so that they can impart an objective methodology to students. Education is not achieved when we transmit a dead subject matter to students, but only when we can stimulate a living process of inquiry and research.

This goal is well appreciated today in some systems of education in the world, and many schools do seek to cultivate reflective intelligence as one of the primary aims. But the task is not complete until we extend our concern to other equally important educative institutions in society. If humanists are to play a role in raising the level of intelligence in society, it is important that we concern ourselves with the media of mass communication—television, radio, the cinema, the press, newspapers, magazines, and book publishing. Television in many countries has replaced the schools as the primary formative influence on children, who spend more time in front of TV than in school (between 5 and 7 hours per day). Regretfully, the media in capitalist countries are controlled by powerful economic interests, whose main concern is profit, and who are interested in entertainment and sensationalism rather than education; in totalitarian societies they are controlled by the state, which is interested in indoctrination, propaganda, and control.

A serious problem with the electronic media, as Marshall McLuhan has pointed out, is that they employ visual images rather than written symbols, immediate impressions instead of sustained analyses. How can we stimulate reflective criticism in viewers? A necessary precondition in my judgment is that the electronic media present a plurality of ideas and be open to dissent. For people will be unable to develop critical thinking unless alternative ideas can be examined in the give and take of argument. Humanism is committed to the free mind—uncontrolled by the church, state, or economic interests; it is committed to free inquiry as the best method of social change.

As humanists, we must for a long time function as critics within our societies, as skeptics dubious of excessive claims and false faiths. Like Socrates, we are gadflies, forever picking holes in the reigning mythologies, including, I might add, those of other humanists as well. For humanism is not a dogma or creed, a fixed set of first principles or values; it is first and foremost a method of intelligent inquiry applied to all beliefs, including its own.

## V

If we are to make progress in reconstructing beliefs, however, we must go further. We must try to satisfy the need for mystery and drama and the hunger for meaning. It is here that I think we have often failed. The growth of education and science in the modern world is a marvel to behold, and we should do whatever we can to assist its development. But we have learned that an increase in the sum of knowledge by itself will not necessarily overturn superstition, dogma, and gullibility, because these are nourished by other sources in the human psyche.

One point often overlooked in satisfying our fascination with mystery and drama is the role of imagination in the sciences. Science can only proceed by being open to creative explorations in thought. The breakthroughs in science are astounding, and they will continue in the future as we probe further into the world of matter and life and into the universe at large. The space age is the beginning of a new epoch for humankind, as we leave our solar system and possibly discover extraterrestrial life.

The arts are essential for humanism — to keep alive the dramatic qualities of experiences. Poetry, music, and literature express our passionate natures. Man does not live by reason alone; and science is often viewed by its critics as merely cold and rational. As such, we seem to be cut off from people who hunger for something more. Our aesthetic impulses, our delight in beauty need cultivation. For the humanist the arts are the deepest expression of our "spiritual" interests, but we need to make a distinction between art and truth. For though we may appreciate aesthetic form, knowledge claims require rigorous testing.

In any case, humanism needs poetry and symbol, creativity and drama; it needs to enhance its message with passion, emotion, love, and devotion. We need to appeal to the whole person, not simply his cerebellum. In this we have been outdone by the traditional religions of ceremony. We need to celebrate life and its potential good, to find joy and happiness as part of it, and to satisfy the quest for meaning. I think it is this craving for meaning that leads to the psychotic disorientation found in the cults of unreason. "Follow me" say the theologies of deity or utopia: "I am the light, the truth, and the way." And people are willing to abandon all standards of critical judgment in the process.

We need to make it clear that humanism has an ethical program. Ethics is autonomous, we say. It is not derived from theology, metaphysics, or ideology. It is created by human beings to fulfill their aspirations. That is the first part of the ethical program we insist upon: the need to develop a new system of values based upon human experience and intelligence. Today, for the first time in the history of humankind we say that it is *we* who are responsible for our destiny, not God or fate or the law of history. We can build a better world here and now for people to enjoy. We need not escape from this into nirvana or utopia.

The key moral virtues for humanists besides intelligence are those of the free, autonomous, independent person, able to use his own powers as best he can, in order to attain the good life. We must do what we can to facilitate growth and actualization so that each person can achieve a sense of his own creative well-being.

In this connection it is important that we develop our *courage*—not to merely be, but to *become*. Man is what he chooses to become in the future. Our model is Prometheus, who stole fire and the arts of civilization from the gods. If the opposite of intelligence is gullibility and ignorance, the opposite of courage is fear and dependence, the refusal to face the world or try to change it.

Life has no meaning independent of it. We cannot look outside ourselves for hope and salvation. The meaning of life is what *we* choose to invest it with. Neither the old religious faiths nor the new cults of unreason are relevant to the contemporary human situation. We need to create a new future for humankind and for ourselves; our saint is not the ascetic who withdraws from life in religious meditation but the activist and doer, who has a lust for life and a determination to create a better world.

The problem of meaning is not to contemplate our essence but to go out into the world and change it. At the present moment in human history we need to build a civilization based upon peace, justice, democracy, freedom, and a genuine world community. Justice does not rest as an absolute standard in the lap of the gods. It is relative to humans. We believe we can create a more humane society, in which equality of consideration and opportunity prevail, a society in which men are free to guide their own destinies and to fulfill their own plans and projects individually and cooperatively. If we are to achieve a just society, democracy is probably the best method available; but it means that we need to democratize all the institutions of society, not simply the state or the economy. A high priority on the humanist agenda at present is the need for economic development of the third world, with assistance from the affluent countries. It is clear to the humanist that no society can develop in isolation from others, that we are all part of a world community.

We will not succeed in expanding humanism if we abandon intelligence or flee in despair to the irrational. Humanism can provide an authentic alternative for humankind. But it will require dedication and devotion to get the message across. Although the development of intelligent skepticism is a necessary precondition if we are to spread humanism, we will not succeed in this venture unless we can at the same time inspire the imagination and provide a deep sense of the meaning of humanist values for life, as well as the importance of our commitment to them.

# 23

# The Original Sins: Gullibility and Nincompoopery

## I

The human species has a perverse streak that runs deep in its nature. It is the capacity for being easily deceived, the tendency to allow wishes, desires, fancies, hopes, or fears color the imagination or influence judgment or beliefs. Bacon identified this as the "idol of the tribe."

"Gullibility" is the best term to describe this tendency; for humanists it is the cardinal sin corrupting human nature. It is the willingness to be lulled or dulled into assenting to a truth claim without adequate evidence or grounds to support it. Gullibility is so widely distributed among humans that few are without it entirely. No one can escape its temptation, though there are obviously degrees of perversity or wickedness; but some, by hard therapeutic efforts of will, can cultivate virtue by means of critical intelligence. The most gullible sinners in our midst are those who are willing to swallow whole whatever they hear or are promised, to gulp it down—hook, line, and sinker. They are, as it were, the sitting gulls, ducks, or pigeons—choose your own metaphor—prey to every huckster at the fair. They are the suckers, if you will, fair game for every con man, willing to gobble down everything fed them, unsophisticated greenhorns, fall guys. In the most extreme form these are the *taugenichts* (good-for-nothings); they may be pleasant, perhaps charming. Yet they are weak-minded yokels, willingly taken in by the proverbial city slicker.

The problem is not so much in the con men—the purveyors of false gods and empty services—who are waiting in the wings for the kill, but in the sitting ducks who are readily given to self-deception in their search for faith and belief. For the foolables, stuffables, deludables, hoodwinkables, bamboozlables, hogwashables, humbuggables, born-yesterdayables, there is almost a psychological need to be duped.

In ordinary life, the plain man of common sense can easily spot both the dupes and the con men, and he is able to guard himself from falling prey to their snares and vices. The opposite of the gullible, he is usually the hard-nosed skeptic. He is the person who can smell a rat a mile away, who takes

---

This article appeared in *Religious Humanism,* Winter 1975.

everything with a grain of salt, and who is often difficult to convince. He is usually "from Missouri," has a look of disbelief when faced with humbug, tends to shrug his shoulders, shake his head, and exclaim "in a pig's eye!" If he is French, he is likely to roll his eyeballs up and, with a sigh of disgust, mutter under his breath, "Merde!" Or if he is from the Bronx the response he emits is popularly known as the raspberry. The contrast between the gullible and skeptical is that between *instant recall* (repeating what you have been taught) and *instant recoil* (being reluctant to assimilate). As Thomas Hobbes said about bitter pills, if swallowed whole they go down easily, but if chewed over, they are instantly spit up.

The skeptical person asks for proof and demands evidence; he tests claims by how well they work out in practice. His antidote for the original sin is critical analysis; it is difficult and demanding, for we are forever prey to temptation. The mind is often weak—how delicious to be gulled into belief. The skeptic is more hoax-proof; but, as I said, it is not easy.

Some people believe that education and a good dose of book learning is the only cure for gullibility. These are important, but there is no guarantee that they will overcome the innate perversity of the will to believe—it depends upon the kind of education we are exposed to. Indeed, some of the most cultivated intellectuals are the most easily gulled by the latest fads and fashions of intellectual snobbery. Men of practical wisdom often are less easily fooled than the sophisticated products of higher learning. There is a kind of native intelligence at work as one goes about the business of living.

Generally people are more easily gulled when they enter unfamiliar ground away from home. There, they are all too willing to throw caution to the wind and leap in, whereas skeptical persons tread carefully, raising difficult, probing questions. It is especially in fields that require a smattering of learning that gullibility is strongest. Historically, the best illustration was religion, though it also applied to science, philosophy, morality, and politics. Nevertheless, religion is notorious because, since it was held sacred, it was especially immune to critical scrutiny by common sense. And there was a great battle between believers and unbelievers—between those who were committed to orthodox dogmas, or received opinions, and the heretics, who were not. Each age has old beliefs deeply ingrained and inculcated generation after generation as the gospel truth by authority and tradition. The gullibles continue to accept received doctrine on the basis of faith and custom. The skeptic questions its veracity.

Historically the term "freethinker" was used to describe a person skeptical of religious claims. The freethinker rejected doctrine that rested upon dogma, revelation, custom, or authority. He held that the individual must investigate—at least in principle—the claims made and then abandon any position whose validity could not be rationally or evidentially demonstrated. A number of epithets, mostly uncomplimentary, have been used by believers to characterize freethinkers in the historic debate. (I should not say "debate," because for a long time they burned freethinkers at the stake.) They were the doubters, dissenters, nonconformists, heretics, agnostics, atheists — or, in stronger language, infidels, apostates, miscreants, recusants (those who refuse to comply with or conform to religious regulations or practices), nullifidians (persons of no faith or religion), minimifidians (irreligious unbelievers), or just plain backsliders.

At the turn of the century the term "rationalist" was often used interchangeably with "freethinker," pointing to those who attempted to ground religious and other beliefs on reason. More recently, the term "humanist" has been used to designate those individuals who are skeptical of religious faith; it is supposed to be a code word or a more polite term for "atheist," a word that is still considered to be in bad taste. Most humanists generally resist the simple equation of atheism and humanism, for atheism connotes a negative rejection, whereas the humanist claims to have a positive ethical philosophy. Indeed some postmodern humanists define humanism preeminently in ethical terms. Nevertheless, I submit that, whatever else he may be, the humanist is at root a skeptic; and his natural tendency is to combat gullibility wherever it occurs.

## II

When I say that the humanist is committed to reason, I mean in two ways: first for judging descriptive, cognitive, or explanatory truth claims; and second — far more controversial — for making normative or ethical evaluative and prescriptive judgments. And, once embodied in one's life and culture it has an attitudinal effect on the whole person, in creating an active disposition.

Humanists, with freethinkers, rationalists, and atheists, have invariably been skeptical about classical religious theism. Thus humanism, more often than not, is in opposition to the claims of supernaturalists concerning the existence of God. Actually, humanists have been skeptical about a whole range of religious phenomena: miracles and revelation, biblical truths, mysticism, immortality of the soul, and personal survival.

In every age there are people of overweening faith, insisting that this, that, or something else is absolutely true, ultimately real, and the source of salvation, even though it transcends the limits of ordinary understanding or evidence. Today, we are deluged by a whole series of new sects, cults, and practices, including demon-possession, exorcism, witchcraft, astrology, occultism, Krishna cults, scientology, dianetics, UFOs, and paranormal phenomena.

People ask: Are we witnessing a revolt against reason? One reads in the *New York Times*:

> The Nichiren Shoshu is one of several Eastern sects that have become popular in this country in the last few years, which teaches that by chanting certain

phrases, the believer can put himself in tune with the basic vibrations of the universe and obtain blessings ranging from spiritual peace to material objects, such as cars and refrigerators . . . The sect claiming 200,000 members in North and South America, numbered less than 100 in 1960. . . . 11,000 persons attended a parade and religious convention in San Diego. . . . [April 14, 1974]

Similarly, in Houston at the Astrodome, the followers of the Maharaj Ji assembled to proclaim his special knowledge; they claim to be eight million strong in the world. Has the progressive, scientific, naturalistic, and humanistic outlook been abandoned? Sir John Eccles, Nobel Prize laureate and brain scientist at the State University of New York at Buffalo, is distressed by the current intellectual scene. He believes we may be experiencing the demise of Western civilization without being aware of it, with the emergence of these cults of unreason. Stephen Toulmin ("The Alexandrian Trap," *Encounter,* January 1974) raises the same fears: After three centuries are we witnessing the end of the Enlightenment and the defeat of science? Or is it rather, as I suspect, that our perverse streak — gullibility — which requires battling in every age, is reappearing? With the collapse of the traditional orthodox religions, many people tend to grasp new faiths and new cults. Still, I find no real difference between the earlier sects of Christianity, Islam, the nineteenth-century Mormonism of Joseph Smith, the Christian Science of Mary Baker Eddy, Jehovah's Witnesses, or Rosicrucians, on the one hand, and some present-day excesses, on the other. What is the difference between a myth based on the life of a poor itinerant carpenter in Galilee and the cult of a teen-age guru in a silver Rolls Royce? A cult is a nontraditional mystery religion or rite for the initiated, one not yet accepted by the establishment. Once it is adopted, it becomes an established religion. But most of today's religions were yesterday's cults; they all strain credulity. I am afraid that cults and sects will probably remain a permanent part of the social landscape, for they seem to fill a deep psychological need: a search for meaning, identity, security, certainty, and hope in a changing and puzzling world.

## III

If the humanist is a skeptic, what are his grounds for belief? My answer is that they are the same as those used by ordinary men in everyday life, as he tests the claims close to him. The scientific method is common sense extended and formalized by scientists and logicians. Yet these are not different in kind, only in elaboration and rigor. I should perhaps use the term "nongullibility" to describe a responsible and objective procedure by which we test truth claims in many areas of life. I mean here that our beliefs should be based on evidence, that they should be logically consistent, and that they should be tested by their predictive consequences.

Where we do not have sufficient supporting data or reasons, we ought to suspend or withhold judgment. We should be doubtful of whatever has not been adequately verified. Skepticism and agnosticism, accordingly, are important responses for areas in which we do not, as yet, have sufficient evidence. On many topics, then, we should have no opinion until all the data are in. That UFOs exist is surely possible; that the earth was visited by intelligent beings from other planets is possible. However, I do not find von Däniken's alleged evidence for this thesis convincing.

Of great importance is the "principle of fallibilism." Beliefs should be taken as tentative hypotheses, no more than probable, open to revision in the light of new evidence. New facts need to be accounted for, and if they cannot then a theory must be modified. The world view of common sense is often mistaken. We should not be restricted by existing scientific or common-sense explanations of the world. Thus we need to be willing to introduce new theories that go beyond the prevailing perspectives, whether in ordinary life or in the sciences. When I refer to common sense, I simply mean that at some point we need to test our hypotheses by hard evidence. Related to this is the need to keep the door open to inquiry. We should be willing to investigate any area. We should not foreclose future investigation on a priori grounds.

We of course always need to be receptive to creative imagination, new hypotheses, alternative explanations, fresh departures in thought. Subjective intuition and introspection may be important as the source of novel ideas. While they may help to originate ideas, however, they cannot at the same time validate them. It is one thing to have a glimmer of a new possibility; it is another to maintain that therefore it is true. I reiterate, we need continually to check the authenticity of ideas by independent evidence.

## IV

Certain objections have been raised to objective thinking. Critics maintain that the logical-empirical method is arbitrary, excluding by definition whatever cannot meet its antecedent criteria, that this closes off glimpses of the "transcendent" or cuts us off from forms of subjective truths that cannot be known in any other way.

I am perplexed by these objections. We should not dogmatically preclude any kind of knowledge. As I have already indicated, we must always leave the door open to unsuspected possibilities; we must always be prepared for new dimensions in experience and thought. Undoubtedly, our knowledge of the universe is meager, given the vast infinity of space and events. Of course, there are many things we do not now know that we will uncover in the future. We must not insist that our present world view or the existing categories of our understanding are final. But when all is said and done, however, we still have the question of where we go from here. What options are proposed? Which beliefs shall we accept? The only approach to take is a practical and responsible one: let us weigh claims as they are introduced. If someone claims to have a new belief or theory, a new body of facts, a new kind of expanded consciousness, let us examine it carefully. Perhaps he *has* discovered something. But then we must examine not only his experience or findings but also his *interpretations* and explanations of them. In all such matters, I would be at a loss to know how to proceed—*unless* the proponent of a "new truth" is clear about what he means and allows us to check his findings by reference to the experience of others. We should always be willing to investigate new visions of the universe and pose new questions, but nothing can be accepted as true until it is supported by responsible evidence. That is all that the skeptic or freethinker or humanist asks of the believer. Is it too much?

Heightened subjective awareness, mystical experiences, feelings of reverence or awe, powerful emotional states are all part of human life, and we should not seek to denude life of them. But we should also not delude ourselves about what they mean unless and until we can certify or validate the claims for them. There is always lurking, as I have said, a danger that our perverse tendency to gullibility will overwhelm us. There are large areas of the unknown that may await further explanation; but let us proceed to investigate them without prematurely announcing what they portend. For example, we should be willing to investigate extrasensory perception and paranormal phenomena—without drawing premature claims, on the basis of sketchy evidence, as to what they mean about man or the universe.

## V

Thus far we have been discussing descriptive claims about the world and examining how to analyze and appraise their veracity. But there is a whole area of life where what is at stake is not what we believe but what we ought to value or do, how we ought to live. Again, humans have a tendency to rush in—to follow astrology, go on a crash diet, enroll in an encounter group or devote one's life to God, country, socialism, or sexual hedonism.

We are living through a moral revolution that in many respects is a humanistic revolution. Among its values are: a new sense of individual freedom and the need to humanize alienating institutions, to actualize human potential, to recognize the equal rights of all groups in society, to extend participatory democracy to a whole range of social institutions, and to build a genuine world community.

Many people representing different points of view today claim to be humanistic in their concern. The question that I want to raise is whether and to what degree reason can intervene. Can objective criteria play a role in warranting value judgments?

This is a highly complex area, for the moral life is full of feeling and passion, impulse and habit.

We surely recognize that there are important uses for reason in ordinary life. Whatever one's values or norms, it is possible to avoid stupid mistakes, foolish or impetuous action, and to use practical reason to control life, moderate desires, mollify passions, and direct activity. Thus we say that some people are reasonable. They have good, plain sense and sound judgment; they manifest prudence and foresight. They are level-headed, sensible, thoughtful, sagacious, experienced, or deliberate in making choices.

On the other hand, gullibility in belief has its counterpart in action. Some people are foolish, irrational, imprudent, impetuous, artless, or inexperienced in their conduct. They manifest a notable lack of wisdom in life. They may bungle and botch, blunder and fumble in their choices. They are, if extreme, muddle-headed, mutton-headed, thickskulled, fatheaded, boneheaded, noodle-headed, or empty-headed! These are the people who cannot see an inch before their noses, or are willing to cut off their nose to spite their face; they don't have enough sense to come in out of the rain, or they invariably put the cart before the horse. They are penny-wise and pound-foolish, don't know their elbow from a hole in the ground, are apt to go on wild-goose chases, have too many irons in the fire, play with fire, buy a pig in a poke, count their chickens before they hatch; they tend to bark up the wrong tree or carry coals to Newcastle. They are, if you will, the nincompoops of this world!

## VI

What I am trying to suggest by this string of synonyms and cliches is that there is a kind of critical intelligence in judging values and making choices: in buying a house, selecting a mate, taking a trip to Florida, or studying for an examination. There is, if you will, a practical logic of decision making that we all recognize. This is analogous, in part, at least, to the use of objective intelligence in formulating beliefs about the world. What are its characteristics in outline?

First, practical intelligence seeks to define values, ends, and goals, to understand wants and needs, to be clear about interests and ideals.

Second, it seeks to ground choices to some extent in a knowledge of the context of action, an inquiry into the circumstances of the situation, the facts of the case. We cannot make intelligent choices unless we know what is at stake, and this includes knowledge of the causal determinants of the present state of affairs.

Third, there is a process of deliberation in which judgments are examined and evaluated, in part by their consistency with other values that we hold.

Fourth, this involves an evaluation of the means at our disposal, the alternatives and available options, as well as an appraisal of the probable consequences of one course of action rather than another. In a deliberative process we calculate costs and efficiencies, anticipate likely results, and then decide whether or not an action is worthwhile. Practical intelligence requires both a realistic appraisal of our powers and opportunities, a willingness to engage in creative experiment, and some sense of our limits and constraints.

There is, then, a significant difference between a choice based upon reflective inquiry and one following capricious or impulsive reaction. If I were to locate a second sin, a perverse streak in human nature, it would be moral *nincompoopery*. The contrasting humanist virtue is to eat of the fruit of knowledge of good and evil. Alas, nincompoopery, like gullibility, is also widely distributed among human beings who stoutly resist moral inquiry.

To be committed to a reflective approach to one's values implies some willingness to change, modify, or reconstruct one's values in the light of new facts. This also implies some tolerance of others, a willingness to learn, appreciate, and respect other viewpoints. Its opposite response is dogmatic, intransigent behavior that is unenlightened, hidebound, opinionated, or, if you will, pigheaded! A person reflective about morality generally does not consider his values absolute and eternal, but recognizes that they are open to criticism and may require reexamination and justification. Hence, moral ideals should be treated as hypotheses or guiding principles, to be judged by experience and reason. When our values are based upon a false picture of the world or are patently inconsistent, we should be willing to modify them. Given such an alternative, we are more apt to be willing to find common ground with others, negotiate differences, and frame a new basis for compromise.

## VII

For the humanist, all of this points to the *autonomy of ethics*. (Sidney Hook, the humanist philosopher, considers this to be the prime definition of humanism.) Moral judgments should not be derived from antecedent theological, metaphysical, or ideological premises but need to be worked out and formulated independently in the light of reflective inquiry. The main quarrel humanists have had with orthodox religionists has been precisely on this point: the need to liberate moral judgment from undue ecclesiastical or political authority, legislative authorities, rules, and laws.

Does humanism have its own unique first principles beyond its commitment to inquiry? I am dubious of first principles, from which we derive basic values. If one rejects false notions of a providential universe and immortality, then the good life and happiness is a human goal; this includes the satisfaction of basic needs and creative actualization. But the humanist does not seek to impose a set of values to suppress individuals. The good and the right begin, as John Stuart Mill said, with existing human desires and wants. Reason, as a constitutive principle, intervenes in the processes of human valuing, seeking to revise them and negotiate possible differences in the light of intelligent appraisals.

Given the great pace of social and technological change in postindustrial society, the old morality cannot always be easily stretched. Only new moral principles, appropriate to present desires and future needs, seem appropriate. Only critical intelligence can help us clear our way into new terrain.

It is apparent that it is possible to be a humanist in the sense of helping develop a new morality without being a humanist in the sense of being a skeptic in religion. Secular humanists have many allies within the churches in their efforts to mold a new morality. Similarly, one can be a skeptic in religion but intransigent in one's moral values; some secular humanists are authoritarian in morality. Thus there are two senses of humanism: one in regard to belief and the other in regard to values. (I must also point out that many so-called ethical humanists often get carried away by emotion. One can be committed to "humanistic values" in an unthinking and fanatic way. I have in mind certain excesses in humanistic psychology and education: for example, those who emphasize affective education and ignore cognitive development, or stress freedom and ignore self-discipline, or are against hangups, yet ignore social responsibility. They are all too often moved more by passion and rhetoric than by reason.)

If, as I have argued, the basic element in the humanist point of view is the use of critical intelligence in belief and action, then there can be no absolute or final values (not even those that we presently defend) but rather a constant process of inquiry. Of central significance is the importance of cognitive and moral education for children and young adults. The schools should attempt to teach children how to think, how to detect deception, how to avoid gullibility, and also how to engage in moral reflection. The most appropriate kind of moral education is that which emphasizes awareness, inquiry, growth, not one that seeks to impose values or inculcate virtues as the be-all and end-all of moral instruction. The colleges and universities have a vital role here too: in education in the liberating arts—humanistic and scientific—in order to keep alive the sense of wonder, to expand the horizons of knowledge, to be able to formulate critical value judgments.

## VIII

Thus humanism is not to be defended simply as the equivalent of a set of epistemological principles. For although an essential characteristic of humanism is its commitment to objective criteria of knowledge, the difference between the statement of epistemological metaethical criteria and humanism is that the latter involves a *commitment* to a set of rules of evidence and validation that is *normative*. In other words humanism is basically, whether in epistemology or ethics proper, a normative *ethical* posture, which seeks to ground knowledge and values on autonomous grounds, to judge all truth claims by reference to independent reasons, and to develop the free mind. If epistemological principles are developed in a purely intellectual sphere, they are apt to lack all conviction. Only when they are embodied in the whole personality and culture, and rooted deeply within the psychology of motivation and action, can they inspire conviction and force. People need to be inoculated against gullibility, but unless reason is ingrained in their psychological makeup they are liable to get tripped.

Humanism, then, is first and foremost a normative ethical posture. In the best sense, this form of ethical humanism expresses high ideals that can move people to aspire. What higher constitutive normative principle of individual and social life is there than a commitment to reason? We need to point out, however, that the commitment to reason in any culture requires continuing efforts and that the achievement of the previous generation will not necessarily prevail in the next, given the powerful natural impulse toward gullibility and nincompoopery.

# 24

# The Psychology of Belief

T here are those who deplore humanism's vigorous criticism of religion and the paranormal. They would prefer humanism to take a more restrained, ecumenical posture. They wish us to be receptive to the "nuances of the religious life," the possibilities of "intuitive and mystical truths," the unlocking of the "paranormal mysteries" of the universe.

One can appreciate their concern. We are committed to the use of reason and evidence in evaluating claims to knowledge, but this does not mean that we can legislate, before inquiry, what is true or false. One must always be open to unsuspected possibilities, novel theories, new kinds of discovery. The history of science vividly demonstrates the fact that revolutions in thought can overturn even well-established beliefs, and that ideas once rejected may eventually be verified.

To recognize the inherent fallibilism of the existing body of knowledge does not mean, however, that one should abandon all caution in appraising truth claims. Nor can one argue that, since some things now held to be true on the basis of conjecture *may* be confirmed in the future, one should be entitled to believe *anything* and also be immune to critical scrutiny.

The attack on rationalism and science as being "oppressive" because it demands support for such truth claims is puzzling. To ask for the abandonment of rational and evidential criteria raises the question of what one would substitute in its place? Faith? Passion? Commitment? Action? We have heard these familiar suggestions before. Faith by itself, in opposition to reason, is irrational. *Whose* faith? One can be deeply committed to a set of ideas, but how does one know that they are true? Passion, commitment, and action are surely part of human life, but they cannot be used to verify beliefs. Surely we need to deal with the whole person, not simply his intellect. Reason is only one part of experience and, as such, should not be allowed to denude or destroy our passionate concerns.

Yet if we are to hold beliefs, we wish them to be reliable; otherwise we are merely deluding ourselves. The creative human imagination is essential for extending the range of knowledge. But we can intuit a virtually unlimited number of fanciful hypotheses. The question is always: Which hypotheses

---

This appeared in *The Humanist,* May/June 1977.

are true, and which false? And the only way to decide is to confront the hypotheses with the standards of evidence and reason. All of this seems quite elementary to students of logic and common sense.

Yet increasingly today we are exposed to the opposite point of view; we are virtually overwhelmed by proreligious and proparanormal propaganda. The voice of the skeptic is all too often drowned out by a vast babble of gullible tongues.

Television, radio, films, and the press pour a steady torrent of fraudulent ideas into the marketplace. The mass media today are the most potent source of information for the American people. Their presentations are often based not on truth but on whether they will sell. A book proclaiming an outrageous belief will be heavily promoted. To increase ratings, television networks sensationalize the occult as additives to their raucous fare of violence, comedies, and game shows.

The continuing astrology craze graphically illustrates the problem. The "Objections to Astrology" statement, signed by 186 leading scientists, including nineteen Nobel Prize recipients (*The Humanist,* Sept./Oct. 1975) was sent to every newspaper in the United States and Canada. It pointed out that there was no empirical basis for popular astrology and that the 1,250 out of 1,500 newspapers in the United States that publish such columns were, in effect, deceiving their readers. Since then, even the leading astrologers' associations in the United States have issued a similar statement agreeing, at least in part, with our indictment. Sun-sign horoscopes, they said, were not reliable. In spite of the fact that both astronomers and astrologers agree, very few (if any) newspapers have dropped their astrology columns; the reason, no doubt, is their popularity with the readers.

A cause for dismay is the fact that superstitious ideas long since thought dead now reappear with a vengeance. The "psychic revolution" exemplifies this. How can beliefs that are actually shown to be false and are grossly contradictory or lack sufficient evidence still exert such an influence? Perhaps we need to know more about the psychology of belief. Beliefs do not function simply as cognitive statements about reality. They are organically interwoven in a psycho-biological context. Beliefs fulfill many human purposes and needs. For many people, it apparently does little good to refute or debunk their beliefs, which may be so deeply ingrained in their makeup that to question these beliefs is to threaten their whole life style. Beliefs become enmeshed in innermost dreams and aspirations, loves and fears, moods and desires. Belief systems, even if inconsistent, may be compelling, breeding psychological states that are self-validating.

Skeptical critiques of patently false beliefs often fall on deaf ears. Although critical intelligence can rid some individuals of false illusions, for others, where there is the passionate desire to believe and to be deceived, such criticism may have little or no effect.

Some ethical humanists are disturbed by what they view as the "negativism" of scientific humanism. This charge should be taken seriously. There has been so much to criticize that it has been difficult to let up on attacks. No doubt we have failed in making our positive positions better known. Ethical humanism has enunciated a whole set of constructive ideals. It has defended the ethics of freedom and tolerance, the moral conviction that life can be good, and the ideas that joyful exuberance is possible and that we can create a more democratic society and a world community. We have consistently worked for human rights, women's liberation, abortion, euthanasia, and other progressive goals. But we need to make our positive values better known.

We cannot abandon our commitment to reason (broadly conceived) as a method of testing our beliefs. For when a society abandons all objective standards of knowledge, it opens the door to the development of ideological cults. It is disturbing to realize that the irrationalism of Nazi Germany was preceded by a vast growth of belief in the occult in the Weimar Republic. Some may consider excursions into the occult as "harmless" and the resurgence of fundamentalism as "innocuous." But these primitive reversions may have far-reaching implications. There is always the danger that once irrationality grows it will spill over into other areas of society. The current retreat from reason may have unintended consequences for the future. In breaking down our critical judgment, it may also break down our resistance to new and unforeseen forms of tyranny. There is no guarantee that a society so infected will be resistant to the most virulent programs of new terrorist sects. If beliefs are merely subjective, we have no guarantee that pernicious doctrines will not be heralded and sold to the public as the ultimate road to salvation, nor that a credulous populace, inundated with one wave of nonsense after another, will be able to distinguish truth from fraud and fakery.

# 25

# Is Parapsychology a Science?

## I

An observer of the current scene cannot help but be struck by the emergence of a bizarre new "paranormal world view." How widely held this view is, whether it has penetrated science proper or is simply part of the popular passing fancy, is difficult to ascertain.

Many of those who are attracted to a paranormal universe express an antiscientific, even occult, approach. Others insist that their hypotheses have been "confirmed in the scientific laboratory." All seem to agree that existing scientific systems of thought do not allow for the paranormal and that these systems must be supplemented or overturned. The chief obstacle to the acceptance of paranormal truths is usually said to be skeptical scientists, who dogmatically resist unconventional explanations. The "scientific establishment," we are told, is afraid to allow free inquiry because its own position and bias would be threatened. New Galileos are waiting in the wings, but supposedly they are being suppressed by the establishment and labeled "pseudoscientific." Yet it is said that by rejecting the paranormal we are resisting a new paradigm of the universe (à la Thomas Kuhn) that will prevail in the future.

Unfortunately, the meaning of the term "paranormal" is often unclear. Literally, it refers to that which is *beyond* the normal range of data or experience. Sometimes "the paranormal" is used as an equivalent of "the bizarre," "the mysterious," or "the unexpected." Some use it to refer to phenomena that have no known natural causes and that transcend normal experience and logic. The term here has been used synonymously with "the supernormal," "the supernatural," or "the miraculous." These definitions, of course, leave little room for science. Granted, there are many areas at the present time that are unknown; yet one cannot on a priori grounds, antecedent to inquiry, seek to define the parameters of investigation by maintaining that something is irreducibly unknowable or inexplicable in any conceivable scientific terms.

Some use the term "paranormal" to refer to that which is abnormal or anomalous, that is, to things that happen infrequently or rarely. But there are

This essay is based on a talk delivered at the Smithsonian Institution, April 1978, and was published in *The Skeptical Inquirer,* Winter 1978.

many accidental or rare events that we wouldn't ordinarily call paranormal—a freak trainwreck, a lightning strike, or a meteor shower.

Some use the term "paranormal" simply to refer to the fact that some phenomena cannot be given a physical or materialistic explanation. In some scientific inquiries, physicalist or reductionist explanations are, indeed, not helpful or directly relevant—as, for example, in many social-science studies, where we are concerned with the function of institutions, or in historical studies, where we may analyze the influence of ideas or values on human affairs. But this surely does not mean that they are "nonnatural," "unnatural," or "paranormal"; for ideas and values have a place in the executive order of nature, as do flowers, stones, and electrons. Although human institutions and cultural systems of beliefs and values may be physical at root, they are not necessarily explainable in function as such. There seem to be levels of organization; at least it is convenient to treat various subject matters in terms of concepts and hypotheses relative to the data at hand. To say this, in no way contravenes the physical laws of nature as uncovered in the natural sciences.

The term "paranormal," however, has also been used in parapsychology, where something seems to contradict some of the most basic assumptions and principles of the physical, biological, or social sciences and a body of expectations based on ordinary life and common sense. C. D. Broad pointed out a number of principles that parapsychologists would apparently wish to overthrow: (1) future events cannot affect the present *before* they happen (backward causation); (2) a person's mind cannot effect a change in the material world without the intervention of some physical energy or force; (3) a person cannot know the content of another person's mind except by the use of inferences based on experience and drawn from observations of his speech or behavior; (4) we cannot directly know what happens at distant points in space without some sensory perception or energy of it transmitted to us; (5) discarnate beings do not exist as persons separable from physical bodies.[1] These general principles have been built up from a mass of observations and should not be abandoned unless and until there is evidence that would make their rejection less likely than their acceptance—if I may paraphrase David Hume.[2] Nevertheless, those who refer to the "paranormal" believe that they have uncovered a body of empirical facts that call into question precisely those principles. Whether or not they do remains to be seen by the course of future inquiry. These scientific principles are not sacred and may one day need to be modified—but only if the empirical evidence makes it necessary.

Some who use the term "paranormal" refer to a range of anomalous events that are inexplicable in terms of our existing scientific concepts and theories. Of course, there are many events not now understood. For example, we do not know fully the cause of cancer, yet we would hardly call it paranormal. There have been many reports of loud explosions off the Atlantic coast that remain unexplained and that some have hinted are "paranormal." (These may be due to methane gas, test flights, or distant sonic booms.) If we were to use the term "paranormal" to refer to that which is inexplicable in terms of current scientific theory, with the addition that it cannot be explained without major revisions of our scientific theory, this would mean that any major advance in science, prior to its acceptance, might be considered "paranormal." But then new developments in quantum theory or relativity theory, the DNA breakthrough, or the germ theory of disease could have been called paranormal before their discovery. There are many puzzles in science and there is a constant need to revise our theories; each new stage in science waiting to be verified surely cannot be called "paranormal."

In actuality, the term "paranormal" is without clear or precise meaning; its use continues to suggest to many the operation of "hidden," "mysterious," or "occult" forces in the universe. But this, in the last analysis, may only be a substitute for our ignorance of the causes at work. Although I have used the term because others have done so, I think it ought to be dispensed with as a meaningless concept.

## II

It is clear that science is continually changing and growing. As new facts are discovered, existing concepts and theories must either be extended to account for them or abandoned in favor of new and more comprehensive explanations.

In the current context, any number of new fields have recently appeared alongside the established sciences. These begin with a number of alleged anomalous events that proponents say cannot be readily explained in terms of the existing sciences. One may ask: Do these subjects qualify as sciences? One must always be open to the birth of new fields of inquiry. At first a new or proto science may be rejected by the existing body of scientific opinion; but in time, if it can make its case, it may be accepted as genuine. This has been a familiar phenomenon, as new branches of inquiry emerge in the natural, social, and behavioral sciences. Unfortunately, not all of the claimants to scientific knowledge are able to withstand critical scrutiny, and many turn out to be pseudo or false sciences.

A classical illustration of this is phrenology, which swept Europe and America in the nineteenth century. It was formulated by F. J. Gall, and developed by his followers J. K. Spurzheim and G. Combe. According to the phrenologist: (1) the brain was the organ of the mind; (2) the mental powers of men could be distinguished and assigned to separate innate faculties; (3) these faculties had their seat in a definite region of the brain surface; (4) the size of each region is the measure to which the faculty forms a constituent element in the character of the individual; (5) the correspondence between the outer surface of the skull and the brain surface beneath it is sufficiently close to permit the scientific observer to ascertain the relative

sizes of these organs by an examination of the head; and (6) such an examination provided a method by which the disposition and character of the
subject could easily be ascertained. The theory was allegedly based on empirical observations from which generalizations were formulated. Gall and his
associates examined the heads of their friends, men of genius, and inmates
of jails and asylums in order to map the "organs" of intelligence, murder, sexual passions, theft, and so on. The theory seems quite silly to us today—not
that behavioral functions may not be correlated in some way with regions of
the brain. But it is ridiculous to assert that they could be mapped by examining the exterior skull. Yet so great a degree of popularity did phrenology
enjoy that in 1832 there were twenty-nine phrenology societies in Great
Britain alone, and several phrenology journals in America and Britain—all
of which have disappeared.[3]

The term "pseudoscience" has been used in many ways. One must be
careful not to indiscriminately apply it to budding fields of inquiry that may
have some merit. Perhaps it should be used for those subjects that clearly
(1) do not utilize rigorous experimental methods in their inquiries, (2) lack
a coherent, testable conceptual framework, (3) assert that they have achieved
positive results, though their tests are highly questionable and their generalizations have not been corroborated by impartial observers.

There are a great number of candidates for pseudoscience today, many
of them ancient specialties that still persist: numerology, palmistry, oneiro-
mancy, moleosophy, aleuromancy, apantomancy, psychometry. And new
ones constantly appear. Perhaps some may in time develop testable and
tested theories.

Astrology—which had all but died out by 1900 and is now very strong—
is a good illustration of a pseudoscience. The principles of astrology remain
largely unchanged from the days of Ptolemy (first century after Christ),
who codified the ancient craft. And astrologers still cast their horoscopes
and do their analyses very much as Ptolemy did, in spite of the fact that its
original premises have been contradicted by modern post-Newtonian
physics and astronomy. Most astrologers have considered astrology to be an
occult field of paranormal study; others have attempted to develop it as a
science. Yet astrology does not use rigorous experimental standards of
inquiry by which it can reach conclusions; it lacks a coherent theory of what
is happening and why; and it draws inferences and makes predictions that
are highly dubious. Michel Gauquelin is a critic of traditional astrology on
these grounds, though he has attempted to develop his own field of astro-
biology. Based on careful statistical analysis, he has attempted to correlate
personality characteristics with planetary configurations. Thus, for example,
he maintains that there is a relationship between the position of Mars and
the time and place of birth of sports champions. Thus far, the results of his
study, in my judgment, are inconclusive, though his procedure is far different
from the usual approach of astrologers.

Biorhythm appears to be another false science. It also claims to have its foundation in empirical data; yet when independent examination is made to see whether its predictions are accurate, the results appear to be negative.

## III

What are we to say about parapsychology? Is it a science or a pseudoscience?

Interest in psychic phenomena appears throughout human history, with reports abounding from ancient times to the present. A fund of anecdotal material—premonitions that seem to come true, apparent telepathic communication between friends or relatives, reports of encounters with discarnate persons, and so on—leads many people to believe that there is some basis for psi phenomena. It has been a century since the Society for Psychical Research was founded in 1882 in England by a distinguished group of psychologists and philosophers (including William James and Henry Sidgwick), who were hopeful of getting results from their careful inquiries. In October 1909, William James, a president of the Society, wrote "The Last Report: Final Impressions of a Psychical Researcher," summarizing his experiences.[4] The Society, he said, was founded with the expectation that if the material of "psychic" research were treated rigorously and experimentally then objective truths would be elicited. James reported:

> Like all founders, Sidgwick hoped for a certain promptitude of results; and I heard him say, the year before his death, that if anyone had told him at the outset that after twenty years he would be in the same identical state of doubt and balance that he started with, he would have deemed the prophecy incredible.

Yet James relates that his experiences had been similar to Sidgwick's.

> For twenty-five years I had been in touch with the literature of psychical research, and have had acquaintance with numerous "researchers." I have also spent a good many hours (though far fewer than I ought to have spent) in witnessing (or trying to witness) phenomena. Yet I am theoretically no "further" than I was at the beginning; and I confess that at times I have been tempted to believe that the Creator had eternally intended this department of nature to remain *baffling,* to prompt our curiosities and hopes and suspicions all in equal measure, so that, although ghosts and clairvoyances, and raps and messages from spirits, are always seeming to exist and can never be fully explained away, they also can never be susceptible of full corroboration.

> The peculiarity of the case is just that there are so many sources of possible deception in most of the observations that the whole lot of them *may* be worthless . . . Science meanwhile needs something more than bare possibilities to build upon; so your genuinely scientific inquirer . . . has to remain unsatisfied. . . . So my deeper belief is that we psychical researchers have been

too precipitate with our hopes, and that we must expect to mark progress not by quarter-centuries, but by half-centuries or whole centuries.

Almost three-quarters of a century have elapsed since James's comments. Has any progress been made? Since that time psychic research has given way to parapsychology, especially under the leadership of J. B. Rhine and the establishment of his experimental laboratory. Where before there were only a handful of researchers, now there are many more. We may ask: Where does parapsychology stand today? I must point out that many researchers, both within and outside the field, are not much further along than before.

One thing is clear: many researchers today at least attempt to apply experimental methods of investigation. This was not always the case; and the field today, as then, has been full of deception—conscious or unconscious—perhaps more than most fields of inquiry. There have been a host of fraudulent psychics and researchers, including the Fox sisters (who were hailed as mediums, in whose presence raps were heard during seances, but who admitted they had learned how to crack their toe knuckles); Blackburn and Smith (who deceived scientists into believing that telepathic communication occurred between them); Margery Crandon and Eustasia Palladino (both shown to be fraudulent mediums); the Soal-Goldney experiments on precognition (experiments now in disrepute); Walter J. Levy (who was exposed for faking the evidence on animal ESP at Durham in 1974); and Uri Geller, Jean Girard, and Ted Serios (whose alleged abilities in psychokinesis and psychic photography are open to charges of trickery). Even some of the most sophisticated scientists have been taken in by illusionists posing as psychics. In spite of this, there *are* many parapsychologists today who are at least *committed* to careful scientific inquiry—as Rhine's work illustrates—and the use of rigorous laboratory methods. Whether they ever achieve it is not always clear, and critics are constantly finding loopholes in their methodology.

What about the results? Are the hypotheses proposed by parapsychology testable? Have they been tested? Here there are also wide areas for dispute. Skeptics are especially unimpressed by the findings and believe that parapsychology has not adequately verified its claims—even though some parapsychologists believe that ESP, precognition, and psychokinesis have been demonstrated and need no further proof. I reiterate that, since the chief claims of parapsychology in these areas contravene the basic principles of both science and ordinary experience, it is not enough to point to a body of data that has been assembled over the years; the data must be *substantial.* This does not deny that there seems to be some evidence that certain individuals in some experiments are able to make correct guesses at above-chance expectations. The basic problem, however, is the *lack of replicability* by other experimenters. Apparently, a few experimenters are able to get similar results, but most are unable to do so. The subject matter is elusive. It is rare for a skeptic to be able to replicate results, but it is even relatively rare for a *believer* in psi to get positive results. The problem of replicability has been dismissed by some parapsychologists who maintain that their findings *have* been replicated. But have they? The point is that we cannot predict *when* or *under what conditions* above-chance calls will be made (with, for example, Zener cards, in precognitive dream labs, in remote-viewing testing situations). There is much more likely to be negative results.

One explanation offered by parapsychologists for the difficulty in replication refers to the well-known "sheep/goat" distinction of Gertrude Schmeidler—that is, that those with a positive attitude toward psi (sheep) will get better results than those with a negative attitude (goats). Similar considerations are said to apply to the attitude of the experimenter. Is the explanation for this that when the experimenter is a believer he is often so committed to the reality of psi that he tends to weaken experimental controls? If so, perhaps we should distinguish between the donkey and the fox. The skeptic is accused of being so stringent that he dampens the enthusiasm of the subject. Yet parapsychologists Adrian Parker and John Beloff report on experiments at the University of Edinburgh by pro-psi experimenters that consistently score negative results. Most parapsychologists want positive results, but few receive them. Most people don't display ESP; or if a few do, they do so infrequently. And those few that allegedly have the ability eventually seem to lose it.

According to John Beloff:

There is still no repeatable experiment on the basis of which any competent investigator can verify a given phenomenon for himself.[5]

The Rhine revolution . . . proved abortive. Rhine succeeded in giving parapsychology everything it needed to become an accredited science except the essential: the know-how to produce results where required.[6]

Adrian Parker writes:

The present crisis in parapsychology is that there appear to be few if any findings which are independent of the experimenter . . . It still remains to be explained why, if the experiment can be determined by experimenter psi, only a few experiments are blessed with success. Most experimenters want positive results, but few obtain them.[7]

Charles Tart says:

One of the major problems in attempting to study and understand paranormal (psi) phenomena is simply that the phenomena don't work strongly or reliably. The average subject seldom shows any individually significant evidence of psi in laboratory experiments, and even gifted subjects, while occasionally able to demonstrate important amounts of psi in the laboratory, are still very erratic and unpredictable in their performance.[8]

Rhine himself says:

> Psi is an incredibly elusive function! This is not merely to say that ESP and PK have been hard phenomena to demonstrate, the hardest perhaps that science has ever encountered . . . Psi has remained an unknown quantity so long . . . because of a definite characteristic of elusiveness inherent in its psychological nature . . . A number of those who have conducted ESP or PK experiments have reported that they found no evidence of psi capacity . . . Then, too, experimenters who were once successful may even then lose their gift. . . . All of the highscoring subjects who have kept on very long have declined . . .[9]

All of this means not only that parapsychology deals with anomalous events but also that it may be a uniquely anomalous "science," for findings depend upon who the experimenter is. But even that is not reliable and cannot be depended upon. If any other science had the same contingent results, we would rule it out of court. For example, a chemist or biologist could not very well claim that he could get results in the laboratory because he believed in his research, whereas his skeptical colleagues could not because they lacked this belief. We say in science that we search for conditional lawlike statements: namely, that if $a$, then $b$; whenever $a$ is present, $b$ will most likely occur. Yet in viewing the findings of parapsychology, the situation seems to be that we are not even certain that $b$ occurs (since there is a dispute about the reliability of the experiments). Moreover, we don't know what $a$ is, or if it is present that $b$ would occur; $b$ may occur sometimes, but only infrequently. A high degree of replicability is essential if parapsychology is to be called a science. Some sciences may be exempt from the replicability criterion, but only if their findings do not contradict the general conceptual framework of scientific knowledge, which parapsychology seems to do. According to the parapsychologist, for example, ESP seems to be independent of space and does not weaken with distance; precognition presupposes backward causation; psychokinesis violates the conservation-of-energy law.

It is not enough for a parapsychologist to tell the skeptic that *he,* the parapsychologist, on occasion has replicated the results. This would be like the American Tobacco Institute insisting that, based on its experiments, cigarette smoking does not cause cancer. The neutral scientist needs to be able to replicate results in his own laboratory. Esoteric, private truth claims need to be rejected in science. Until any scientist under similar conditions can get the same results, then we must indeed be skeptical. Viewing what some parapsychologists have considered to be replication often raises all sorts of doubts. In the 1930s, S. G. Soal attempted to replicate the findings of Dr. Rhine in Britain in regard to clairvoyance and telepathy. He tested 160 subjects, always with negative results, indeed with results far below mean-chance expectations. After the tests were completed, he reviewed the data and thought he had found a displacement effect in two cases, which he considered evidence for precognition (that is, above-chance runs in regard to one or two cards before and after the target). Soal then went on to test these two subjects, Basil Shackleton and Gloria Stewart, with what seemed to be amazing results. These results have often been cited in the parapsychological literature as providing strong proof for the existence of ESP. In 1941, in collaboration with the Society for Psychical Research, Soal designed an experiment with Shackleton that included forty sittings over a two-year period. Among the people who participated were C. D. Broad, professor of philosophy at Cambridge, H. H. Price of Oxford, C. A. Mace, C. E. M. Hansel, and others. Broad described the experiment as follows:

> . . . Dr. Soal's results are outstanding. The precautions taken to prevent deliberate fraud or the unwitting conveyance of information by normal means . . . [are] seen to be absolutely water-tight.[10]

> There can be no doubt that the events described happened and were correctly reported; that the odds against chance-coincidence piled up to billions to one . . .[11]

On the basis of his work in precognitive research, Soal was awarded a doctorate of science from the University of London. Even Rhine described the Soal-Goldney experiment as "one of the most outstanding researches yet made in the field . . . Soal's work was a milestone in ESP research."[12]

C. E. M. Hansel found, on the contrary, that the Soal-Goldney experiments were full of holes, and he suggested the high results might be due to collusion between the experimenters and/or the participants, especially in the scoring procedures.[13] Broad responded to "Hansel and Gretel," denying the possibility of fraud. It now seems clear that Hansel was correct. And even parapsychologists now doubt the authenticity of these famous experiments. In a recent publication of the Society for Psychical Research, Betty Markwick reported that there is substantial evidence that extra digits were inserted into the "random number" sequences prepared by Soal to determine the targets in the Shackleton tests. These insertions coincided with Shackleton's guesses and apparently accounted for the high scores on the record sheets. Interestingly, Soal was present at every session in which the subject recorded high scores. When Soal was absent, Shackleton did poorly and the results were null.[14]

Thus the classical tests usually cited as "proof" of ESP employed improper shuffling and scoring techniques or had other flaws in the protocol. Since then parapsychologists have attempted to tighten test conditions and automate the selection of targets. They now use random-number generators and ganzfeld procedures and design ingenious dream research and remote-viewing experiments.

One might consider the use of random generators in testing situations to be an advance over previous methods, except for the fact that it is still the experimenter who designs and interprets the experiment. Walter J. Levy, who fudged his results, used machines in his testing. No wonder the critic is still skeptical of some recent claims made in this area. Great results have been heralded in ESP dream research. Yet here, too, there are many examples of failed replication. For example, David Foulkes, R. E. L. Masters, and Jean Houston attempted to repeat the results obtained at the Maimonides laboratory with Robert van Castle, a high-scoring subject, but they met with no success at all. Charles Honorton has reported what he considers to be impressive results using ganzfeld techniques (where subjects are deprived of sensory stimulation). To date there have been upward of twenty-five published studies. Approximately a third have been significant, a third ambiguous, and a third nonsignificant. This may sound convincing. But given the sad experience in the past with other alleged breakthroughs, we should be cautious until we can replicate results ourselves. Moreover, we do not know how many negative results go unreported. (I should say that I have never had positive results in any testing of my students over the years.) Parker, Miller, and Beloff in 1976 used the ganzfeld method to test the relation of altered states of consciousness and ESP and reported nonsignificant results:

> A total of over 30 independent tests were conducted on the data without a single significance emerging. Whatever way we look at the results, they not only detract from the reliability of the ganzfeld, but also argue against the view that psychological conditions are the sole mediating variable of the experimenter effect.[15]

Similarly, Targ and Puthoff at the Stanford Research Institute, in widely reported remote-viewing experiments, have allegedly achieved results that have been replicated. But the critic has many unanswered questions about the method of target selection and the procedures for grading "hits." Given their shockingly sloppy work with Uri Geller, Ingo Swann, and other "superpsychics" in the laboratory, the skeptic cannot help but be unconvinced about their claimed results.

## IV

These accounts have been introduced as a general comment on the field of parapsychological research. If parapsychology is to progress, then it will need to answer the concerns of its critics about the reliability of the evidence and the replicability of the results.

But difficulties become even more pronounced when we examine other kinds of inquiries that go on in this field; parapsychological literature contains incredibly naive research reports along with sophisticated ones. A perusal of the parapsychological literature reveals the following topics: clairvoyance, telepathy, precognition, psychokinesis, levitation, poltergeists, materialization, dematerialization, psychic healing, psychometry, psychic surgery, psychic photography, aura readings, out-of-body experiences, reincarnation, retrocognition, tape recordings of the voices of the dead, hauntings, apparitions, life after life, regression to an earlier age, and so on.

We now face a puzzling situation. There has been a marked proliferation of claims of the paranormal in recent years, many of them highly fanciful. Presumably, scientific researchers should not be held responsible for the dramatization of results by fiction writers. Yet in my view some parapsychologists have aided, whether consciously or unconsciously, the breakdown in critical judgment about the paranormal. I have not seen many parapsychologists attempt to discourage hasty generalizations based on their work. There are often extraordinary claims made about psychic phenomena, yet there are no easily determinable objective standards for testing them. Because parapsychologists are interested in a topic and do some research, it is said by some that, ipso facto, it is validated by science. (Lest one think that I am exaggerating, one should consult the *Handbook of Parapsychology,* the most recent comprehensive compilation in the field, which includes discussions of psychic photography, psychic healing, reincarnation, discarnate survival, and poltergeists, among other topics.) Professor Ian Stevenson, for example, of the University of Virginia, is well known for his study of reincarnation. After discussing the case of a young child who his parents think is a reincarnation of someone who had recently died, Stevenson says:

> Before 1960, few parapsychologists would have been willing to consider reincarnation as a serious interpretation of cases of this type . . . Today probably most parapsychologists would agree that reincarnation is at least entitled to inclusion in any list of possible interpretations of the cases, but not many would believe it the most probable interpretation.[16]

Rhine is much more cautious in his judgment and implies that only clairvoyance, precognition, and psychokinesis have been established and that adequate test designs have not been worked out for other areas. If one asks if parapsychology is a genuine science or a pseudoscience, it is important that we know if one is referring to the overall field or to particular areas. Surely the critic is disturbed at the willingness to leap to "occult" explanations in the name of science in some kinds of inquiry.

Although I have no doubt that Rhine is committed to an objective experimental methodology, I have substantive doubts about his views on clairvoyance, precognition, and PK. The problem is that one may question not only the reliability and significance of the data but also the conceptual framework itself. Rhine and others have performed tests in which they maintain that they have achieved above-chance runs. What are we to conclude? Simply *that* and no more. ESP is not a proven fact, only a theory used to explain above-chance runs encountered in the laboratory. Here I submit that the most we can do is simply fall back on an operational definition: ESP is itself an elusive entity; it has no identifiable meaning beyond an operational interpretation. Some researchers prefer the more neutral term "psi," but this still suggests a psychic reality. Of special concern is the concept that parapsychologists often refer to in trying to explain the fact that some subjects have significant below-chance runs — "negative ESP" or "psi-missing" — as if there is a mysterious entity or faculty responsible for both above-chance and below-chance guessing. All this seems to me to beg the question. If ESP is some special function of the mind, then we need *independent* verification that it exists, that is, replicable predictions.

One of the problems with ESP is that parapsychologists have noted a "decline" effect; namely, that even gifted subjects in time lose their alleged ESP ability. At this point, I must confess that I am unable to explain why there are significant above-chance or below-chance runs: to maintain that these are due to psi, present or absent, is precisely what is at issue. A problem for me is how many validated cases we actually have of significant below-chance runs in the laboratory. Rhine mentions some. But are they as numerous as above-chance runs? If so, perhaps the overall statistical frequencies begin to reduce, particularly if parapsychologists stop testing those who have shown psychic ability once they lose their alleged powers. We still need to come up with possible alternative explanations. Some that have been suggested are bias, poor experimental design, fraud, and chance. There may be others.

Rhine's reluctance to accept telepathy because of the difficulty in establishing test conditions is surprising to some. Of all the alleged psi abilities, this seems the most likely. Ordinary experience seems to suggest spontaneous telepathy, especially between persons who know each other very well or live together. If telepathy is ever established, I would want to find the mechanism for it — perhaps some form of energy transmission, though most parapsychologists reject this suggestion, possibly because they are already committed to a mentalistic interpretation of the phenomenon.

There are, as Rhine notes, very serious scientific objections to precognition — the notion that the future can be known beforehand (without reference to normal experience, inference, or imagination). The skeptical scientist believes that, where premonitions come true, coincidence is most likely the explanation. If one examined the number of times premonitions do not come true, the statistics would flatten out. The conceptual difficulty with precognition is that, although allegedly we can know the future by precognition, we can also intervene so that future events may not occur.

Louisa Rhine cites the following case to illustrate this:

It concerns a mother who dreamed that two hours later a violent storm would loosen a heavy chandelier to fall directly on her baby's head lying in a crib below it; in the dream she saw her baby killed dead. She awoke her husband who said it was a silly dream and that she should go back to sleep as she then did. The weather was so calm the dream did appear ridiculous and she could have gone back to sleep. But she did not. She went and brought the baby back to her own bed. Two hours later just at the time she specified, a storm caused the heavy light fixture to fall right on where the baby's head had been — but the baby was not there to be killed by it. [17]

If the future is veridically precognized, how could one act to change it? There are profound logical difficulties with this concept. Some parapsychologists discuss a possible alternative explanation for the event; one parapsychologist suggests (without accepting it himself) that the dream itself might have contained enormous energy that forced the calm weather to change into a storm, which cracked the ceiling holding the light fixture. "This alternative, then, is not precognitive but of the mind-over-matter, or PK variety." [18]

This illustrates a basic problem endemic to parapsychology: the lack of a clearly worked out conceptual framework. Without such a causal theory, parapsychologists can slip from one ad hoc explanation to another. In some cases we cannot say that telepathy is operating; it may be clairvoyance; and in others, if it is not precognition, then psychokinesis may be responsible. I fear that the central hypothesis of parapsychology — that mind is separable from the body and that the "ghost in the machine" can act in uncanny ways — often makes it difficult to determine precisely what, if anything, is happening.

A number of familiar conceptual problems also concern psychokinesis. What would happen to the conservation-of-energy principle if PK were a fact? How can a mental entity cause a physical change in the state of matter? Comparing the alleged evidence for PK with the need to overthrow a basic, well-documented principle of physics is questionable. We read about Rhine's above-chance results in his die-rolling test: the results seem inconclusive. Recently a number of superpsychics, such as Uri Geller and Jean Girard, have made extraordinary claims for PK ability. Unfortunately, they have been uncritically welcomed by some parapsychologists and paraphysicists. Yet such superpsychics have been discredited; what seems to be operating is probably magic and illusion, not psi.

Rhine at times expresses an underlying religious motive:

What parapsychology has found out about man most directly affects religion. By supporting on the basis of experiment the psychocentric concept of personality which the religions have taken for granted, parapsychology has already demonstrated its importance for the field of religion . . . If there were no ESP and PK capacities in human beings it would be hard to conceive of the possibility of survival and certainly its discovery would be impossible . . . The only kind of perception that would be possible in a discarnate state would be extrasensory, and psychokinesis would be the only method of influencing any part of the physical universe . . . Telepathy would seem to be the only means of intercommunication discarnate personalities would have.[19]

Unfortunately, many parapsychologists appear to be committed to belief in psi on the basis of a metaphysical or spiritual world view that they wish to vindicate. Charles Tart, a former president of the American Parapsychological Association, admits this motive. Giving an autobiographical account of why he became interested in parapsychology, he says:

> I found it hard to believe that science could have *totally* ignored the spiritual dimensions of human existence . . . Parapsychology validated the existence of basic phenomena that could partially account for, and fit in with, some of the spiritual views of the universe.[20]

Of course, parapsychologists will accuse the skeptic of being biased in favor of a materialist or physicalist viewpoint and claim that this inhibits him from looking at the evidence for psi or accepting its revolutionary implications. Unfortunately, this has all too often been the case; some skeptics have been unwilling to look at the evidence. This is indefensible. A priori negativism is as open to criticism as a priori wish fulfillment. On the other hand, some constructive skepticism is essential in science. All that a constructive skeptic asks of the parapsychologist is genuine confirmation of his findings and theories, no more and no less.

I should make it clear that I am not denying the possible existence of psi phenomena, remote viewing, precognition, or PK. I am merely saying that, since these claims contravene a substantial body of existing scientific knowledge, in order for us to modify our basic principles—and we must be prepared to do so—the evidence must be *extremely strong*. Unfortunately it is not.

In the last analysis, the only resolution of the impasse between parapsychologists and their critics would come from the *evidence* itself. I submit that parapsychologists urgently need to bring their claims to the most hardheaded group of skeptics they can find. In a recent review, C. P. Snow forcefully argues for this strategy. He admits that there are a good many natural phenomena we don't begin to understand and ought to investigate. Moreover, phenomena exist that have not yet been explained by natural science but which do not contradict it. It is when such phenomena allegedly do so that we should take a hard look. Snow says:

> An abnormal number of all reported paranormal phenomena appear to have happened to holy idiots, fools, or crooks. I say this brutally, for a precise reason. We ought to consider how a sensible and intelligent man would actually behave if he believed that he possessed genuine paranormal powers. He would realize that the matter was one of transcendental significance. He would want to establish his powers before persons whose opinions would be trusted by the intellectual world. If he was certain, for example, that his mind could, without

any physical agency, lift a heavy table several feet, or his own body even more feet, or could twist a bar of metal, then he would want to prove this beyond, as they say in court, any reasonable doubt.

What he would not do is set up as a magician or illusionist, and do conjuring tricks. He would desire to prove his case before the most severe enquiry achievable. It might take a long time before he was believed. But men with great powers often take a long time for those powers to be believed. If this man had the powers which I am stipulating, it probably wouldn't take him any longer to be accepted than it did Henry Moore to make his name as sculptor.

Any intelligent man would realize that it was worth all the serious effort in the world. The rewards would be enormous—money would accrue, if he was interested in money, but in fact he would realize that that was trivial beside having the chance to change the thinking of mankind.

It would now be entirely possible for such a man to have his claims considered with the utmost energy and rigor. For a number of eminent Americans of the highest reputation for integrity and intellectual achievement have set themselves to examine any part of the paranormal campaigns. The group includes first-class philosophers, astronomers, other kinds of scientists and professional illusionists. They are skeptical as they should be. This is too important a matter to leave to people who want to believe. So there they are, the challenge is down. It will be interesting to see if any sensible and intelligent man picks it up.[21]

This, then, is an invitation and a challenge to parapsychologists to bring their findings to the most thoroughgoing skeptics they can locate and have them examine their claims of the paranormal under the most stringent test conditions. If parapsychologists can convince the skeptics, then they will have satisfied an essential criterion of a genuine science: the ability to replicate hypotheses in any and all laboratories and under standard experimental conditions. Until they can do that, their claims will continue to be held suspect by a large body of scientists.

## NOTES

1. C. D. Broad, "The Relevance of Psychical Research to Philosophy," *Philosophy* 24 (1949), pp. 291–309.

2. David Hume, *A Treatise of Human Nature*, 1739; *Enquiry Concerning Human Understanding*, 1748; *The Dialogues Concerning Natural Religion*, 1779.

3. Encyclopaedia Britannica, 11th ed., pp. 534 ff.

4. Gardner Murphy and Robert O. Ballou, eds., *William James on Psychical Research* (New York: Viking, 1960), p. 310.

5. John Beloff, "Parapsychology and Philosophy," *Handbook of Parapsychology*, ed. B. Wolman (New York: Van Nostrand, 1977), p. 759.

6. ——, *Psychological Sciences: A Review of Modern Psychology* (New York: Barnes & Noble, 1973).

7. Adrian Parker, "A Holistic Methodology in Psi Research," *Parapsychology Review* 9 (March–April 1978), pp. 4–5.

8. Charles Tart, "Drug-Induced States of Consciousness," *Handbook of Parapsychology*, p. 500.

9. J. B. Rhine, *The Reach of Mind* (New York: William Sloane, 1947), pp. 187–89.

10. C. D. Broad, "The Experimental Establishment of Telepathic Precognition," *Philosophy* 19 (1944), p. 261.

11. ——, "The Relevance of Psychical Research to Philosophy," reprinted in *Philosophy and Parapsychology*, ed. Jan Ludwig (Buffalo, N.Y.: Prometheus Books, 1978), p. 44.

12. J. B. Rhine, *The Reach of Mind*, p. 168.

13. C. E. M. Hansel, *ESP: A Scientific Evaluation* (New York: Scribner, 1966).

14. Betty Markwick, "The Soal-Goldney Experiments with Basil Shackleton: New Evidence of Data Manipulation," *Proceedings of the Society for Psychical Research* 56 (1978), pp. 250–78; D. J. West, "Checks on ESP Experimenters," *Journal of the Society for Psychical Research* 49 (Sept. 1978), pp. 897–99.

15. Adrian Parker, "A Holistic Methodology in Psi Research," p. 4.

16. Ian Stevenson, "Reincarnation: Field Studies and Theoretical Issues," *Handbook of Parapsychology*, p. 657.

17. L. E. Rhine, "Frequency of Types of Experience in Spontaneous Precognition," *Journal of Parapsychology* 18, no. 2 (1954), p. 199.

18. Douglas Dean, "Precognition and Retrocognition," *Edgar D. Mitchell, Psychic Explorations: A Challenge for Science*, ed. John White (New York: Putnam, 1974), p. 155.

19. J. B. Rhine, *The Reach of Mind*, pp. 209, 214.

20. Charles Tart, *Psi: Scientific Studies of the Psychic Realm* (New York: E. P. Dutton, 1977), pp. vii–viii.

21. C. P. Snow, "Passing Beyond Belief" (a review of *Natural and Supernatural: A History of the Paranormal* by Brian Inglis), *Financial Times*, London (Jan. 28, 1978).

# 26

# The Scientific Attitude versus Antiscience and Pseudoscience

I

There has been a long-standing conflict in the history of culture between science and religion, reason and passion. Theologians have incessantly argued that there are "limits" to scientific inquiry and that it cannot penetrate the "transcendental realm"; and poets have decried deductive logic and the experimental method, which they claim denude experience of its sensuous qualities. The running controversy between the two cultures of science and the humanities is thus familiar.

The classic critique notwithstanding, the scientific enterprise has made remarkable progress in the past three centuries, resolving problems that were allegedly beyond the reach of its methodology; and the scientific revolution, which first began in the natural sciences, has been extended to the biological, social, and behavioral sciences, with enormous benefits to humankind. Since the Enlightenment, it has been commonly believed that with the achievement of universal education the scientific outlook would eventually triumph and would emancipate humankind from superstition. Progress was thought to be correlative with the growth of science.

This confidence in science, however, has been badly shaken in recent years. Even supposedly advanced societies are inundated by cults of unreason and other forms of nonsense. Earlier in this century we witnessed the emergence of fanatic ideological cults, such as Nazism and Stalinism. Today, Western democratic societies are being swept by other forms of irrationalism, often blatantly antiscientific and pseudoscientific in character. There are various manifestations of this new assault on reason.

A good illustration of the trend is the growth of astrology, but it is only the tip of the iceberg. For if one surveys the current state of belief, one finds that large numbers of people are apparently ready to believe in a wide variety of things, however outrageous, without sufficient proof. Even a random cataloging of some of the bizarre cults and gurus illustrates the point: Krishna consciousness, the Maharaj Ji, Aikido, the Maharishi Mahesh Yogi and various forms of transcendental meditation, the Unification Church,

---

This is based on a speech delivered at the founding meeting of the Committee for the Scientific Investigation of Claims of the Paranormal and was published in *The Humanist*, July/Aug. 1976.

the Process, Gurjievians, Zen, Arica, the Children of God and the I-Ching. From the standpoint of the skeptical, scientific humanist, these cults are no more irrational than orthodox religious groups. Why are the preachings of the latest guru more nonsensical than a dead and risen deity, Mohammed's visitation by the angel Gabriel, Joseph Smith and his trek westward, Mary Baker Eddy and Christian Science, Theosophy, the Rosicrucians, or the canonization of saints for alleged miracles? The traditional religions strain the credulity as much as or more than the newer exotic religions imported from Asia, but the former have been around longer and are considered to be part of the established social system. What is apparent is the tenacious endurance of irrational beliefs throughout history down to the present day—and in spite of the scientific revolution.

Take the phenomenon of "nouveau witches," as Marcello Truzzi has called them, and the revival of interest in exorcism. Only a few years ago it would have been rare to have encountered any college student who believed in witches. Yet today, belief in a host of witches and demons, even the devil, has become fashionable in some circles. This is the age of monsters, in which Frankenstein, Dracula, and werewolves become real for impressionable minds. The novel and the film *The Exorcist* stimulated belief in exorcism; and some people were unable to distinguish truth from fiction. Thus we are confronted with a plethora of flourishing myths, cultivated by a profit-seeking publishing and media industry.

All this is symptomatic of the current rejection of reason and objectivity. Whereas a decade ago there was a general consensus that at least some rules of evidence existed, today the very existence of objective criteria for judging truth claims is seriously questioned. One hears over and over again that "one belief is as good as the next" and that there is a kind of "subjective truth" immune to rational or evidential criticism. One even finds proponents of forms of subjectivity among the philosophers of science, those who claim that historical conditions or psychological factors are largely responsible for revolutions in scientific thinking.

The reaction against rigorous standards assumed another form in the 1960s in the assault of the New Left and the counterculture upon the intellect. The current growth of cults of unreason is perhaps only a consequence of that phenomenon. We were told then that we needed to break loose from the demands of logic and evidence, and to "expand our consciousness" by drugs and other methods. Theodore Roszak spelled out such a position in his widely read books *Making of a Counter-Culture* (New York: Doubleday, 1969) and *Unfinished Animal: The Aquarian Frontier and the Evolution of Consciousness* (New York: Harper & Row, 1975).

The counterculture insisted that objectivity was impossible either because of class or professional biases or because we were locked into the categories of our scientific world view. One doesn't hear much criticism today of Marxism but one does hear that the existing scientific outlook is confining.

And so there is an attempt to break out by means of new forms of experience, of which the occult is only a part: mantras, meditation, bioenergetics, yoga, organic gardening, Kirlian photography, and extrasensory perception.

This exists beside another mood that is increasingly evident today—an aversion to technological culture itself. Science and technology are often indiscriminately blamed for the present world situation. We hear on all sides about the dangers of technology: the destruction of the natural ecology, pollution, resource depletion, the misuses of energy, the threat of nuclear power plants, and so on. Many of these concerns are legitimate. Yet the critical stance is often not simply against technology but also against science and scientific research. There are those on the fundamentalist right who still vehemently oppose, on ethical or religious grounds, the teaching of theories of evolution, comparative social-studies courses, and sexual education. But in addition, the scientist is often viewed by some on the left as a kind of demon—if he engages in human experimentation or behavior modification, or if he participates in genetic research or wishes to test the genetic basis of I.Q. And there is a growing body of opinion that views medical doctors and psychiatrists as evil high priests or voodoo men.

We are confronted today with a form of moral righteousness and anti-intellectualism—often bordering on hysteria—that indicts science as dehumanizing, brutalizing, and destructive of human freedom and value. This attitude is paradoxical, for it seems to occur most virulently in affluent societies, where the greatest strides in scientific research and technology have been made.

Should we assume that the scientific revolution, which began in the sixteenth century, is continuous? Or will it be overwhelmed by the forces of unreason? However, the picture I am drawing must not be overstated. Alongside the critics of science are its defenders. And vast resources are plowed into scientific education, research, organizations, and publications. Science is still highly regarded by much of the public.

Indeed, the fact that science is essential to our technological civilization is well recognized by some of the critics of science—which brings me to still another dimension of the growth of irrationality: the proliferation of pseudoscience. Those who are not tempted by the occult can always find chariots of the gods, UFOs, Bermuda triangles, or lost continents to beguile them. The new prophets seek to have their speculative theories cloaked in the mantle of scientific legitimacy; they include von Däniken and those associated with dianetics, Scientology, and recent efforts to develop a "scientific astrology."

The growth of pseudoscience can be seen in many other areas. There is, for example, an effort to explore the so-called parapsychological realm. Psychic phenomena, which were carefully studied in the late nineteenth century by the Society for Psychical Research in England, and parapsychology, which was researched for many years by J. B. Rhine at Duke University, have now become the rage. Uri Geller has been examined by "scientific experts" and found to possess amazing "psychic powers," but his feats can be duplicated easily by magicians such as James Randi, using traditional magic tricks. Students and professors alike announce new investigations of clairvoyance, precognition, dream telepathy, out-of-body experiences, reincarnation, communication with spirits of the dead, psychic healing, poltergeists, and auras. Some enthusiasts claim to have discovered "leaks from the transcendental realm" and new dimensions of reality. The enemy is always the "behaviorist," "experimentalist," or "mechanist," who is allegedly closed to such inquiries. We are, some maintain, at a revolutionary stage in the history of science, which has seen the emergence of new paradigms of explanation. Critics insist that our usual scientific categories and methods are too narrow and limiting.

I am not denying the constant need to examine evidence and to maintain an open mind. Indeed, I would insist that it is essential that scientists be willing to investigate claims of new phenomena. Science cannot be censorial and intolerant, nor cut itself off from new discoveries by making judgments antecedent to inquiry. Extreme forms of scientism can be as dogmatic as subjectivism. There is a difference, however, between the careful use of research methods on the one hand, and the tendency to hasty generalizations based upon slender evidence on the other. Regretfully, there is all too often a tendency for the credulous to latch onto the most meager data and frame vast conjectures, or to insist that their speculations have been conclusively confirmed, when they have not.

## II

Serious questions can be raised about the current scene. Is the level of irrationality greater or less than in previous times, or has the level of nonsense remained fairly constant in human culture and only assumed different forms? Why does irrationality persist, even in advanced societies?

No doubt, many sociological and cultural hypotheses can explain the growth of irrational beliefs. In recent years the mass media have grown in influence: the image of the scientist is often drawn by journalists, novelists, and dramatists, not always by scientists themselves; and what science is or does has sometimes been misconstrued and given a bad name. Or again, it is estimated that half of all the support in the world for scientific research is for weapons development, and most of the rest is for industrial and pragmatic purposes. Scientific research all too often has been controlled by private interests for their profit or by governments for indoctrination and control. The free, creative scientific inquirer often has to depend for his financial support on the power structure; and what happens to the fruits of his labor is beyond his control.

These explanations are no doubt valid. But there are also, in my judgment, profound psychological factors at work; and there is much confusion about the meaning of science itself. The persistence of irrationality in modern culture reveals something about the peculiar nature of the human species. There is a tendency in the human animal toward gullibility—that is, a psychological readiness to accept untested beliefs, to be gulled into assent. This tendency seems to be so deeply ingrained in human behavior that few are without it in some measure. We are tempted to swallow as the gospel truth what others offer us. I am not talking simply of stupidity and ignorance but of uncritical naivete about some matters.

Undoubtedly there are individuals who specialize in deceiving others; they purvey false gods and empty services. But there are no doubt also sincere believers who delude themselves, who are willing to believe ideas without adequate evidence, and who seek to convert others to their misconceptions. What is at work here is not conscious fraud, but self-deception. The curious thing is that, sometimes if a psychotic repeats himself often enough, in time others come to believe and follow him. Moreover, if an untruth is exaggerated sufficiently, some people are more apt to believe it. Moreover, the heretic always risks being burned at the stake, especially after the new mythology becomes institutionalized as official doctrine.

There is, I think, still another tendency in human behavior that feeds on gullibility—the fascination with mystery and drama. Life for many persons is humdrum and boring. Overcome by ennui and the tyranny of trivia, they may seek to escape this world by the use of drugs or alcohol, by dulling or suppressing their consciousness. Release into nothingness is their goal.

Another method of diversion is the quest for hedonistic pleasures and thrills. Still another is the use of the imagination. The arts of literature and drama give free play to the creative imagination, as does religion. It is difficult for some individuals to distinguish truth from falsity, fiction from reality. The cults of unreason and the paranormal attract and fascinate. They enable one to skirt the boundaries of the unknown. For the ordinary person, there is the everyday world—and the possibility of escape to another. And so they look elsewhere—for another universe and another reality.

Thus there is a search that is fundamental to our being: the quest for meaning. The human mind has a genuine desire to plumb the depths of the unspoken, to find deeper significance and truth, to reach out to another realm of existence. Life is without meaning for many, especially for the poor, the sick, the forsaken, and those who have failed or have little hope. The imagination offers salvation from the trials and tribulations encountered in this life. Thus, belief in reincarnation or personal survival, even if unproven, offers solace to individuals in the face of tragedy, death, and the existence of evil. For ideological reasons, the means of salvation is the utopian vision of the perfect society in the future. The soul cries out for something more, farther beyond, deeper, more lasting, and more perfect than our transient world of experience.

Accordingly, the persistence of faith may be explained in part by characteristics within our nature: gullibility, the lure of mystery, the quest for meaning. People will take the least shred of evidence and construct a mythological system. They will pervert their logic and abandon their senses, all for the Promised Land. Some will gladly barter their freedom to the most authoritarian of systems in order to achieve comfort and security. The cults of unreason promise solace; they seek to invest the solitary individual, who often feels estranged and alone, with an important role in the universe.

## III

What can science say about such human needs? Have we perhaps left the domain of science entirely and moved into that of philosophy? Science should have something to say, for what is at stake is the nature of science itself.

There are many meanings of the word "science." Some who talk about science refer to specialties in a specific field, such as endocrinology, microbiology, or econometrics. Others who talk about science have in mind the technological and experimental applications of scientific theories to concrete problems. Yet these views of science are overly narrow; for it is possible for a society to make massive progress in certain narrowly technical fields and yet miss the whole point of the scientific enterprise. The totalitarian societies of our time have invested vast sums in technical research and have achieved a high level of scientific competence in certain fields, but the scientific outlook has not prevailed in them. Merely training people to be scientific specialists is not enough. A culture can be full of scientific technicians, yet still be dominated by the irrational. We must distinguish science as a narrow technical enterprise from the *scientific attitude.* It is here that I think we have not established an important goal. Unfortunately, to have scientific credentials in one field does not mean that a person will incorporate a scientific attitude into other parts of his life.

The best therapy for gullibility and unbridled imagination is the development of the scientific attitude, as it applies not only to one's specialized field of expertise but also to the wider questions of life itself. But we have failed in our society to develop and spread the scientific attitude. It is evident that one can be a scientific specialist but a cultural barbarian, an expert technologist in a particular field but ignorant outside it.

If we are to meet the growth of irrationality, we need to develop an appreciation for the scientific attitude as part of culture. We must make it clear that the key methodological principle of science is that one is not justified in affirming a truth claim unless one can support it by evidence or reason. It is not enough to be inwardly convinced of the truth of one's beliefs. They must at some point be objectively verifiable by impartial investigators. A belief that is warranted is not so because it is "subjectively true," as Kierkegaard thought; if it is true, it is so because it has been confirmed by a community of inquirers. To believe validly that something is true is to relate one's beliefs to a rational justification; it is to make a claim about the world, independent of one's wishes.

Although the specific criteria for testing a belief depend upon the subject under consideration, there are certain general criteria. We need to examine the *evidence*. Here I am referring to observation of data that are reproducible by independent observers and that can be examined experimentally in test cases. This is familiarly called the empiricist or experimentalist criterion. A belief is true if, and only if, it has been confirmed, directly or indirectly, by reference to observable evidence. A belief is also validated by offering supporting *reasons*. Here there are logical considerations that are relevant. A belief is related to a set of other beliefs that have been established by previous inquiries. This criterion is that of logical consistency. A belief is invalid if it contradicts other well-grounded beliefs within a framework. We also evaluate our beliefs in part by their observed *consequences* in practice and by their effect upon conduct. This is the utilitarian or pragmatic criterion: the utility of a belief is judged by reference to its function and its value. However, one cannot claim that a belief is true simply because it has utility; independent evidence and rational considerations are essential. Nevertheless, reference to the results of a belief, particularly to those of a normative belief, is important.

These general criteria are, of course, familiar in logic and the philosophy of science. It is the hypothetical-deductive method of testing hypotheses that I am talking about. But this method should not be narrowly construed, for the scientific method employs common sense; it is not some esoteric art available only to the initiated. Science employs the same methods of critical intelligence that the ordinary man uses in formulating beliefs about his practical world; and it is the method he has to use, to some extent, if he is to live and function, to make plans and choices. To deviate from objective thinking is to be out of touch with cognitive reality; and we cannot avoid using it if we are to deal with the concrete problems we encounter in the world.

The paradox is that so many people are willing to abandon their practical intelligence when they enter fields of religion or ethics, or to throw caution to the wind when they flirt with so-called transcendental matters.

In any case there is a need to develop a general scientific attitude for all or most areas in life, to use, as far as possible, our critical intelligence to appraise beliefs, and to insist that they be based upon evidential grounds. The chief corollary to this is the criterion that *where we do not have sufficient evidence, we ought to suspend judgment.* Our beliefs should be considered tentative hypotheses based on degrees of probability. They should not be considered absolute or final. We ought to be committed to the principle of fallibilism, which considers that our beliefs can be erroneous. We should be willing to revise them, if need be, in the light of new evidence and new theories.

The scientific attitude thus does not foreclose on a priori grounds an examination of claims about the transcendental. It is committed to free and open inquiry. It cannot refuse to engage in research, say, for example, into paranormal phenomena. But it does claim the right to ask that such research be responsible and carefully conducted, that the evidence not be outstripped by conjecture, nor the conclusions based upon the will to believe.

## IV

The basic question is: How can we cultivate the scientific attitude? The most vital institution in society for developing an appreciation for the scientific attitude is the school. It is not enough, however, for educational institutions to simply inform young people of the facts or to disseminate a body of knowledge. Education of that sort may be nothing more than rote learning or indoctrination. Rather, a key purpose of education should be to develop within individuals the use of *critical intelligence* and *skepticism*. It is not enough to get students to memorize a subject matter, amass facts, pass examinations, or even to master a specialty or profession or be trained as citizens. If we do that and nothing more, we have not educated fully; the central task is to cultivate the ability to test beliefs, evaluate hypotheses, appraise arguments—in short, to develop an attitude of objectivity and impartiality. The tremendous information explosion today has bombarded us with competing truth claims. It is vital that individuals develop some understanding of the effective criteria for judging these claims. I refer not only to our ability to examine claims of knowledge about the world but also to our ability to develop some skills in appraising value judgments and ethical principles. The goal of education should be to develop reflective persons—skeptical yet receptive to new ideas, always willing to examine new departures in thought, yet insisting that they be tested before they are accepted.

Education is not achieved when we transmit a finished subject matter or discipline to students—only when we stimulate a living process of inquiry. This goal is appreciated today in some educational institutions that do attempt to cultivate reflective intelligence. But education is not complete unless we can extend our concern to other important educative institutions in society. If we are to raise the level of critical intelligence and promote the scientific attitude, it is important that we concern ourselves with the media of mass communication. An especially serious problem with the electronic media is that they employ visual images rather than written symbols, disseminate immediate impressions instead of sustained analyses. How can we stimulate reflective criticism in viewers given this form of information?

I have no easy solution to offer. What I do wish to suggest is that we ought not to assume, simply because ours is an advanced scientific-technological society, that irrational thinking will be overcome. The evidence suggests that that is far from being the case. Indeed, there is always the danger that science itself may be engulfed by forces of unreason.

If we are to deal with the problem, what we need, at the very least, is to be clear about the nature of the scientific enterprise itself and to recognize that it presupposes a basic attitude about evidential criteria. Unless we can impart through the educational institutions in society some sense of the skeptical approach to life—as therapeutic and corrective—then I am afraid we will be constantly confronted by new forms of "know-nothingism."

If we are to make progress in overcoming irrationality, however, we must go still further. We must perhaps try to satisfy the need for mystery and drama and the hunger for meaning. The growth of education and science in the modern world is a marvel to behold, and we should do whatever we can to further its development. But we have learned that an increase in the sum of knowledge by itself will not necessarily overturn superstition, dogma, and gullibility, because these are nourished by other sources in the human psyche.

One point often overlooked in satisfying our fascination with mystery and drama is the possible role of imagination in the sciences. Science can only proceed by being open to creative explorations in thought. The breakthroughs in science are astounding, and they will continue as we probe further into the microworld of matter and life and into the universe at large. The space age is the beginning of a new epoch for humankind, as we leave our solar system and explore the universe for extraterrestrial life. We need to disseminate an appreciation for the adventure of the scientific enterprise. Unfortunately, for some, science fiction is a substitute for science. The religion of the future may be a space-age religion, in which the new prophets are not the scientists but the science-fiction writers.

Science has thus a double focus: objectivity and creativity. The arts are essential in keeping alive the dramatic qualities of experience; poetry, music, and literature express our passionate natures. Man does not live by reason alone; and science is often viewed by its critics as cold and rational. People hunger for something more. Our aesthetic impulses and our delight in beauty need cultivation. The arts are the deepest expression of our "spiritual" interests, but we need to make a distinction between art and truth.

In any case, we need to satisfy the quest for meaning. It is this craving for ethereal meaning that, I think, leads to the psychotic disorientation found in the cults of unreason. "Follow me," say the cults of irrationality. "I am the light, the truth, and the way." And people are willing to abandon all standards of critical judgment in the process.

I wish to make it clear that there is a need today for developing alternative normative institutions. I would suggest that such a program would not build systems with beliefs that are patently false or irrational or that violate the evidence of the sciences; yet it would seek to address itself to the other dimensions of human experience, and it would give the arts, philosophy, and ethics powerful roles in helping fulfill our human needs.

# 27

# The New Censors of Science

I

The freedom of scientific research, a basic principle essential for scientific inquiry, is undergoing considerable criticism in contemporary society. Indeed, so sustained has the assault become in some areas that we may be reaching a situation of clear and present danger in which the very viability of the scientific enterprise is thrown into question. Accordingly, it is important that the ethical justification for scientific research be clarified, particularly since the new censors usually claim the right to restrict scientific research on ethical grounds.

Many of us grew up believing that science and the quest for truth were positive goods. We assumed, moreover, that the growth of scientific knowledge was progressive and that in time we would be able to extend significantly the boundaries of our understanding of nature and life. Indeed, this attitude has characterized the outlook of wide sections of the educated classes for the past three centuries. The scientific revolution of the sixteenth and seventeenth centuries, first developed in physics and astronomy, was later applied to chemistry and biology, and in the nineteenth and twentieth centuries to the social and behavioral sciences. Many of us were educated in a climate that was highly favorable to the scientific approach, which held the belief that scientific research ought to be pursued unencumbered by political, religious, economic, or social pressures. This point of view involved the conviction that reason and science ought to be applied to human affairs and that, with the growth of universal learning and education, we would be able to solve the problems besetting humankind and contribute to the common good.

The development of the scientific outlook was not made without opposition from many quarters. There was the notorious conflict between science and the established ecclesiastical forces at the beginning of the modern era and when Bruno and Galileo were martyred to the cause of free inquiry. Physics and astronomy were eventually vindicated by their demonstrated success in explaining a wide range of previously inexplicable phenomena.

This article is reprinted from *History, Religion and Spiritual Democracy,* ed. Maurice Wohlgelernter (New York: Columbia University Press, 1980).

Even in the twentieth century, biologists who proposed theories of evolution to account for the origin of species had to contend with opposing religious doctrines of creation, and the rise of behavior psychology precipitated an outcry in some quarters that it had destroyed the soul. Similar objections were voiced against Freudian theories of psychoanalysis. By and large, however, these religious objections eventually dissipated—or at least we thought so—and most educated people were willing to accept the findings of the sciences.

Demands for the censorship of science historically have come from other quarters as well: political and economic repression is familiar. Vested interests have often found scientific discoveries dangerous; totalitarian regimes, in particular, have sought to impose an ideological straitjacket on creative scientific inquiry and have proscribed scientific theories if they were contrary to the prevailing status quo. Nazi racial doctrines made non-Aryan science *verboten,* and Lysenkoian environmentalism inveighed against genetics. One cannot perform scientific research if there is fear of reprisal. The principle is, or at least it was until recently, well understood in democracies. Even dictators have recognized that if their scientists are to be effective they must be allowed some degree of autonomy.

## II

It is disturbing, therefore, to find that there are today new calls for the limitations of scientific research. Indeed, much to the surprise of scientists in many fields of inquiry, their investigations increasingly are being condemned, and there are all sorts of pressures to police, stifle, even prohibit their research. The paradox is that the great hue and cry is not made on religious or political grounds—blasphemy or sedition—but rather on alleged ethical grounds. The indictment usually is that some areas ought *not* to be studied, are intrinsically evil to know about, or that the research will have harmful consequences to individuals or to society. The new censors of science today are, above all, moralists. One might say that the censor has always been a closet moralist in disguise; today he is out in the open and his sense of moral righteousness has become intensified.

We may ask if scientific research is ethically justifiable and if so under what conditions. Is the quest for truth less important than the attainment of justice, virtue, or goodness?

It is clear that scientific research is no longer simply the work of an isolated individual in a secluded study or laboratory, but now has wide social implications. Accordingly, we are told that what the scientist does must be carefully regulated by society. If the medieval church opposed research on human cadavers, modern moralists have their own "thou shalt nots." Usually, they insist that legal restrictions be enacted to enforce their moral concern. Since scientists often need governmental or foundation support, regulation at the source becomes especially threatening to the kinds of research they wish to pursue. There is an ever-increasing catalogue of projects that various groups seek to proscribe.

Many moralists a generation ago condemned physicists for their work on nuclear energy. The development of nuclear weapons, and their capacity for the destruction of life on this planet, was attributed by some critics to a lack of social conscience.

More recently, biologists and geneticists have been seriously criticized for engaging in genetic engineering. This is considered to be dangerous. Geneticists are opening up a Pandora's box, we are told, by cloning, by interfering with the natural processes of evolution, or by participating in DNA recombinant research—which, we are warned, could unleash highly resistant strains of E. coli bacteria and destroy humankind. In some cases this has reached the proportions of moral hysteria. The public outcry is growing: city councils, state legislatures, Congress, even some concerned scientists are outdoing themselves in seeking to regulate this research.[1]

Geneticists have also been attacked by some groups for focusing on the hereditary factors in behavior and minimizing environmental conditions. This is said to be "conservative" or "reactionary," for it undermines efforts at social reform. Similar charges have been leveled against sociobiologists.

Astronomers have been cautioned about bringing virulent strains of life from other planets. Some have said that efforts to communicate with extra-terrestrial intelligences by means of radio astronomy could also be detrimental to the human species. Why inform possible hostile forces in the universe about our presence?

Medical researchers have also been censured for various forms of human experimentation and drug therapy. Many disciples of the "right to life" have sought to prohibit any form of fetal research, and, in fact, the federal government banned fetal research for several months pending the recommendations of a commission set up to investigate its "morality."

Psychiatrists have been heavily indicted for engaging in "brainwashing," performing lobotomies, implanting electrodes, or for seeking to control and thus "dehumanize" personality. Psychologists have also received their share of criticism. Some critics have maintained, for example, that it is wrong to investigate the subject of I.Q. as it relates to race or publish findings that may be injurious to certain racial or ethnic groups. Jensen and Eysenck have been called racists for their work in this area. Extreme critics of the behaviorists have characterized them as "totalitarian oppressors," objecting to their use of behavior modification, or to their "depersonalized" approach to human subjects. New regulations governing the study of human subjects are restrictive and require the establishment of special ethical-review boards.[2] Research involving prisoners has been made very difficult, if not virtually impossible; the same restriction has been applied to children, who cannot grant informed consent, and to retarded and handicapped persons.

Some have objected strenuously to research with animals. There is a developing movement for the protection of animal rights. Frederick Wiseman produced a film, widely shown on educational television, portraying scientists studying the sexual behavior of primates as questionable; and Peter Singer, the philosopher, in a much discussed book, *Animal Liberation,* has criticized the use of animals for scientific research. The antivivisectionists believe that animal rights should transcend the interests of the research scientist.

I have touched only on some of the recent efforts to limit research, and many other illustrations could be offered. The merits of each of these cases need to be discussed in detail and on their own terms, something I cannot attempt to do here. What I wish to identify, however, is an emerging trend. We may, indeed, have passed a critical turning point in society's appraisal of the ethical case for scientific research.

### III

Clearly, at present, the public has a very deep mistrust of certain aspects of science. This distrust is shared by the communications media, some intellectuals, and some scientists. It has assumed many dimensions.

There is a profound suspicion that science and technology are responsible for many of the serious problems of the contemporary world. It is believed that, since the results of scientific research are often harmful rather than beneficial, society needs to regulate what scientists do. This antiscience attitude must, of course, be put in proper perspective. There is also a deep appreciation for the positive uses of science and technology by modern society, and the whole structure of industry rests upon scientific research. The critique of scientific research on moral grounds must be related to two other disturbing trends.

There appears to be a growing breakdown in the conviction that there are objective scientific criteria for judging truth. This argument assumes many forms but, taken in its extreme, it claims that knowledge, in the last analysis, is "subjective." This view is prevalent in the current generation of college students, who often call upon us to justify the scientific method itself. Many people today fail to understand even the most elementary canons of inquiry; for example, they believe that merely to formulate a speculative hypothesis (perhaps von Däniken's "chariots of the gods," or Uri Geller's psychokinesis) is sufficient to make it true, requiring no additional supporting evidence or the criteria of logical consistency. Clearly, this attitude is symptomatic of a broader mood in society, a mood that usually has two contradictory aspects. In an extreme form it is held that we ought to be tolerant of different points of view and that since one view is as good as the next, no one is entitled to criticize a contrary view. Or, contrariwise, that one's system of beliefs or values is absolutely true and immune to criticism (a view generally held by the various cults of unreason). The point is, we have failed to define the tentative and hypothetical, yet objective, character of scientific inquiry.

Unfortunately, this rejection of objectivity can be found among some of the most sophisticated philosophers of science, who (following Kuhn, for example) argue that the logical positivistic view of science is mistaken, that there are no clearly definable criteria of the logic of scientific validation, but that the methods by which we judge theories and the models themselves are a function of social and historical forces. These are very serious criticisms. Clearly we cannot deny the sociohistorical context of scientific research. Yet scientific inquiry, if nothing else, rests upon a set of epistemological assumptions. If one abandons these, then one throws the scientific program into serious jeopardy, for there may then seem to be little reason to assume that science is any truer than religion, art, poetry, or feeling. If the scientific program is to succeed, we must recognize that there are at least *some* objective standards of verification and validation, however much we may quibble about certain aspects of these criteria.

Science is also criticized today by those who would reject its naturalistic or materialistic "world view." We are told by many critics that scientists are biased because they automatically exclude data that do not fit their preconceived categories. These critics maintain, for example, that scientists neglect to consider a whole range of paranormal phenomena that transcend the usual boundaries of evidence and logic. Telekinesis, remote viewing, clairvoyance, astral projection, precognition, and other kinds of experience are said to give glimpses of a "new vision of reality." There are those who claim to be doing "hard research" in these areas, but I am extremely skeptical about their rigor and find that their activities more often than not border on pseudoscience. In any case, many of the concepts of behavioral science have been discarded. I might add that the newest discoveries in physics and astronomy (black holes, antimatter, quarks, and charms) and the frequent inability of physicists and astronomers to interpret their theories immediately invite speculation about the possible "psychical" implications of their findings. Similarly, the probability that there are other forms of intelligent life in the universe invites science-fiction extravagance. My response to all of this is, of course, that science is not unalterably committed to any world view per se—whether materialist, mechanist, or naturalist. Science is, however, committed to the use of the hypothetical-deductive method as a way of verifying its hypotheses, and it should be open to any and all new theories that are proposed.

Whatever the reasons, this is the age in which there has been a proliferation of unsubstantiated claims; faith healing, exorcism, astrology, auras, fortune telling, transcendental meditation, and the resurgence of fundamentalism are all symptomatic of a spiritualist-psychic world view that has descended upon us. One might ask: Are we "opening up to a new dimension of reality," as the proponents of the paranormal claim? Or are these signs that the scientific revolution which began in the sixteenth and seventeenth centuries is reaching an end and that we shall be overwhelmed by new forms of irrationalism? I don't mean to be overly pessimistic. One cannot predict historical trends. Perhaps what we have been witnessing is simply a return to the normal state of human credulity, in which gullibility and the will to illusion prevail. Every age needs to develop critical intellligence as therapy against nonsense, and perhaps we have been failing in that endeavor.

Nevertheless, one should not simply minimize or dismiss the significance of what has been happening in the past decade. Science is basically an affair of a relatively small percentage of the total population. Even those who claim to be scientists may be narrow specialists in their fields, failing to understand the nature of scientific intelligence or the scientific outlook and not extending it to other domains.

Whatever the causes, a strong antiscience mood seems to have developed. Today, the scientist is considered in some circles to be a kind of moral monster who, if left to his own devices, is likely to alter human beings radically or destroy the world. Doomsday prophecies abound. Much of the indictment is against technology; scientific research has given us powerful tools for understanding and controlling nature, but the same research has had harmful fallouts (for example, ecological pollution, environmental carcinogens, the dangers of biochemical and nuclear warfare). What is often taken for granted is that scientific technology has provided many boons to humankind: the green revolution, the marvellous therapies of medical science, the increase of literacy and education, improved communication and travel, the electronic and computer revolution, and so on.

All of this brings me back to my original theme. The attack on science has not only involved skepticism about its methodology, its world view (if there is such a thing), and the deleterious effects of an uncontrolled technology, but there has also been an assault on free scientific research itself.

## IV

Should scientific research be limited on ethical grounds, as its critics maintain? That is, are there certain things that we should not inquire into or know because it would be evil to do so? Or, should we insist upon the principle of free research without external controls? Can an ethical case be made for scientific freedom? An unfortunate aspect of recent discussions is the impression that there is an opposition between ethics and scientific research. Often it is assumed that scientists are *a*-ethical, and the burden of proof is thus placed upon *them* to show why they should be allowed to investigate in a field where the rights of others are at stake.

Another illustration of the prevalent tendency to cut off research is seen in the *Report and Recommendations: Research Involving Prisoners,* published by the National Commission for the Protection of Human Subjects of Biomedical and Behavioral Research.[3] The *Report* recognizes that "since the 1960's, the ethical propriety of participation by prisoners in research has increasingly been questioned in this country. . . . Eight states and the Federal Bureau of Prisons have formally moved to abandon research in prisons." Following this, the Health Subcommittee of the Senate Committee on Labor and Public Welfare held hearings in late 1973. In 1975 the House Subcommittee on Courts, Civil Liberties, and the Administration of Justice held hearings on whether to prohibit medical research in federal prisons or in prisons of states receiving federal grants. After these hearings, the director of the Federal Bureau of Prisons mandated that "continued use of prisoners in any medical experimentation should not be permitted" and he ordered that such participation be phased out.

With this as background, the commission was called upon to make recommendations. It concluded: "In the course of its investigations and review of evidence presented to it, the Commission did not find in prisons the conditions requisite for a sufficiently high degree of voluntariness and openness, notwithstanding that prisoners currently participating in research consider, in nearly all instances, that they do so voluntarily and want the research to continue."[4]

The commission therefore recommends that research be conducted, but only if certain restrictive standards are met. The *Report* states: "Compliances with these requirements must be certified by the highest responsible federal official, assisted by a national ethical review body. The Commission has concluded that *the burden of proof that all the requirements are satisfied should be on those who wish to conduct the research.*"[5] [Italics mine.]

The *Report* then recommends that a number of requirements be satisfied: studies of the causes and effects of incarceration, studies of prisons, and studies improving the health or well-being of individual prisoners can be carried on provided they present minimal or no risk to the subjects. The commission then recommends that any other type of research involving prisoners should *not* be conducted unless: (1) "the type of research fulfills an important social and scientific need, and the reasons for involving prisoners in the type of research are compelling," (2) "the involvement of prisoners in the type of research satisfies conditions of equity," (3) "a high degree of voluntariness . . . and openness . . ." and other provisions, such as "provisions for effective redress of grievances," are fulfilled. It is further recommended that "the head of the responsible federal department or agency should determine . . . the competence of the investigator."[6] Moreover:

All research involving prisoners should be reviewed by at least one human subject review committee or institutional review board *comprised of men and women of diverse racial and cultural backgrounds* and that includes among its members prisoners or prisoner advocates and such other persons as community representatives, clergy, behavioral scientists and medical personnel not associated with the conduct of the research or the penal institution.[7] [Italics mine.]

One may ask why there should be equal board representation on a quota basis and why community representatives and clergymen, who have no scientific qualifications, should serve. Unfortunately, what is often alleged to be an ethical issue becomes politicized and is taken up as part of an ideological battle. The concern for prisoner's rights—as important as it is—has become for some groups basically a political, not an ethical, issue. Prisoners have become the folk heroes of society, oppressed because of class or race. Critics ask, in effect: How dare the establishment experiment with the poor victims of society? Even if prisoners themselves voluntarily agree to participate in research (which is almost always the case) the paternalistic moralists, claiming to believe in the right of individual consent, will not permit it.

Clearly, prisoners' rights should not be violated nor should prisoners be harmed. The *Report* indicated two basic ethical principles to safeguard prisoners: (1) "the principle of justice," which required that prisoners and groups be treated fairly, and (2) "the principle of respect for persons," which requires that the autonomy of prisoners be promoted and protected. I disagree with neither of these; it is merely a question of emphasis.

Public-interest lawyers have argued that prisoners cannot really give free and informed consent because of the constraints implicit in their incarceration; therefore, one should not be allowed to conduct medical, social, or psychological research on prisoners. But actually prisoners often face greater risks in the prison yard from other inmates or guards than from research projects. It is absurd to allow a narrow application of the risk-benefits principle to prohibit research. Raymond B. Cattell argues that had this principle been observed at the time of Columbus, funding for his voyage to America would not have been approved because of the dangerous risks to certain Portuguese seamen.[8]

Those who argue for drastically restricting research offer moral arguments. The following statements, for example, appear in the Appendix to the *Report,* and are illustrative of the case against research: "Scientific progress is grand, but even it must bow before the altar of human rights; scientific progress is progress only if it legitimately respects the value and dignity of persons."[9]

"Experimentation with prisoners is not scientifically necessary for the good of society. . . . To continue experimentation with prisoners under the present circumstances would violate and erode our sense of what we are as a society; a community constituted by mutual regard for other's equal, intrinsic dignity."[10]

But may we not question, on a more fundamental level, the lower priority given to another basic ethical principle, namely, that the right to free inquiry ought to prevail in society? What we have are competing principles and rights. Which ones ought to prevail?

Often the principle of informed consent, if pushed to an extreme, can become ridiculous in its interference with bona fide research, as Bernard Davis of Harvard Medical School points out:

> An example of silly interference has arisen in connection with some research on cell genetics in man that depends on cultivating human cells in test tubes. . . . A convenient source is foreskins from newborns, a byproduct of circumcision. This material has been used now for a number of years. An investigator at MIT recently had his regular supply of foreskins from the Boston Women's Hospital cut off . . . because the doctor was afraid that he would have to have written informed consent from both the father and the mother. He didn't know what some Massachusetts prosecutors might do.[11]

It is sometimes even necessary today to have written informed consent in order for scientific investigators to use waste products that are collected from hospital patients.

But there are many less amusing incidents of repression. John L. Horn, professor of psychology at the University of Denver, relates how a research proposal that he submitted in 1974 to the Small Grants Section of the National Institute of Mental Health was rejected. The proposal was "to construct tests that would be more nearly culture-fair than existing tests and yet would measure important aspects of intelligence." Involved in the project was the analysis of data that had been gathered by another investigator some five years earlier from 624 middle-class urban white children and 209 lower-class rural black children. Although the SGS review committee that had evaluated the proposal judged it to be adequate on scientific grounds, it was rejected for reasons concerning "the ethics of research." According to the letter of rejection, the reasons were as follows:

> 1. The reviewers were seriously concerned about the potential risks both to the subjects in the study and to the classes of persons represented by the subjects. In regards to the former, *no information was given in the proposal that the childrens' parents gave consent to have their children's test performance used for research purposes of this kind.* . . .
> 2. Even more seriously, the reviewers felt that this study was *liable to potential social and political misuse.* They were aware that you had intentionally confounded race and class in an attempt to prevent invidious comparisons between groups, but given today's climate, the reviewers were not sure that any precautions could be successful in that respect. . . .[12] [Italics mine.]

Both of these reasons are highly suspect. To require researchers to obtain informed consent from parents for possible use of the data by other researchers at some future date would make research cumbersome, if not impossible. No one can foresee all of the secondary analyses which will be made of one's studies.

To extend the notion of risk beyond the individuals originally involved in the study to a "class or group risk" is equally dubious. It is an impossible burden to ask that the scientist anticipate all of the social consequences of his inquiry and whether or not the results might be used adversely against some group at a later date.

Horn relates that not only was his proposal rejected but also a government official wrote to his university about the proposal, suggesting ethical improprieties on Horn's part—a subtle form of coercion.

## V

I submit that we need to recognize the freedom of inquiry as a general *prima facie* ethical principle that ought to be respected by society. Such a principle serves as a guide for decision. Can this principle be justified, and on what grounds?

Many arguments can be adduced in its favor. First, the quest for truth is among the highest of human values, expressing an enduring human interest and the intrinsically worthwhile nature of the search for knowledge. People have always cherished new discoveries about nature and life. They have wished to ferret out what is genuine from what is false, to understand the cause of things, to unravel and comprehend their complexity.

In this regard, science has emerged as the most powerful tool invented to reveal causal relationships. The search for knowledge is unending. It requires constant care and attention, nourishment, and cultivation. No one can anticipate what new ideas will emerge or new hypotheses will develop. There are always surprises in the course of inquiry.

If the creative "mind" of man is to proceed, it requires conditions of freedom. Fear of sanction or reprisal will destroy the quest for truth. Thus, a society which prizes knowledge and allows its scientists, philosophers, humanists, poets, artists, and ordinary people to live and breathe in a context of freedom is more likely to come closer to discovering truth. We cannot add to the fund of knowledge if the censor or moralist is permitted to prohibit the free expression of our cognitive talents.

In the tradition of Western civilization, the use of our rational capacities has been considered to be the highest good and a significant source of happiness. Perhaps this tradition has underestimated the emotional satisfaction of other needs essential to the good life. Nevertheless, the rational life (as broadly interpreted) is among the deepest expressions of human power, and is what distinguishes humans, in some senses, from other forms of life on earth.

The quest for knowledge needs no justification. This quest is ethically significant in its own terms as the most developed expression of our potentialities, the most eloquent source of enrichment, the noblest fulfillment of human excellence.

We need not apologize because we are curious, inquisitive, or wish to find what is the case and why. Those who oppose the continuing human search—for whatever lofty moral principles—are, in the last analysis, the enemies of humankind. These persons seek to suppress our deepest instincts to know. It is they, not those who seek knowledge, who are behaving unethically.

There is also a second argument in support of free scientific inquiry: the utilitarian justification. Knowledge is an instrument of action and of life. Basic research can be applied in practice and can stimulate invention and technology; it can help cure suffering and disease, eliminate poverty, and create a better life for humanity.

One never knows beforehand what the full consequences of scientific research will be. Hence, to seek to limit any area of inquiry on the basis of present-day knowledge is to cut off the possibilities of new applications that may be beneficial to humankind. We cannot anticipate the results of free inquiry; however, we must encourage continuing investigation. A progressive society is one in which innovation and ingenuity, imagination and intellect, should have free play.

Hence, even though there may be some abuses in the quest for knowledge, the long-range advantages of free inquiry far outweigh any immediate disadvantages. We need to balance possible short-range dangers with long-range results. We may thus maintain that "the right to knowledge and the free use thereof" has, overall, long-range utility for the good of society at large. No doubt, there will be hazards and mistakes, but it is far better to risk possible abuses than to adopt a policy of short-sighted censorship.

However, in arguing on both intrinsic and consequential grounds that the "right to free scientific research" is a prima facie principle that ought to prevail, I do not wish to assume the mantle of the absolutist. No right is absolute and there may be exceptions to the application of general ethical principles. We are, in general, opposed to killing, yet in some situations—for example, in self-defense or euthanasia—killing may be ethically justifiable. A prima facie duty is not an absolutely binding one. We ought, in general, to keep our promises, but we can imagine cases in which we are released from an obligation to do so, particularly if keeping a promise would have destructive consequences. Thus, although we ought to recognize the general right of scientists to seek the truth, we may in certain situations reluctantly, and only as a last resort, decide to limit the application of that right.

But the salient point is that *the burden of proof should be upon those who wish to restrain the quest for knowledge and not on those committed to it.* I fear that what is happening now is that scientists are increasingly being put on the defensive and being called upon to vindicate their commitment. The public is becoming suspicious of their motives and goals. However, it is precisely those groups which wish to abrogate the right to knowledge that need to justify their call for constraints, and their reasons must be compelling. There must be an overwhelmingly clear and present danger for us to restrict such inquiry.

We may add to this still another consideration. The freedom of scientific research ought to be explicitly protected as a First-Amendment right. I cannot understand why censors in recent years have transgressed this right with impunity. It should have full constitutional protection. Perhaps someone should make a case against the secretary of HEW and the new "boards of inquisition" now being established. The right to scientific research is intrinsically related to freedom of belief, speech, and publication – as is academic freedom. And we are well aware that there have been many attempts in the past to abrogate academic freedom; inquisitorial congressional committees and militant disruptions of classrooms and speakers are recent instances of such abrogation. The committees and the militants have violated First-Amendment rights.

I am not unaware of the distinction between knowledge and action. I concede that, although society ought not in principle to limit knowledge, it can in some situations restrict actions, especially where such actions invade the rights of others. In a sense, this distinction is false, for all knowledge is a form of behavior, not an inner "mentalistic" state. Still, a distinction can be made in degree if not in kind. However, knowledge, even if it involves no overt action, may have consequences which someone may interpret to be "harmful." It is on the basis of these considerations that some have called for a moratorium on research into I.Q. and race for fear of injuring minority groups. But if we were to argue in this way, then Linus Pauling should not be permitted to publish his findings about the alleged benefits of Vitamin C. Nor should the proponents of Vitamin E be allowed to publish their research until the evidence is conclusive, because of possible hazards to a class of users. But clearly, in an open society, all points of view should contend; if someone's views are mistaken this can be pointed out by their critics. To restrict any and all knowledge which may be "harmful" is excessive moral zeal, which in the last analysis is counterproductive, and, if generalized, would make the attainment of truth virtually impossible.

Nevertheless, I think that a democratic society *can* limit certain forms of technology. Many products of industry are so noxious to health and to the environment that it is perfectly within the jurisdiction of the community to establish standards to curb their production. There should be, of course, sufficient evidence for these decisions. The fact that the products of technology and industry need greater scrutiny and control is surely not at issue here. The right to knowledge does not mean the right to manufacture goods that will poison the atmosphere or pollute the streams. (Though I would here take a libertarian position and allow, wherever possible, individuals to have the free choice to purchase products that may harm them, so long as these products are properly labelled.)

The very process of conducting scientific research may, in some instances, have overt public consequences. This seems to be the case with recombinant DNA research (though I might add that I am not convinced of the clear and present danger to public safety which the opponents of DNA research have portrayed.) Thus, the scientific researcher does not always passively view his subject; indeed, he may manipulate, change, even harm the subject. When should he be prevented from doing that?

I would suggest the following guideline: the right to inquire should be respected. It is so intrinsically and instrumentally valuable that it should be curtailed only after critical, reflective inquiry. I reiterate: the person who wishes to suppress inquiry—not those devoted to it—should ultimately be required to demonstrate his case.

Still, one cannot say that the scientist is exempt from the laws governing society. Nazi doctors experimented with their patients, tortured them, and violated their rights. There is the unfortunate Tuskegee study, in which researchers withheld treatment from some black patients with syphilis. Scientists who perform such acts cannot expect to occupy a privileged place in society, immune from the law. Scientists do not have a right to place in excessive risk the health and well-being of subjects under study—unless the subjects agree. The right to seek the truth does not mean that scientists are entitled to kill or maim subjects in the process. But I fear that the principle of informed consent can be construed in such a way as to impair legitimate scientific research.

The principle of informed consent should not be interpreted as universally binding. If we were to permit this interpretation, we might seriously impede much research that can be highly significant for society. Indeed, some kinds of research may be invalidated if the subjects are aware that they are being tested. Withholding some information may be necessary— not to injure or harm subjects, but in order to investigate their behavior accurately, without their preestablished attitudes intervening.

Similarly, there are many kinds of tests, in schools or other institutions, which we should be able to do with children without the consent of their parents being required. Bureaucracies—whether police departments, hospitals, corporations, government agencies, churches, or schools—are notoriously cautious. There seems to be developing a generalized apprehension that, since certain forms of research might be adverse to the institution's reputation or to the subjects involved, the institution should not participate in it. There is a growing fear by administrators and scientists of possible legal proceedings being brought against them.

My chief concern here, however, is not the topic of informed consent. I have used it only by way of illustration. I am concerned, I reiterate, with the broader question: the undermining of scientific research in general, of which this is only one aspect. That is why I have argued that we need to be aware of our obligation to it as a general ethical principle.

## VI

I think it is important that we now call a halt to the enroachments of governments and other external bodies that wish to regulate scientific research.

We should instead allow for responsible peer review by those within the profession. It is true that professionals may disagree and moral choices are often difficult to make. Nonetheless, it would be a mistake for scientists to look outside for political or legal adjudication. To move in the direction of government control will set an unfortunate precedent and may hopelessly impair future scientific investigation. The danger is that scientists will barter away their creativity to unqualified review boards, which are being asked to pass on the merits of an inquiry or the competence of the researchers and may destroy daring innovations and discoveries. Such boards may hamper research, functioning instead as inquisitional bodies. If such boards had existed in the days during which Freud developed his theories of psychoanalysis, they might have prohibited publication of case studies about patients (without their consent) as a violation of their right to privacy (or as sexually prurient). They might have condemned Galileo's experiments as immoral, since they challenged religious beliefs. Marx's inquiries might have been censored because they would lead to violent revolution and harm some individuals in the process. These boards might have forbidden the work of such scientists as Pasteur, Ehrlich, and Koch and might have made difficult the discoveries of vaccines for yellow fever, poliomyelitis, or other dread diseases. The entire field of nuclear research, like recombinant DNA today, might have been proscribed because of the dangers of nuclear contamination.

In the current context, I believe that scientists are faced with an urgent problem: to make clear to themselves and to society the humanistic character of their enterprise. Scientists must demonstrate that, far from there being an opposition between science and ethics, science is among the highest of human endeavors, and that to seek to restrict or prohibit it is a most drastic step that itself requires justification. There is today within society an excessive, brooding, pessimistic fear of the unknown that we might unmask. Yet, only by intensified research can we hope to discover not only new and exciting forms of truth but also the safeguards that can be applied in the process of research. To close the door to research is to prevent not only positive results from being known but also the means of guarding ourselves against possible misadventures.

In the last analysis, the best safeguard against the undermining of scientific research is an informed, intelligent public. The larger task facing scientists is to help educate the public about the nature of the scientific method and the roles of science and research in human progress. We have been failing to accomplish this task, and the rising tide of subjectivism and the assault on scientific research are symptomatic of a failure by the broader public to appreciate how society has benefited from the untrammelled search for knowledge.

The freedom of scientific inquiry ultimately depends upon a public enlightenment that must be nurtured not only in the schools but through all media of communication. The task is heavy and unremitting and seems sometimes like the labors of Sisyphus. But it must be shouldered by all who have faith that human freedom can be furthered by the arts of intelligence.

## NOTES

1. The Carter administration proposed legislation that would give the secretary of HEW the power to license and regulate research projects doing controversial genetic studies. Violators of the licensing or other provisions of the law could be assessed penalties of up to $5,000 and as much as a year's imprisonment. (*Chronicle of Higher Education,* April 11, 1977, p. 3.)

2. Congress has enacted legislation to regulate research on human subjects in order to protect their rights. The National Research Act and the Public Health Service Act charges HEW with responsibility for such regulations: "The Secretary shall by regulation require that each entity which applies for a grant or contract under this Act for any project or program which involves the conduct of biomedical or behavioral research involving human subjects submit in or with its application for such grants or contract assurances satisfactory to the Secretary that it has established (in accordance with regulations which the Secretary shall prescribe) a board (to be known as "Institutional Review Board") to review biomedical and behavioral research involving human subjects conducted at or sponsored by such entity in order to protect the rights of human subjects of such research." (*Federal Register,* 40, no. 50, part II, Protection of Human Subjects, Technical Amendments [March 13, 1975], p. 11854.)

3. National Commission for the Protection of Human Subjects of Biomedical and Behavioral Research, *Report and Recommendations: Research Involving Prisoners,* Bethesda, Md., October 1976.

4. Ibid., p. 12.

5. Ibid., p. 13.

6. Ibid., pp. 16, 20.

7. Ibid., p. 20.

8. Raymond B. Cattell, *A New Morality from Science: Beyondism* (New York: Pergamon, 1972).

9. Cornell West, "Philosophical Perspectives on the Participation of Prisoners in Experimental Research," *Report and Recommendations,* pp. 2–14.

10. Roy Branson, "Philosophical Perspectives on Experimentation with Prisoners," *Report and Recommendations,* pp. 1–28.

11. Bernard Davis, "The Scientific versus the Adversary Approach in Bio-Medical Research," *The Ethics of Teaching and Scientific Research,* ed. Sidney Hook et al. (Buffalo, N.Y.: Prometheus Books, 1977), p. 168.

12. John L. Horn, "The Ethics of Research: A Case History and Its Lessons," *The Ethics of Teaching and Scientific Research,* p. 137.

*PART FIVE*
# In Focus

# 28

# *Reason* Interview

REASON: You've been generating some heat from members of the Moral Majority. Could you tell us a little bit about the idea behind your magazine, *Free Inquiry*?

KURTZ: Well, the Moral Majority and the fundamentalist right, if that is the word to use, have been attacking secular humanism for several years now. This has built up in intensity, and I was dismayed at the fact that there did not seem to be an adequate response. I thought they were attacking certain central values in Western civilization, in particular, the value of freedom, which is my basic commitment, and also the idea of a secular society and the separation of church and state. It seemed to me that it was important that there be a response, so that is what prompted me and others associated with me to found *Free Inquiry*—as an intellectual, serious magazine concerned with exploring and debating issues, pro and con, concerning freedom and the secular society, and with a commitment also to democracy.

REASON: What is the history of secular humanism in the United States, and what are its essential features?

KURTZ: "Secular humanism" is a fairly recent term, and we have been trying to trace where it came from. Apparently it appeared in a footnote in the sixties in a Supreme Court decision, cited, I believe, by Justice Black in the Torcaso case. It was taken up by the fundamentalists, who claim that secular humanism has been established as a religion in the United States. I'm willing to use that term, but I consider the basic term to be "humanism." And of course humanism is the oldest philosophical, ethical, and scientific tradition of Western civilization. I trace humanism to Socrates, Aristotle—to the Greeks—and through classical Roman civilization.

Humanism, as I view it, is first a commitment to free inquiry, to the free mind. It's a philosophical and ethical point of view that is opposed to any kind of repression by social institutions—the state, the church, or other dominating institutions. So the central value of humanism is the freedom of

---

This interview for *Reason* magazine was conducted by two philosophers, Tibor Machan and Lansing Pollock, and appeared March 1982.

the individual. Now the secular aspect, of course, was prominent in ancient Athens, when Socrates was condemned to death by the Athenians for irreligion, and in the *Euthyphro,* a very important dialogue, in which Plato tries to distinguish morality from religion. But there is this whole notion that morality can be independent of religious foundations, and there's an autonomy about moral judgment and that you do not have to deduce moral principles and values from either a metaphysical or a theological principle.

Secularism and secular values appeared in the Renaissance as people rediscovered the great classics. And the scientific revolution, as I view it, as well as modern literature, are all part of the secular development of independence of thought and art and of an effort to find the good life here and now for human beings.

REASON: It has been suggested that leaders of the fundamentalist right and the Moral Majority are hostile toward secular humanism because humanism is associated with Karl Marx, who wanted it to replace religion as an ethical mode.

KURTZ: There are many different kinds of humanists, of course. Marx was a humanist in the sense that he was critical of religion—he was an atheist, it's true. He also had a concern with the human condition and improvement of the human lot. But I think that certain forms of Marxism are a betrayal of humanism and that Marxism as it has developed is the enemy of humanism. I consider Marxism and some of its variations—Stalinism, Leninism—to be the major opposition to humanism in the world, not fundamentalism or Christianity, which is another problem. The early Marx was perhaps not totally unappreciative of the role of freedom, but those forms of Marxism that emphasize the principles of equality and the collective betray humanism in the deeper sense. Any humanism that ignores freedom of the individual in its analysis is *anti*humanism.

REASON: Has there been an evolution in your political thinking?

KURTZ: At the moment I am a libertarian democratic secular humanist— that's an awkward combination of terms, I know. At one time I was a democratic socialist. In the thirties and particularly the forties, the influence of Marx was very strong. But I soon abandoned that, and it seems to me that Marxism is predicated on a basic fallacy about the nature of man and the nature of the good society. So I moved from democratic socialism, which I no longer accept, and I now believe that economic freedom is an essential condition of the good society. That's why I'm a libertarian, or a modified libertarian. So many people in my generation did not appreciate the need for economic freedom and freedom of the marketplace. Political freedom is central, of course, and this is why I'm so opposed to Marxist communism. But political freedom is not enough without economic freedom, in my view. And surely we have empirical evidence from the past sixty or seventy years that, where a society abandons economic liberty, where there is a monopoly not only of political power but of economic power, then you have no freedom. You don't have intellectual freedom, or religious freedom, or any other. If we don't learn from experience, how else do we learn? We have to test theories by how they work out in practice.

REASON: This brings to mind a rather different topic—this issue of the teaching of evolution versus creationism in the public schools. One of the charges that has been leveled at you and secular humanism in general by members of the New Right is that in fact the promulgation of the evolutionist theory is just as dogmatic as any kind of creationism. There is, according to them, no evidence that fully sustains the evolutionist thesis. How would you respond to this charge?

KURTZ: Oh, I think there have been dogmatists on both sides. I'm not going to defend everyone who has taken a position in this controversy. My argument is that what is taught in biology courses should be matter of peer review, should be determined by the biology teacher and scientists in general. I am disturbed about vigilante parents' groups or the use of the state to compel scientists to use certain textbooks and to develop a certain kind of curriculum. What I find most paradoxical about the fundamentalist right is their abandonment of freedom. They are contradictory. Do they believe in freedom or not? They are the ones who want to use the legislature to dictate to the schools.

Now if biologists decide, on the basis of scientific inquiry, that the creationists' hypothesis is meaningful, and they decide to introduce it in the textbooks, I'm certainly not going to oppose that. But biologists do not do that. And that's why I think that it's a kind of censorship and a very dangerous assault on the process of free inquiry within the sciences. Darwin's explanations of how evolution occurred are open to criticism. I don't know that anyone accepts the complete Darwinian theory. But evolution seems to be strongly supported by many of the sciences—not simply biology but geology, astronomy, the life sciences. So there's a whole range of evidence, and if you want to question or assault this basic principle of science, you undermine not only biology but all these other sciences as well.

I have no objection, incidentally, to creationism being taught in a history of ideas or a history course if the historians decide to do it. I think that's part of human culture to learn about attitudes and beliefs that people have held. What I'm objecting to is the imposition on science by extrascientific methods and by the power of the state.

REASON: *A Secular Humanist Declaration,* which you authored, states that it is the duty of public education to deal with moral values. Whose moral values should be taught in public schools?

KURTZ: That's a very good question. I think all education is moral. Even if you're teaching reading, writing, and arithmetic, you teach neatness, punctuality, politeness, honesty; and these are values. I don't see how you can have any educational program without values. What I had in mind there, of course, is Aristotle and his *Nicomachean Ethics*: that it is essential in any society to develop character and virtue and certain principles of excellence. And I think the schools have a role to play in this—private schools as well as public schools. To say that the schools should not teach morality would be to rob the schools of any kind of education. So you teach morality; there's no question about that. What kind of morality? It seems to me the common, human values shared by people, the common human decencies, the virtues. It seems to me that one of the great tasks of education is not only to get children to think critically—that seems to be a common human value—but also to grow *and* to appreciate the needs of others to grow, morally, by cultivating independence of moral judgment.

REASON: Murray Rothbard has commented on the controversy involving secular humanism and the Moral Majority. One of the things he pointed out is that, once you do have a public-education system, it is somewhat odd to be surprised that the overwhelming majority—which in this country does happen to be Christian or in the Judeo-Christian tradition—should then wish to have *its* values taught in public schools rather than the values of an intellectual elite, which the secular humanist group is identified as. What is your response to this?

KURTZ: I don't think that secular humanism is being taught in the schools. I think that's a conspiracy theory. What *is* being taught in the schools is modern science, literature, the arts; the whole curriculum is the curriculum of the modern world. And what the Moral Majority wants to do, as I see it, is repeal the modern world and return to a kind of simplistic view of the universe. So this notion of a group of conspirators that have taken over the schools seems to me to be completely false.

REASON: In all fairness, it doesn't have to be a conspiracy in the sense of a consciously designed program perpetrated by a few people. It could be simply that, by natural accretion, intellectuals who have gotten their education from sophisticated thinkers in various universities have come to dominate what is taught in the schools. And for a while, they could maintain that they were the experts at this, and people would tolerate it. But now the rank and file are saying, "No, get rid of this bunch of kooks and get us back to fundamental Christian values."

KURTZ: Yes, and now what they want to do, as we know, is burn books in a campaign to purify the libraries and the schools of literature that they consider to be offensive or obscene or immoral. They want to impose creationism as an alternative theory, with equal time, in the science courses. They are opposed to philosophy—and this is a very deep, essential point. They are opposed to the teaching of courses in morals and ethics in colleges, universities, and public schools because this is independent of religious tradition. So really the critique is of the whole modern curriculum. Now, look, I don't agree with many libertarians who want to get rid of the public schools. I believe in freedom and pluralism, and I think there ought to be a diversity of institutions.

REASON: But if you do have this *public* institution, isn't it then up to a democratic assembly to dictate its content?

KURTZ: No. It seems to me that the appropriate authorities, educators qualified in the field, should determine what ought to be taught. A large percentage of people in the United States believe that astrology is true, so should astrology be in the curriculum in every school? If Christian Scientists were a predominant part of American society, should the medical schools teach Christian Science? I mean, where do you draw the line? You break down all professional standards. I'm a philosopher; I teach at a university. Should people in the community examine my textbooks and say, "No, no, no, you should not teach Aristotle"? Tim LaHaye [founder of Christian Heritage College, president of Californians for Biblical Morality, chairman of the Conservative Council in Washington, D.C.] is opposed to the teaching of Aristotle. Aristotle is one of the most wicked men of the history of thought, in this battle of the mind. You can't teach Aristotle; you have to teach whom they want, you see. So it seems to me that there are institutions that exist and they have a role and function to play, and I would allow the qualified people within a field to be the best judge of what is to be taught.

REASON: Aren't you confronted, as a secular humanist committed to democracy, with a dilemma? This is what Murray Rothbard was trying to get at. The dilemma is: either you have public education and then you have democracy invading the classroom; or you have free inquiry but you don't have public education, because the public domain is in fact under democratic control. You cannot be for both unlimited democracy and free inquiry, because unlimited democracy, as even Aristotle taught, would ultimately overrun free inquiry.

KURTZ: I'm not for unlimited democracy. What would unlimited democracy mean in the university? The janitors and secretaries would outvote the faculty? That's mobocracy.

I'm a little disturbed about what I would consider the tyranny of principles. The great danger in the world today, as I see it, is rampant egalitarian collectivism—the effort to take a principle and to drive it all the way, destroying initiative and freedom and any sense of justice and fairness. On the other hand, it seems to me that extreme libertarianism, which takes the freedom principle and is not willing to recognize the application of principle *in context,* could also lead to a kind of tyranny.

Should we get rid of the public schools? It seems to me that something should be said in defense of the public school. It was the melting pot of democracy, and people learned from different ethnic, religious, racial backgrounds.

REASON: Actually, did you know that public schools started in New England in response to the fact that some private schools started to admit blacks into their classes, whereupon the civil community got so upset that they instituted their own public-education system, which kept blacks out of the system? This is documented very early back in the 1600s in New England. *This* is how public education started.

KURTZ: I realize that, yes. But it was early in the nineteenth century that the public-school movement really developed. And the idea was universal education. So, should we get rid of the public schools? But in any case the assault on secular humanism is an assault also on the private-school curriculum, where you have the same thing happen. The questions are: Don't we want to give our children the best education? Should one narrow ideological group in the society dictate what should be in the curriculum, as they are intending to do?

REASON: One of the complaints of people like Jerry Falwell is, "Look, you have got this view of what a modern education should be, but we don't believe all that." In other words, you are saying, "They want to impose their values on us. We're not going to stand for it." Falwell and his crowd are saying, "You're imposing your values on us, and we're not going to stand for it." What's the difference between them and you?

KURTZ: There's a real difference. I don't want to impose my values on anyone. I want historians and philosophers and scientists and critics and artists, all participating in the schools, qualified in their fields, to teach the subject matter they think is appropriate. What I'm raising a question about is this effort to denude the curriculum and to impoverish education in the modern world.

REASON: We heard that you have had some rather peculiar experiences with your opponents on the right. When some people said they wanted to give a fair shake to secular humanism, you consented and you were videotaped and there was some strange development—

KURTZ: Yes. You are referring to the fact that the 700 Club of the Christian Broadcasting Network, which is one of the largest religious enterprises in the country, contacted me. Pat Robertson and his sympathizers had been attacking secular humanism vigorously, and I was surprised and really appalled at the fact that they never presented the other point of view. Then one day I was called by one of the producers, who asked me if I would consent to do a documentary on humanism. He said they thought that secular humanism was being attacked unfairly and their viewers ought to have a chance to hear the other point of view. So they came to the State University of New York in Buffalo and spent eight hours, and he said it would be a fair documentary, pro and con. And I had a very good rapport with the crew that came up. So I was absolutely flabbergasted when I began hearing from all over the country that this tape was playing over and over again, and they had apparently sold thousands, and it was playing in many churches throughout the country. Finally, I got a chance to see one. It seemed to me a blatant distortion and unfair caricature of my position.

REASON: What sort of thing did they do?

KURTZ: You know, what they are really doing—this is a point that I think readers of *Reason* should be aware of—is attacking the libertarian aspect of secular humanism, wherein secular humanists believe in moral freedom of choice and the right of an individual to lead his own life as he sees fit as long as he doesn't harm others. That's the basic principle I was defending, along with the need to cultivate moral growth and development and the use of critical reason.

But in any case, I said that there is a great moral tradition, which goes back to the Greeks, that you can lead a noble life without necessarily going to church or adopting a specific religious code. But they began to saddle me with situation ethics. I said that I think there are general moral principles based on human experience—sincerity, truth, honesty, trust—that I'm prepared to accept.

"Are there no exceptions?" they asked.

And I said, "There are exceptions, of course."

"Do you think you should always tell the truth?"

And I said to them, "Yes, I believe truth telling is the general principle. However, there are exceptions. Sometimes you may lie. A man is in a hospital. He has had a heart attack, and you visit him, and he asks you how serious it is. If you tell him the truth, then he is liable to have another heart attack; so you withhold the information from him."

They took these statements out of context. Do I believe in abortion? I said I believe in the right of freedom of choice of the individual and that the state ought not to regulate that. "However," I said, "abortion should not be used as a method of birth control, and in my view women ought not have it after the fourth month." But they cut all that. I said, "I believe in the right of abortion," and they showed dead fetuses in the can.

REASON: They showed this on film?

KURTZ: On film, yes. And I said, "I believe in freedom, moral freedom of the individual to his own life," and then they showed gay disco bars and a kid dead of an overdose of drugs.

REASON: So fairness is not a Judeo-Christian virtue, accepted by the Moral Majority?

KURTZ: Apparently not. I thought it was an immoral use of the media.

REASON: If you look at the people who have endorsed the *Secular Humanist Declaration,* you see people like B. F. Skinner and Antony Flew, and it can give the impression that there really are no clear tenets here. Is this a grouping of people who really don't share much in common?

KURTZ: No, there *are* certain principles, it seems to me, that secular humanists are willing to defend. The first principle is a commitment to freedom, to freedom of inquiry, the free mind, and against all efforts to repress that. The second is a commitment to a rational process of inquiry. And the third principle is the view that ethical values in some sense are related to human experience and human needs and do not have to be derived either from an ideology or from a theological foundation. Now we may disagree on many other principles, but it's a commitment to a free society and to democracy.

REASON: What about the secular humanists, or at least people who are secularists, who are maintaining nowadays that there are no widely valid methods for reaching truths, for reaching understanding? For example, the prominent philosopher Paul Feyerabend maintains that the Western rationalist position, coming down from Socrates, is just one of many, many equally valid approaches that human beings can take to their lives. So tea-leaf reading, astrology, turning to medicine men, or anything else—if it suits you, fine.

KURTZ: I disagree. But the fact that Feyerabend is or is not a secularist is independent. I think that one of the major problems we face in the world—it's a worldwide problem—is the retreat from reason. It's not simply the retreat from freedom, which we all deplore in our effort to cultivate and develop a free society, but the retreat from reason. Many commentators in the universities today are appalled by the fact that subjectivism is widespread and there seems to be a breakdown of any notion that there are standards of reason or evidence to test hypotheses or judgments. The growth of the paranormal is illustrative of this immediacy and subjectivity as a foundation of belief. The growth of fundamentalism, in my view, and some of the cults of unreason are also symptomatic of this. And also the growth of ideological religions in the world.

REASON: One of the things that is difficult for many of the people who also value free inquiry—and Feyerabend certainly does that—is to reconcile that commitment to freedom with what they would probably call the dogmatism of reason.

KURTZ: There certainly have been dogmatic rationalists. And although it seems to me that there are some objective criteria for judging truth claims, I shouldn't leave out the fact that skepticism ought to be a component of any objective method of inquiry. One has to be skeptical of all things, in a constructive, positive way, including any dogmatic application of reason.

REASON: Is it in this general skeptical vein that you have been involved in efforts to debunk claims regarding phenomena like ESP, psychic powers, UFOs, astrology, and so on?

KURTZ: I think "debunking" is maybe too strong a term. What we want to do is provide a scientific investigation of the claims. I think it is unfortunate that the proparanormal point of view has been purveyed in the mass media without any criticism. The electronic media, particularly television and the movies, have led the way, and publishers and magazines and so on have been presenting this material as true, without question. A great number of scientists in these fields who have looked at the evidence are very skeptical about it. We are trying to develop, in a very modest way, some appreciation for critical intelligence, which involves skepticism about things that have not been tested.

REASON: When you say "we".

KURTZ: I founded the Committee for the Scientific Investigation of Claims of the Paranormal. We are going into our eighth year, and we publish a journal, *The Skeptical Inquirer.* The committee includes about a hundred scientists.

REASON: Hasn't your group actually been able to explain some of this? You take somebody like Uri Geller, who has been on television supposedly displaying his extraordinary powers. Haven't you been able to expose exactly what he's up to and how he does it?

KURTZ: Well, there's so much—every day there's something new. There are so many claims that it's hard to deal with them all. What we're trying to do is simply crystallize critical skepticism in the public. Members of our committee, and others, have attempted to examine, for example, whether Uri Geller uses psychokinesis to bend metal. We don't think there have been any objective tests where this has been proven. We have magicians on our committee who can bend metal when you're not looking, and we think that's what Uri Geller does.

REASON: One final question. You are a professor of philosophy and at the same time you have strongly expressed commitments in various areas of public life, personal morality, and so forth. The philosopher Leo Strauss once wrote a piece on the relationship between having a "subjective certainty," he called it, with respect to some issues and maintaining one's philosophical commitment to being open-minded and regarding every major issue as problematic, never to have the door quite closed on it. How, in your personal life, have you managed to live with these two things?

KURTZ: My model of philosophy is Socrates, and my mentor in the twentieth century might be John Dewey, but more particularly Sidney Hook. And I believe philosophy has a role in the marketplace of ideas. The thing that is interesting and unfortunate is that the university is no longer the "sacred" institution. Ideas, education, and the *process* of inquiry have moved to other institutions in society—the media, the press. Philosophical inquiry is fundamental, an important activity, and it ought to be done in the larger market of ideas. So I try to apply philosophy to practice. But at the same time that I am committed to certain positions, I am committed to being skeptical. The role of the committee and *Free Inquiry,* in one sense, is to develop an appreciation for critical intelligence, for the skeptical attitude and outlook.